W9-BKA-483

welcome to
claire's

claire criscuolo

35 Years of Recipes and Reflections from
the Landmark Vegetarian Restaurant

Photographs by Julie Bidwell

LYONS PRESS
Guilford, Connecticut
An Imprint of Globe Pequot Press

Throughout this book you will see the following symbols next to the recipes. This will guide you as to which recipes are gluten-free, include a gluten-free option, are vegan, or include a vegan option.

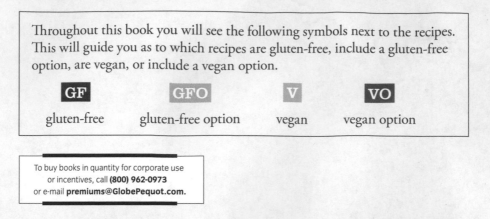

GF
gluten-free

GFO
gluten-free option

V
vegan

VO
vegan option

To buy books in quantity for corporate use or incentives, call **(800) 962-0973** or e-mail **premiums@GlobePequot.com.**

Copyright © 2012 by Claire Criscuolo

ALL RIGHTS RESERVED. No part of this book may be reproduced or transmitted in any form by any means, electronic or mechanical, including photocopying and recording, or by any information storage and retrieval system, except as may be expressly permitted in writing from the publisher. Requests for permission should be addressed to Globe Pequot Press, Attn: Rights and Permissions Department, P.O. Box 480, Guilford, CT 06437.

Lyons Press is an imprint of Globe Pequot Press

All photographs © Julie Bidwell except the photos licensed by Shutterstock.com that can be found on pages x, 2 (center), 67, 74, 76, 78, 88, 97, 98, 102, 121, 122, 134, 140, 144, 147, 157, 163, 173, 196, 201, 209, 215, 223, 229, 241, 262, 283, 293, 299, 306, 312, 317, 321, and 331; the photo on page 8 courtesy of David and Michelle Benivegna; the photo on page 23 courtesy of David Jenkins and Mary Barnett; and the photo on page 360 courtesy of Alex and Alison Rivera.

Text design: Diana Nuhn
Layout artist: Nancy Freeborn
Project editors: Gregory Hyman and Tracee Williams

Library of Congress Cataloging-in-Publication Data

Criscuolo, Claire.
  Welcome to Claire's : 35 years of recipes and reflections from the landmark vegetarian restaurant / Claire Criscuolo.
      p. cm.
  Includes indexes.
  ISBN 978-0-7627-7446-3
  1. Vegetarian cooking. 2. Claire's Corner Copia (Restaurant) I. Title.
  TX837.C77226 2012
  641.5'636—dc23

                                                                              2011033003

Printed in the United States of America

10 9 8 7 6 5 4 3 2 1

I dedicate this book with great love to my husband, Frank, the love of my life.

contents

introduction

This book is really a love story. That is because everything about Claire's has to do with love— love for others, love for community, love for organic and sustainable foods, and love for the past, the present, and the future. Really, it's as simple as that.

Since September 17, 1975, Claire's Corner Copia has been located at 1000 Chapel Street. It's at the corner of College Street in New Haven, Connecticut, right across the street from the old campus at Yale University, and diagonally across from the historic New Haven Green. This location is undeniably the most beautiful corner in the city. It's the place where you can see the first daffodils of spring as they pop up from the land surrounding the Yale campus; it's the place where you can see the reflection of the majestic steeple from the Trinity Church on the Green through our windows; and it's the place where you can feel like you're in the center of the city, surrounded by the warmth and comfort that comes from a place of love.

Shortly after my husband Frank and I were married, we knew that we wanted to work together, and I knew that I wanted to spend my days cooking simple and fresh foods, the way my mother made food for my brothers and me growing up. After attending college and

not enjoying college food so much, I was certain that, like me, folks were longing for those slow-cooked soups, homemade breads, homemade dressings for bountiful salads, and made-from-scratch desserts. And I was certain that I wanted to help make these foods available for those who missed that care.

Today, we've been in business—right here on this corner—accomplishing that goal for over thirty-five years, and each year is as memorable as the one before.

At Claire's, our commitment to using organic and local foods remains strong, and we continue to source as many organic ingredients as we can. We follow the recommendations from the Environmental Working Group so that we always know the highest and lowest pesticide residues in foods. This allows us to make good choices for ourselves and for our customers.

We continue to learn from our treasured staff members, who cook and bake, assist our customers each and every day, and keep us focused on our mission of using only the best ingredients. We learn from our customers, who inspire us to do better each day. Whether it's finding a more sustainable way to handle our energy needs or taking an opportunity to grow our own organic heirloom tomatoes, herbs, and arugula (which we do each year in my backyard), we continue to seek ways to be better shepherds of the land we borrow from our future generations.

At Claire's, our local commitments go beyond food, as well. As always, our hearts and support go out to those in need, and each year we try to think of new and creative ways to offer our support to our community. Please feel free to check back in with us on our website (www.claires cornercopia.com) from time to time for regular updates of these local events. As Margaret Mead once said, "Never doubt that a small group of thoughtful, committed citizens can change the world. . . . Indeed, it is the only thing that ever has."

And so with this book, we celebrate over thirty-five years of committing to changing the world, one Lithuanian Coffee Cake at a time. This book—our love story—is a collection of our favorite recipes and, of course, we've included our Claire's Classics, the recipes that our beloved customers keep coming back for, some daily and others faithfully during their reunions and during business trips back to the city. We've also included some personal essays written by me, as well as Claire's Corner Voices, reflections written by some of our favorite customers and former staff. If you come to Claire's, we hope the experience will bring you fond memories. And if you have yet to visit us, we hope a future visit will make you feel like you have always been here and perhaps encourage you to visit us more often.

We've been given so much from so many, and this is us trying to give back to you. And that is sustainable!

breakfast

It's always the same scenario: Our schedules get hectic and instead of feeding our bodies with extra nutrients to compensate for the added stress, we tend to grab the quickest, and usually the least nutritious, foods. And we tend to skip what is still the most important meal of the day—breakfast, the meal that refuels and repairs our bodies after a night of sleep, and the absence of any food for several hours. It doesn't make sense, yet this is what so many of us do.

The motto *Be Prepared* works for the Boy Scouts, and this doctrine is vital when it comes to healthy eating.

So how do you prepare for a good start to your day? With a good breakfast. This includes the same basic rules of good nutrition that you need to think about for every meal. You need good protein to build, repair, and maintain body cells; to transport vitamins and minerals; and to build muscle. Vegetarian sources for good protein include beans, whole grains, nuts, and dairy. Complex carbohydrates help to sustain your blood sugar levels so you'll have the energy throughout the day to keep up with your tasks at hand. Aim for six to eleven servings a day. Good sources include whole grains like quinoa, brown rice, wheat berries, whole barley, oats, and whole wheat. And whole grains contain healthy doses of fiber, which helps your body absorb the energy from these good grains more slowly. This allows for fewer peaks and slumps of energy—we've all had the 10:00 a.m. energy drain after a nutrient-deficient breakfast or no breakfast at all.

Diets high in fiber are associated with reduced rates of heart disease and the prevention of some cancers. So be sure to include 28 grams in your daily diet, along with plenty of vitamins and minerals to help protect and strengthen your body to prevent illness. Fruits and vegetables are beautiful and delicious and, along with soy and low-fat dairy products, are invaluable toward the goal of eating a healthful diet. Set a goal to eat nine servings of fruits and vegetables, and three to five servings of soy or low-fat dairy, each day. Good fats, such as those from olive, canola, and nut oils and from flax, provide a good source of energy, help to lower cholesterol, provide us with antioxidants, and simply make food taste good. You'll want to limit your fat intake to less than 30 percent of your total calories each day, with no more than 10 percent of those fat calories from saturated fats.

I'm always in a rush on workdays—who isn't?—and I often turn to smoothies for my breakfast before I leave for work. They are delicious and beautiful, and at the same time they provide a fast and efficient way to maintain my goal of eating well. On my days off from work, I love to make a cooked breakfast, such as eggs, pancakes, oatmeal, or quinoa, not so much because I have more time to cook, but because I have more time to relax and enjoy the cooked meal.

So with all of this knowledge in hand, let's make some breakfast!

Fresh Fruit Smoothies

Smoothies are a popular way to enjoy two or more fruits. At home, I serve them in my favorite wine glasses. Children will enjoy being included when you're relaxing with these "cocktails."

Makes 3 or 4 smoothies

2½ cups pineapple juice

2 ice cubes

8–10 strawberries

2 tablespoons wheat germ

   Or:

2½ cups grapefruit juice

2 ice cubes

3 kiwi, peeled and quartered

2 tablespoons wheat germ

Place all ingredients in a blender. Process on high speed about 30 seconds, until blended. Serve immediately, or reblend for 5 seconds just before serving.

Back-to-School Smoothie

This is a basic recipe to allow for loads of creativity and for the seasonal availability of fruits.

Serves 2

2 cups organic soy milk, almond milk, or organic dairy milk

1 citrus fruit, peeled, seeded, and cut into slices

1 cup organic low-fat plain yogurt or dairy-free "yogurt," or 2 servings of protein powder

1 cup fresh or frozen organic fruit pieces: strawberries, raspberries, blueberries, bananas, mango, pineapple, papaya, apples, pears, ripe persimmons, seedless watermelon, or other

2 teaspoons organic flax oil

2 tablespoons pure maple syrup, organic agave, local honey, or other sweetener (optional)

2 tablespoons organic wheat germ

Combine ingredients in a blender cup. Cover and blend on high speed for about 45 seconds or until blended smooth.

Tip: Omit the wheat germ to make this recipe gluten free.

Mango Lassi GF

Many years ago, a young woman, Anjul Dutt, was visiting her brother, who was in graduate school at Yale. She really wanted to work at Claire's during her summer visit, but we didn't have an opening that year. Over the next few summers, she repeated her request. When she appealed to me for a summer job during her brother's last year at school, I couldn't resist her determination—she had even called me from Wales, where she had been living at the time. So I hired her. This turned out to be one of the best decisions ever, as she's kind, friendly, and smart, and she really, really loves good food! We stay in contact to this day. She taught me about lassi drinks from her homeland in India, and this lassi, a mango lassi, remains one of our most popular drinks. We make it with our homemade yogurt and it's my favorite "go-to" drink at Claire's, too.

Makes about 1½ cups

½ cup small ice cubes, or 5–6 larger cubes

1 cup plain low-fat or fat-free yogurt

½ cup frozen mango chunks

1 tablespoon honey

1 teaspoon ground cardamom

Combine the ingredients in a blender cup. Cover and blend for about 15 seconds until smooth and creamy.

Vita Mita GF

We're always in awe of our customers and how they share their unbridled excitement for good food. Keo, a young man from Brazil, was visiting Yale for a month and during this time, he ate at Claire's almost daily. He brought his guitar, and when we called out names as we delivered the food to our guests in the dining room, Keo would make up a song using the customer's name. Really! It was so much fun. Keo shared this recipe with us for a smoothie he enjoyed in his homeland of Brazil. It's a really delicious and healthy smoothie, loaded with vitamin A, omega-3 fatty acids, potassium, antioxidants, and protein.

Makes a little over 2 cups

½ cup small ice cubes, or 5–6 larger cubes

½ avocado, pitted and skin removed

1 banana

1 cup plain soy milk

1 tablespoon honey

Combine the ingredients in a blender cup. Cover and blend on high speed for about 15 seconds until smooth and creamy. It will be somewhat thick and lovely.

Jazzed-Up Oatmeal

This embellished oatmeal takes only minutes to prepare and adds even more cholesterol-lowering fiber to an already healthful breakfast.

Serves 4

1¾ cups organic soy milk, plus additional as desired when serving

1¾ cups water

1 organic apple, Pink Lady or other, cored and coarsely chopped

¼ cup dried apricots, sliced

¼ cup dried cranberries

¼ cup sliced almonds

2 cups organic rolled oats

¼ cup local pure maple syrup

2 teaspoons cinnamon

2 organic bananas, sliced

1. Bring the soy milk and water to a boil in a heavy pot over high heat. Add the apple, apricots, cranberries, almonds, and oats. Stir to combine.

2. Lower the heat to medium and cook for about 3–5 minutes, stirring occasionally until the oats are cooked and thickened to your preference. Remove from the heat and stir in the maple syrup, cinnamon, and bananas. Serve with additional soy milk as desired.

Claire's Classic

Maple-Nut Granola V

Pure maple syrup gives this granola its delicious flavor. Please don't be tempted by imitation maple syrup. It's not even close in flavor or contents. Over the years, our granola has become so popular that we sell it "to go" for your snacks or breakfast at home.

Serves 8

6 cups rolled oats

½ cup chopped walnuts

½ cup sliced almonds

½ cup wheat germ

2 teaspoons cinnamon

1 cup pure maple syrup

2 tablespoons soybean or vegetable oil

½ cup chopped dried figs

½ cup chopped dried apple rings

1. Preheat the oven to 250°F. In a bowl, combine the oats, walnuts, almonds, wheat germ, and cinnamon. In another bowl, whisk together the maple syrup and oil: pour this mixture over the oat mixture all at once. Toss well.

2. Spread evenly in a shallow baking dish or on a cookie sheet. Bake for about 1½ hours, stirring every 15 minutes.

3. Stir in the figs and apples. Continue baking about 30 minutes, until the mixture feels dry. Cool to room temperature. Store in a covered container at room temperature for up to 1 week.

Hot

ESPRESSO DRINKS

RUSSIAN FRUIT TEA

HOMEMADE HOT CHOCOLATE
- WITH PEPPERMINT
- WITH MAPLE
- MEXICAN

HOMEMADE CHAI LATTE

ORGANIC APPLE CIDER

ORGANIC BIGELOW TEAS

TEA LATTES

Cold

- HOMEMADE LEMONADE
- FRESH-BREWED ICED TEA
- ARNOLD PALMER
- RUSSIAN FRUIT LEMONA
- ICED COFFEE
- ICED CHAI LATTE
- JUICES
- MANGO LASSI
- LEMONADE FREEZE

Quinoa Breakfast Bowl V GFO

Quinoa is an ancient grain that originated in the Andes, grown by the Incas. It is rich in protein and fiber and has a nutty flavor. When paired with fresh fruits and soy milk, it makes for a most wonderfully delicious and healthful breakfast. Quinoa is readily available in supermarkets.

Serves 4

1 cup organic quinoa

1 cup orange juice, freshly squeezed if possible

1 cup organic soy milk

2 tablespoons pure maple syrup

1 teaspoon cinnamon

1 teaspoon cardamom

3 organic peaches, pitted and cut into medium dice

1 cup blueberries

¼ cup sliced almonds

4 teaspoons organic flax oil (optional)

Additional soy milk for pouring over quinoa

1. Measure the quinoa into a medium-size pot. Add the orange juice, soy milk, maple syrup, cinnamon, and cardamom into the pot. Stir to combine. Cover and bring to a boil over high heat. When the mixture reaches a boil, reduce the heat to low. Cover and simmer for about 12 minutes, or until the liquid is absorbed and the quinoa grains are tender.

2. Spoon into individual bowls. Divide the peaches, blueberries, and almonds evenly and place on the quinoa. Drizzle a teaspoon of organic flax oil over the top of each. Serve additional soy milk to thin as you please.

Tip: Use gluten-free soy milk to make this recipe gluten free.

> "I am so comforted by the commitment of the Criscuolos to the values of consistency, hard work, and heart-healthy cuisine. No matter how unpredictable the world is, I know I can go to Claire's and her carrot cake will still taste as magnificent as it was in 1978 the first time I tasted it, just like home."
>
> —Sara (Sylvester) Hernandez, former weekend manager at Claire's Corner Copia

Claire's Classic

Breakfast Baked Apples GF

I enjoy these baked apples any time of day. They're rich-tasting with or without the butter.

Serves 6

6 large baking apples (Rome, Pink Lady, or McIntosh are my favorites)

2 cups cider (fresh-pressed, if possible)

Cinnamon for sprinkling

4 tablespoons (½ stick) butter, cut into 6 pats (optional)

2 teaspoons vanilla extract

3 cups plain nonfat yogurt

2 tablespoons honey

1 teaspoon cinnamon

1. Preheat the oven to 425°F. Cut a 1-inch top off each apple, and core the apples. Arrange the apples cut side up in a glass baking pan 2 or 3 inches deep and large enough to hold the apples in a single layer. Pour the cider over the apples. Sprinkle each apple with cinnamon. If desired, top each apple with a pat of butter. Pour ¼ teaspoon vanilla extract on top of each apple and pour the remaining ½ teaspoon into the cider in the pan. Cover tightly with foil.

2. Bake for 30 minutes, then uncover and baste. Replace the foil and continue baking for 15 to 30 minutes, until cooked to the desired softness.

3. Combine the yogurt, honey, and cinnamon, transfer the apples to individual bowls, and top the apples with the yogurt mixture.

Apple-Maple Muffins

Use organic apples and local maple syrup for a delicious way to help support your community.

Makes 1 dozen

1 cup organic unbleached all-purpose flour

½ cup organic whole wheat flour

½ cup organic granulated cane sugar

½ teaspoon sea salt

1 teaspoon baking soda

2 teaspoons cinnamon

½ teaspoon ground cardamom

3 organic eggs or equivalent vegan substitute

½ cup olive oil

¼ cup maple syrup

1 teaspoon pure vanilla extract

2 small local apples, cored and finely chopped

¾ cup chopped walnuts

1. Center the oven rack. Preheat the oven to 375°F. In a large bowl, measure the flours, sugar, salt, baking soda, cinnamon, and cardamom. Sift this into another bowl.

2. In a separate bowl, whisk together the eggs, oil, maple syrup, and vanilla until well blended. Pour this over the dry ingredients all at once, using a rubber spatula to scrape the bowl and mixing lightly with a spoon to combine. Add the chopped apples and walnuts and stir well to combine.

3. Spray a muffin tin with nonstick cooking spray. Spoon about ⅓ cup batter into each muffin tin. Bake on the center rack of the preheated oven for about 22 minutes, until a cake tester inserted into the center of a muffin comes out clean.

4. Remove from the oven and turn out onto a platter. Cool to room temperature before storing in a covered container for up to 2 days.

Claire's Classic

Chocolate Chip and Walnut Scones

We bake these scones at Claire's for breakfast, but you can also enjoy them midmorning with coffee for a break from work or studies. The scones are good plain or with raspberry jam.

Makes 8 large scones

2 cups unbleached flour

1 cup whole wheat flour

¼ cup sugar

4 teaspoons baking powder

¼ teaspoon salt

2 tablespoons freshly grated orange zest

12 tablespoons (1½ sticks) butter, cut into 12 pieces

1 egg, lightly beaten

1 cup buttermilk or sour milk

½ teaspoon vanilla extract

½ cup chocolate chips

¼ cup chopped walnuts

1. Preheat the oven to 375°F. In a bowl, sift together the unbleached flour, whole wheat flour, sugar, baking powder, and salt. Stir in the orange zest. Using two knives, cut the butter into the flour mixture until it resembles coarse crumbs.

2. In a separate bowl, whisk together the egg, buttermilk or sour milk, and vanilla extract. Pour the liquid over the flour mixture all at once and stir just to combine. Stir in the chocolate chips and walnuts.

3. Line a cookie sheet with parchment paper or grease lightly. Drop the scone batter by heaping spoonfuls onto the cookie sheet, leaving as much space as possible to allow for spreading. Bake for 40 minutes on the center rack of the oven. The scones are done when a cake tester inserted into the center of each comes out clean.

Yogurt Parfait GF

This parfait is beautiful and healthful. And it's easy to bring along to eat at your desk, or for the kids to eat while waiting for the school bus. Plan on using an ice pack to keep the yogurt fresh and safe if you are packing the parfait to travel.

Serves 4

4 cups organic low-fat yogurt

2 cups whole grain, fruit, and nut granola

2 cups assorted organic berries, fresh or defrosted if frozen

½ cup raw pumpkin seeds

4 teaspoons organic flax oil (optional)

4–8 teaspoons local honey

1. Line up 4 bowls or glasses (or biodegradable, disposable cups if you'll be taking your yogurt parfaits "to go"). Into each bowl, spoon ½ cup of yogurt, ¼ cup of granola, ¼ cup of berries, and 1 tablespoon pumpkin seeds. Repeat to make another layer.

2. Drizzle a teaspoon of the flax oil onto each parfait. Top with 1–2 teaspoons of honey, depending on the sweetness you want. Enjoy!

Claire's Classic

French (Italian) Toast

My mom has always had a knack for turning leftovers into marvelous new meals. This delicious French toast is made with leftover Italian bread. During the week, our day-old bread was used for stuffing peppers, zucchini, or eggplant or for making garlic croutons or bread pudding, but the Italian bread left over from Saturday was used for this special French toast, and my brothers and I always looked forward to it. Although I mainly eat whole-grain breads today, I sometimes buy a loaf of Italian bread on Saturday and save it for the next day, just to make this wonderful French toast. I serve it with pure maple syrup and homemade applesauce or top it with lightly sautéed slices of banana.

Serves 4

4 eggs, slightly beaten

3 tablespoons low-fat or soy milk

½ teaspoon cinnamon

½ teaspoon vanilla extract

Pinch of nutmeg

8 1-inch slices day-old Italian bread

1 tablespoon butter or trans fat–free organic margarine

1. In a large bowl, whisk together the eggs, milk, cinnamon, vanilla extract, and nutmeg. Add the slices of bread and completely coat each slice. Let soak for 10 minutes.

2. Melt butter in a large nonstick skillet over medium-low heat. Using a fork, lift out the slices of bread one at a time and arrange them in the skillet. Cook for 2 or 3 minutes, until golden brown. Using a plastic spatula, turn and cook the other side until golden brown.

I love breakfast. There's something about starting your day with a piping-hot cup of coffee and some sweet or savory goodness . . . and no one has better breakfast than Claire's. If you've ever been to the restaurant as it's opening, you know what I'm talking about—the sometimes bombastic symphony of Beethoven, pots and pans clanging, and staff laughing; the aromatic beckoning of the morning's muffins and treats; and the light breeze that lifts those delicious smells into the air and down College and Chapel Streets. Whether I'm there for business or leisure, Claire's is always enjoyable, and I daresay it's because she's created an environment where everything is beautiful and delicious.

—**Emily Byrne, executive director of New Haven Promise**

Oatmeal-Blueberry-Pecan Buttermilk Pancakes

Is there anything more pleasant than having the free time (sometimes you just have to make the time) to enjoy a cooked breakfast of pancakes and pure maple syrup? These pancakes are rich in fiber, complex carbohydrates, protein, vitamins, minerals, and antioxidants—and they are incredibly delicious.

Serves 4–6

2 cups rolled organic oats

1¾ cups buttermilk

¼ cup freshly squeezed organic orange juice

2 organic eggs, lightly beaten

4 tablespoons organic dairy-free buttery spread, melted

½ cup organic whole wheat flour

1 tablespoon organic turbinado sugar

2 teaspoons finely grated orange zest, from about 1 organic orange

1 teaspoon baking powder

1 teaspoon baking soda

¼ teaspoon cinnamon

¼ teaspoon cardamom

1 cup blueberries

¼ cup chopped pecans

Almond oil or other high-heat-tolerant oil for brushing the griddle pan

¾–1 cup pure maple syrup

1. In a bowl, combine the oats, buttermilk, and orange juice. Set aside for about 15 minutes until the oats soften. Add the eggs and melted spread, and beat with a spoon for about 30 seconds until well combined. Add the flour, sugar, orange zest, baking powder, baking soda, cinnamon, and cardamom. Stir well to mix until the dry ingredients are fully incorporated. Gently fold in the berries and pecans.

2. Heat a griddle pan over medium heat. Brush the pan lightly with the almond oil. Pour the batter in ¼ cupfuls onto the heated griddle, allowing for space in between for turning. Cook until golden brown, about 2 minutes, then flip gently with a sturdy spatula. Cook the other side until golden brown, about 2 minutes. Serve with maple syrup.

Eggs in Bread (AKA Toads in a Hole)

Serves 4

4 1-inch slices whole wheat Italian bread

1 tablespoon extra-virgin olive oil

Nonstick organic olive oil or canola oil spray

4 organic eggs

Sea salt and pepper

1. Using your fingers, create a cavity in the center of each slice of bread, making a depression but not going all the way through. The cavity should be about 2 inches long and 1 inch wide. (We like to drizzle the bread that we take out with a little local honey and then eat it.) Brush both sides of the bread with the olive oil.

2. Heat a large skillet over medium heat, then carefully remove the skillet from the stove and spray it with nonstick organic olive oil spray. Return the hot, sprayed skillet to the medium heat. Arrange the slices of bread in the skillet in a single layer, leaving as much space as possible between slices to make it easier to turn them later.

3. Crack one egg at a time into a small bowl, then turn it into the cavity in the bread, repeating until every slice of bread is filled with an egg. Sprinkle each with a little sea salt and pepper. Cook for about 4 minutes, until the egg begins to set and the underside of the bread is toasted to your preference; check by lifting with a metal spatula.

4. Carefully turn each slice of bread, sprinkle with sea salt and pepper, then cook the other side for about 4 minutes, until the egg is fully set and the underside of the bread is nicely toasted. Transfer the Eggs in Bread to a platter. Serve hot, at room temperature, or chilled.

soups, stews & sandwiches

When I was growing up, soups were the foundation of most of my family's lunches and suppers, and my brothers and I loved them. Naturally, when my husband, Frank, and I opened Claire's Corner Copia, soup became the foundation of the restaurant, and that practice continues to this day. The soup of the day is our most sought-after item.

Soup is a wonderful way to eat well at Claire's, particularly because most of our soups include beans and/or vegetables and have little or no cholesterol. That is not to say that we don't indulge in a rich, creamy bisque or chowder now and then, but we restrain ourselves because we want our beloved customers to eat well.

I'd like to offer a few tips regarding soup-making. Use a heavy, stainless steel pot with a thick aluminum core for even heating and to help prevent sticking. Don't use a lightweight stockpot for making soups or you will run the risk of burning your soup. Sort your beans for any stones or foreign matter—leaves and such—and rinse your beans before using to be sure no dirt remains. After all, beans are grown in dirt, too, just like vegetables. It's also wise to use the best oils, beans, grains, herbs, and vegetables for your soups—the results can only be as good as the ingredients.

In addition to soups, sandwiches have always been popular at Claire's. And they've risen even more in popularity over the past couple of years, both for our customers and for me at home. Sometimes I just want a sandwich and a nice bowl of soup for supper on a weekday. Our customers must agree; soup and a half-sandwich is one of our most popular lunch items, second only to our SSB—our soup, salad, and bread. The latter combination has been on our menu since 1975 and like us, it's still going strong. I guess it goes back to our philosophy that if you use the finest organic and sustainable ingredients and you prepare the foods with love for ourselves, our earth, and others, you just cannot go wrong.

Another way to further that philosophy is to share your soup with a neighbor, particularly an elderly neighbor. He or she will really appreciate it, and you'll feel good knowing that you shared something good.

Have fun making soup and sandwiches for yourself, your family and friends, and your neighbors.

White Bean Soup with Sweet Potato V GF

We look forward to serving this soup every fall and enjoy it through the winter at Claire's. It is so popular that we have customers who nearly cross the state to come and enjoy it!

Serves 6

4 quarts water

1 pound Great Northern beans, picked over

2 bay leaves

¾ cup olive oil

10 cloves garlic, chopped

1 cup chopped parsley

6 medium sweet potatoes, peeled and diced

¼ teaspoon dried basil or 10 leaves fresh basil, chopped

Salt, to taste

1 teaspoon black pepper

1. Bring the water to a boil in a large covered pot. Add the beans and bay leaves. Cook, uncovered, over medium heat for 1½ to 2 hours, stirring occasionally, until the beans are soft.

2. Meanwhile, in a large skillet, heat the olive oil over low heat. Add the garlic and cook, stirring frequently, for 5 minutes. Add the parsley, sweet potatoes, and basil. Sprinkle with salt and pepper. Cook, uncovered, over low heat for 20 minutes, stirring frequently, until the sweet potatoes are tender.

3. Spoon the sweet potato mixture into the pot with the beans. Continue cooking for 30 minutes, stirring frequently. Taste for seasoning.

> "Claire's friendly faces, welcoming environment, and delicious food make a perfect home-away-from-home. Like home, it always has what I need. When I crave a nutritious meal to push me through my studying, I grab a hearty bowl of soup and a piece of Lithuanian Coffee Cake with extra frosting. When I want to catch up with a friend, I indulge in a steaming piece of Mexican lasagna and a piece of Lithuanian Coffee Cake with extra frosting. When I am particularly stressed, I snag a piece of double-layer chocolate cake and a piece of Lithuanian Coffee Cake with extra frosting. There is no place like home, and for me there certainly is no place like Claire's."
>
> —Sam Gardenswartz, Yale Class of 2013 and frequent Claire's Corner Copia visitor

Asopao with Pigeon Peas and Plantains

When Frank and I visited Puerto Rico during a vacation, I fell in love with this soup and ate it every day. I couldn't go without it once I got home, so I went to work making this recipe, which has become very popular. And plantains are available in nearly every supermarket.

Serves 6

1 small white organic onion, coarsely chopped

2 cloves garlic, sliced

3 small organic bell peppers, seeded and coarsely chopped

½ cup coarsely chopped cilantro

3 tablespoons extra-virgin olive oil

¼ cup sliced pimento-stuffed green olives, drained

1 4-ounce package soy pepperoni

1 28-ounce can crushed tomatoes

3 quarts water

1 bay leaf

1 teaspoon dried oregano

2 teaspoons paprika

Pinch of saffron

Salt and pepper, to taste

1 12-ounce bag pigeon peas, sorted for stones

3 large organic bell peppers, seeded and coarsely chopped

2 large organic potatoes, cut into large dice, set in a bowl covered with water to prevent them from darkening

3 large green plantains, peeled and cut into ½-inch slices, set in a bowl covered with water to prevent them from darkening

1½ cups cooked organic brown rice

1. Place the onion, garlic, chopped small peppers, and cilantro into the bowl of a food processor fitted with a metal blade. Cover and process for about a minute until finely minced.

2. Heat the olive oil in a heavy 8-quart pot over low-medium heat. Add the minced mixture, called *soffrito*, and cook for about a minute, stirring frequently to flavor the oil. Add the olives. Separate the slices of soy pepperoni and add them to the pot. Stir to combine. Add the crushed tomatoes, water, bay leaf, oregano, paprika, saffron, salt, and pepper. Cover, raise the heat to high, and bring to a boil, which should take about 15 minutes.

3. When mixture reaches a boil, lower the heat to medium and stir in the sorted pigeon peas. Cover and continue cooking at a medium boil, stirring occasionally, for about 1 hour or until the pigeon peas are barely tender. Add the chopped large bell peppers. Drain the potatoes and plantains and add them to the pot. Cover and continue cooking for about 30 minutes until the pigeon peas, potatoes, and plantains are soft. Stir in the cooked rice. Taste for seasonings.

Cuban Black Bean Soup Ⓥ GF

This is one of our oldest and most popular soups at Claire's. Serve this filling soup with a sprinkling of finely chopped red onion.

Serves 8

4½ quarts water

12 ounces black beans, picked over

½ cup plus 1 tablespoon olive oil

10 clove garlic cloves, minced

½ teaspoon crushed red pepper flakes

½ teaspoon fennel seeds

1 bay leaf

1 cup chopped parsley

1 28-ounce can whole tomatoes in juice, crushed with your hands

½ cup brown rice, uncooked

Salt, to taste

1 teaspoon black pepper

1. Bring the water to a boil in a large covered pot. Add the beans, olive oil, garlic, red pepper flakes, fennel seeds, bay leaf, and parsley. Cook over medium heat, uncovered, for 1 hour, stirring frequently.

2. Add the tomatoes and continue cooking for 30 minutes. Add the rice, salt, and pepper. Lower the heat and simmer for 1 hour, stirring frequently until the beans are very soft. Taste for seasoning.

Spanish Black Bean Soup V GF

This delicious soup is rich in protein, fiber, vitamins C and A, and iron.

Serves 8

4 quarts water

1 pound organic black beans, picked over for stones

¼ cup extra-virgin olive oil

6 cloves garlic, coarsely chopped

1 large onion, coarsely chopped

3 organic bell peppers, seeded and coarsely chopped

4 small carrots, sliced

1 14-ounce can chopped tomatoes in juice or cherry tomatoes in juice, crushed by hand

1 small bunch organic Italian flat-leaf parsley, coarsely chopped (about a cup)

1 teaspoon fennel seeds

1 tablespoon smoked sweet paprika

Sea salt and pepper, to taste

1. Bring the water to a boil in a large covered pot over high heat. Add the beans, olive oil, garlic, and onion. Cover and reduce the heat to medium-high. Cook at a medium-high boil for about 30 minutes, stirring occasionally.

2. Add the remaining ingredients, cover and cook at a medium-high boil, stirring occasionally for about an hour and a quarter, or until the beans are tender to your preference. Taste for seasonings.

Spanish Butterbean and Vegetable Soup V GF

I love the flavors of Spanish foods, and this Spanish-style soup sings the praises of fennel seeds, smoked paprika, tomatoes, bell peppers, and saffron, with the health benefits of protein, fiber, and vitamin C. I serve this soup with my Parmesan-Herb Garlic Bread (page 82).

Serves 6

2½ quarts (10 cups) water

1 cup (½ pound) dry organic lima beans, sorted for stones and rinsed

2 organic bay leaves

6 cloves organic garlic, sliced

1 medium organic yellow onion, coarsely chopped

2 tablespoons organic Spanish extra-virgin olive oil

2 tablespoons organic butter or organic vegan buttery spread

1 cup chopped organic Italian flat-leaf parsley

3 large organic red bell peppers, seeded and cut into large dice

Sea salt and pepper

1 28-ounce can organic or San Marzano whole peeled tomatoes in juice, crushed by hand

2 teaspoons smoked paprika

1 teaspoon organic fennel seeds

A generous pinch of saffron, about 1 teaspoon

1 cup white wine

Finely grated zest from 1 organic orange

Freshly squeezed juice from 1 organic orange

1. Measure the water, the sorted lima beans, and the bay leaves into a large, heavy pot. Cover and set over high heat and bring to a boil. When it reaches a boil, reduce the heat to medium and cook at a medium boil for about 45 minutes, stirring occasionally, until the lima beans are crisp-tender when tested with a fork (scoop a bean into a big spoon, then test it with a fork).

2. Add the remaining ingredients, cover, and continue cooking (it will return to a boil in about 15 minutes), stirring occasionally for about 45 minutes to an hour, until the beans and peppers are tender-soft. Taste for seasonings.

Moroccan Chickpea Soup V GF

Serve this fiber- and flavor-packed soup with lemon wedges and warm wheat pita bread.

Serves 6

2 quarts water

1 pound dried organic chickpeas

3 tablespoons Moroccan or other olive oil

2 medium organic onions, coarsely chopped

1 teaspoon each ground coriander,
   cinnamon, and ground ginger

Pinch of saffron

2 28-ounce cans organic chopped tomatoes
   in juice

¼ cup chopped organic Italian flat-leaf
   parsley

Grated zest from 2 lemons

Salt and pepper, to taste

¼ cup organic brown rice

1. Combine all the ingredients except the brown rice in a large, heavy pot. Cover and place over high heat. Bring to a boil, then reduce the heat to medium. Cover and cook at a medium boil for 2 hours, stirring occasionally until the chickpeas are just tender.

2. Add the brown rice, cover, and continue cooking for about ½ hour, stirring occasionally until chickpeas and rice are tender. Taste for seasonings.

Egyptian Lentil Soup V GF

One of the best parts of our location across from a world-class university is that we are blessed with customers and staff from so many countries. They share their recipes, which gives us a peek into their traditions, and we love this. This flavorful soup is a perfectly delicious example.

Serves 6

3 quarts water

2 bay leaves

7 cloves garlic, coarsely chopped

1 pound lentils, sorted for stones

¼ cup extra-virgin olive oil

3 large yellow onions, cut in half, then sliced thin

1 tablespoon coriander

1 tablespoon cinnamon

Sea salt and pepper

1. Place the water, bay leaves, and garlic in a heavy pot over high heat; cover and bring to a boil. Add the lentils and reduce the heat to medium. Cover and cook the lentils at a medium boil, stirring occasionally, for about 45 minutes to an hour, until the lentils are tender. Meanwhile, heat the olive oil in a large skillet over medium heat. Add the onions and stir to coat with the oil. Cover and cook, for about 10 minutes, stirring frequently until the onions are tender and golden.

2. Stir in the coriander, cinnamon, and a little salt and pepper. Cover and continue cooking for a minute, stirring once or twice to prevent sticking. Turn the onions and any juices into the lentils, using a rubber spatula to scrape the juices from the skillet. Stir well to combine. Cover and continue cooking for about 5 minutes, stirring frequently until the lentils are soft-tender. Taste for seasoning.

> **"Claire, you taught people so much on how to eat. You have helped shaped people's lives."**
>
> —Jennifer Hughes, a longtime, favorite customer

Lentil Soup with Broccoli, Asparagus, and Escarole V GF

We make lentil soup every week at Claire's and we vary the ingredients, something that keeps both our customers and our soup-makers happy.

Serves 12

4 quarts water

1 pound organic green or brown lentils, picked over for stones

2 organic bay leaves

$1/3$ cup extra-virgin olive oil

5 large cloves organic garlic, sliced

2 large organic yellow onions, coarsely chopped

16 baby organic carrots, cut into quarters

1 28-ounce can organic whole peeled tomatoes in juice, crushed with your hands

1 teaspoon dried organic basil

3 teaspoons sea salt

1 large head organic escarole, well washed and chopped

1 large bunch organic asparagus, tough ends trimmed and discarded (or saved to make a broth), stalks and tips cut into ½-inch pieces

2 organic broccoli crowns, chopped

1. Place the water, lentils, and bay leaves in a large, heavy-bottomed pot. Cover and bring to a boil over high heat. When the mixture reaches a boil, reduce the heat to medium and add the olive oil, garlic, and onions. Stir well to combine. Cover and cook at a medium boil, stirring occasionally, for about 30 minutes, then add the carrots, tomatoes, basil, sea salt, and escarole. Stir to combine, cover, and continue cooking at a medium boil for about 20 minutes, stirring occasionally, until the lentils are nearly tender to your preference.

2. Add the cut asparagus and broccoli, stir to combine, cover, and continue cooking at a medium boil for about 20 minutes, stirring frequently, until the lentils and the vegetables are tender. Taste for seasonings.

Pasta e Fagioli *(Pasta and Bean Soup)* V GFO

Every Italian family has its own favorite recipe for *pasta e fagioli,* or "macaroni and beans," as my mom called it. This delicious dish is pureed smooth after it's cooked, and it tastes best with a slice of bread spread with a thin layer of peanut butter—this sounds unusual, but trust me on this one, it is truly wonderful and it's the way my father-in-law, and now my husband, eats his.

Serves 8

4 quarts water

1 pound dried Great Northern beans, picked over

3 tablespoons extra-virgin olive oil

4 large cloves garlic, coarsely chopped

½ cup finely chopped fresh sage

1 teaspoon dried sage

Salt and pepper, to taste

1 6-ounce can tomato paste

8 ounces ziti, cooked according to package directions

1. Measure the water and beans into a stockpot. Cover and bring to a boil over high heat. Lower the heat to medium-low and cook, covered, at a medium boil for 1 hour, stirring occasionally. Add the oil, garlic, fresh and dried sage, salt, pepper, and tomato paste. Stir well to combine. Cover and continue cooking at a medium boil, stirring occasionally, for another 1½ hours, or until the beans are soft.

2. Taste for seasonings. If you have a hand blender, use it to puree the soup until smooth. Or puree the soup in a food processor, being careful not to burn yourself. Return the pureed soup to the pot and reheat over low heat if desired.

3. To serve, ladle the soup into eight soup bowls and top each serving with one-eighth of the cooked ziti, using a spoon to push the ziti down into the soup. Sprinkle with freshly ground black pepper.

Tip: Use gluten-free pasta to make this recipe gluten free.

Escarole e Fagioli *(Escarole and Bean Soup)* V GF

This quintessentially Italian soup remains ever popular on our menu, something I'm happy for given it's so rich in protein, fiber, vitamins, and minerals. A bowl of this soup with good bread is all you need for a most satisfying lunch. It's how our beloved customers do it nearly every day at Claire's.

Serves 8

4 quarts water

12 ounces dry cannellini beans, picked over for stones and rinsed

8 large cloves garlic, sliced

½ small head Savoy cabbage, chopped

½ bunch organic celery, chopped

1 large fresh tomato, chopped, include juices

1 cup chopped Italian flat-leaf parsley

1 teaspoon fennel seeds

½ teaspoon crushed red pepper flakes

12 fresh basil leaves, chopped

⅓ cup extra-virgin olive oil

Salt and pepper

3 large heads escarole, well washed to remove any grit, and coarsely chopped

1. Bring the water to a boil in a large covered pot over high heat. Add the beans, garlic, cabbage, celery, tomato, parsley, fennel seeds, red pepper flakes, basil, olive oil, salt, and pepper. Stir well to combine. Cover and return to a boil, then reduce the heat to medium and cook, covered, for about 1½ hours, stirring occasionally, until the beans are barely tender.

2. Stir in the escarole, cover and continue cooking for about 30–45 minutes, stirring frequently, until the escarole and the beans are tender to your preference. Taste for seasonings. Before serving, set aside 4 cups of the soup for Panecotto (see note below).

Note: Panecotto (page 253) is a satisfying dish made using leftover Escarole e Fagioli and hard bread, a perfect example of the Italian way to never waste good food.

Claire's Classic

Escarole and Bean Soup V GF

Escarole can be found in the produce section of most supermarkets. The entire head (minus the stem) is delicious in soups. The tender pale green inner leaves also make a delicious salad.

Serves 8

4 quarts water

12 ounces Great Northern beans, picked over

8 large cloves garlic, minced

½ small head green cabbage, chopped

1 cup chopped parsley

1 teaspoon fennel seeds

½ teaspoon crushed red pepper flakes

10 leaves fresh basil, chopped or ½ teaspoon dried basil

½ cup plus 1 tablespoon olive oil

2 medium potatoes, diced

1 teaspoon black pepper

2 large heads escarole, chopped

Salt, to taste

1. Bring the water to a boil in a large covered pot. Add the beans, garlic, cabbage, parsley, fennel seeds, red pepper flakes, basil, and olive oil. Return to a boil, then lower the heat to medium and cook, uncovered, for 1½ hours, stirring every 5–10 minutes.

2. Add the potatoes, pepper, escarole and salt. Continue cooking over medium-low heat for 1 hour, stirring frequently, until the beans are soft and the broth is creamy. Taste for seasoning.

Spinach and Vegetable Soup
with Pastina V GFO

This soup pairs lots of incredibly healthy organic spinach with the little pasta stars of my childhood in a delicious soup that's on the table in about an hour. And for an extra treat and added nourishment, beat 3 eggs with about ¼ cup of grated Parmesan cheese and stir it into the soup during the last minute of cooking. Either way, it's a wonderful soup, my "go-to" soup for comfort.

Serves 6

3 tablespoons organic butter, buttery spread, or extra-virgin olive oil

2 shallots, coarsely chopped

3 cloves garlic, sliced

2 carrots, finely chopped

1 medium red onion, coarsely chopped

2 ripe tomatoes, coarsely chopped, including any juices

2 pounds organic baby spinach, rinsed and drained

Sea salt and black pepper

3 quarts water

1½ cups uncooked pastina (tiny star pasta)

Freshly grated Parmesan or pecorino Romano cheese (optional)

1. Melt the butter or buttery spread (or heat the olive oil) in a heavy pot over medium heat. Add the shallots, garlic, carrots, onion, and tomatoes with their juices. Cover and cook for about 5 minutes, stirring frequently until the vegetables soften a bit.

2. Add the spinach, and sprinkle with a little salt and pepper. Using two wooden spoons, toss to coat with the liquids. Cover and cook for about 10 minutes, stirring frequently until the spinach is wilted and has released most of its liquids.

3. Stir in the water and raise the heat to high. Cover and bring to a boil, stirring frequently. When it reaches a boil, after about 10 minutes, reduce the heat to low-medium and cook at a low-medium boil for about 20 minutes, stirring occasionally until a flavorful broth is achieved. Add the pastina into the boiling soup, stirring well to combine. Cook, uncovered, stirring frequently for about 10 minutes until the pastina is tender and the soup has thickened a bit.

4. Taste for seasonings. Serve with additional black pepper and grated Parmesan or Romano cheese on top, if desired.

   Tip: Use gluten-free pasta to make this recipe gluten free.

Claire's Classic

Minestrone I V

In our house, minestrone is always made with odd lots of vegetables—three or four carrots left in the bin, two or three remaining ribs of celery, a quarter head of cabbage—whatever vegetables we have on hand. Our minestrone is always delicious and interesting and contains an abundance of healthful, colorful vegetables.

Serves 8

¼ cup olive oil

1 small yellow onion, finely chopped

4 large cloves garlic, coarsely chopped

1 medium leek, white and pale green parts only, well washed and cut into ½-inch pieces

3 medium carrots, peeled and chopped

3 ribs celery, chopped

3 quarts water

1 12-ounce package navy pea beans, picked over

1 6-ounce can tomato paste

½ cup coarsely chopped Italian flat-leaf parsley

10 large fresh basil leaves

2 large bay leaves

1 tablespoon chopped fresh oregano or ½ teaspoon dried oregano

Salt and pepper

3 medium baking potatoes, peeled and cut into ½-inch cubes

2 small zucchini, cut into ½-inch pieces

¼ medium head green cabbage, coarsely chopped

12 green beans, trimmed and cut into 1-inch lengths

1 small head escarole (about 12 ounces), coarsely chopped

¼ cup pastina (tiny pasta bits)

1. Heat the oil in a large pot over medium-low heat. Add the onions, garlic, leek, carrots, and celery. Stir to coat the vegetables with the oil. Cover and cook, stirring occasionally, for 5 minutes, or until the vegetables have softened and released some of their moisture. Add the water and the navy pea beans. Cover, raise the heat to high, and bring to a boil. Lower the heat to medium-low, cover, and cook at a medium boil for 30 minutes, stirring occasionally.

2. Add the tomato paste, parsley, basil, bay leaves, oregano, a little salt, and pepper. Cover and continue cooking, stirring occasionally, for 30 minutes, or until the beans are barely tender. Add the potatoes, zucchini, cabbage, green beans, and escarole. Stir well to mix. Cover and continue cooking, stirring occasionally, for about 50 minutes, or until the beans are tender.

3. Stir in the pastina. Cover and continue cooking, stirring occasionally, for 6–10 minutes or until the pastina is soft. Taste for seasonings.

Claire's Classic

Minestrone II Ⅴ

Minestrones are tasty and robust and can be made with any number of different vegetable and beans. We sometimes add green peas, fresh corn, spinach, or kale, or use only chickpeas or navy (pea) beans. Serve with fresh crusty bread.

Serves 8

4 quarts water

½ pound red kidney beans, picked over

½ pound Great Northern beans, picked over

¼ pound lentils, picked over

1 small onion, chopped

6 cloves garlic, chopped

¼ cup chopped parsley

½ small cabbage, chopped

1 8-ounce can whole tomatoes, crushed with your hands

1 cup olive oil

¼ teaspoon dried oregano

¼ teaspoon dried basil

3 carrots, diced

½ bunch celery, diced

1 zucchini, diced

1 potato, diced

1 cup chopped broccoli florets

Salt, to taste

1 teaspoon black pepper

½ cup cooked tubettini (little pasta tubes)

1. Bring the water to a boil in a large pot. Add the kidney beans and cook, uncovered, over medium heat for 30 minutes. Add the Great Northern beans and continue cooking, stirring occasionally, for 1 hour. Add the lentils, onion, garlic, parsley, cabbage, tomatoes, olive oil, oregano, basil, carrots, and celery and continue cooking, uncovered, for 1 hour.

2. When the kidney beans are soft, add the zucchini, potato, broccoli, salt, and pepper and continue cooking over low heat for 30 minutes. Stir in the pasta and taste for seasoning.

Soy Chicken Minestrone with Barley ▣

This soup is really a whole-meal soup with enough substance for supper. It has it all—protein, complex carbohydrates, vitamins, and minerals, with lots of veggies so that you're bound to satisfy everyone.

Serves 8

¼ cup extra-virgin olive oil

1 large sweet onion, coarsely chopped

5 large cloves garlic, sliced

3 medium carrots, chopped

5 ribs organic celery, chopped

1 cup chopped Italian flat-leaf parsley

1 bay leaf

12 fresh basil leaves

2 tablespoons fresh leaves oregano or
   ½ teaspoon dried

Salt and pepper

1 28-ounce can whole peeled tomatoes
   in juice

2 quarts water

1 cup hulled barley

2 potatoes, cut into ½-inch cubes

½ head Savoy cabbage, chopped

12 green beans, cut into 1-inch lengths

2 small zucchini, cut into ½-inch pieces

1 12-ounce can organic kidney beans,
   drained

1 6-ounce package meatless chicken strips

1. Heat the oil in a large pot over medium-low heat. Add the onion, garlic, carrots, celery, parsley, bay leaf, basil, and oregano. Sprinkle with salt and pepper. Cover and cook, stirring occasionally, for about 5 minutes or until the vegetables have softened and released some of their moisture.

2. Put the tomatoes and juice into a blender cup, cover, and blend for about 10 seconds until nearly smooth. Add this and the water to the pot. Cover and raise the heat to high, and bring to a boil. Add the barley. Lower the heat to medium-low. Cover and cook at a medium boil for 30 minutes, stirring occasionally, until the barley is barely tender. Add the potatoes, cabbage, green beans, and zucchini. Stir well to mix. Cover and continue cooking, stirring occasionally, for about 25 minutes, until the potatoes are just tender.

3. Stir in the drained beans and the soy chicken strips. Cover and cook for about 3 minutes, stirring occasionally, until the beans and soy chicken strips are heated through. Taste for seasonings.

Irish Stew ⓥ

We often reserve this recipe (which uses traditional Irish ingredients of potatoes, cabbage, and bacon) and our Irish Soda Bread (page 324) for Saint Patrick's Day, and honestly we cannot figure out why. It's delicious, and our customers like it fine. Every year, we say "Let's make this dish throughout the year." Yet the recipe goes back into the box. This year we'll try again, hopefully with success.

Serves 6

2 tablespoons extra-virgin olive oil

2 tablespoons trans fat–free margarine or organic butter

2 large sweet organic onions, peeled and cut into quarters, then separated

4 medium carrots, cut into ½-inch slices

6 large organic Red Bliss potatoes, quartered

Salt and pepper, to taste

2 teaspoons dried sage

1 bay leaf

1 medium head Savoy cabbage, cored and coarsely chopped

2 5-ounce packages vegetarian Canadian bacon slices, cut into strips, separated

3 cups water

1. Heat the oil and the margarine or butter in an 8-quart Dutch oven or deep sauté pan over low heat. Add the onions, carrots, and potatoes. Sprinkle with salt, pepper, and sage. Add the bay leaf. Cover and cook for 20 minutes, stirring occasionally until the vegetables have released some of their liquids.

2. Add the cabbage, the vegetarian bacon, and 3 cups of water. Raise the heat to high, cover, and bring to a boil. (This will take about 8 minutes.) Lower the heat to medium-low and cook, covered, at a low boil, stirring occasionally, for about 20 minutes or until the potatoes are tender. Taste for seasonings.

French Peasant Soup GF

This is a hearty and savory stewlike soup. After thirty-five years, it remains a weekly favorite.

Serves 8

12 ounces Great Northern beans, picked over

1 small onion, chopped

8 cloves garlic, minced

½ cup olive oil

¼ teaspoon dried thyme

1 bay leaf

¼ teaspoon dried basil

6 carrots, chopped

½ bunch celery, chopped

¼ cup chopped parsley

4 tablespoons (½ stick) butter

1 small head green cabbage, chopped

5 medium potatoes, diced

Salt, to taste

1 teaspoon black pepper

1. Bring 4 quarts water to a boil in a large covered pot. Add the beans, reduce the heat to medium, and cook, uncovered, for 30 minutes, stirring frequently.

2. Add the onion, garlic, olive oil, thyme, bay leaf, basil, carrots, celery, parsley, butter, and cabbage. Bring to a boil, then reduce the heat to low and simmer for 1½ hours, stirring frequently, until the beans are nearly tender.

3. Add the potatoes, salt, and pepper. Continue simmering for 30–45 minutes, until the beans are very soft and the soup is thick. Taste for seasoning.

French Vegetable Bisque GF

This is our vegetarian version of a rich lobster bisque, and it is a favorite among the staff. Everyone loves its flavor—creamy and spicy.

Serves 6

8 tablespoons (1 stick) butter, cut into pieces

1 large onion, chopped

4 shallots, chopped

¼ cup chopped parsley

½ teaspoon dried thyme

4 carrots, chopped

½ bunch celery, chopped

1 large potato, diced

1 cup white wine

2 28-ounce cans whole tomatoes, crushed with your hands

1 zucchini, chopped

1 cup brown rice, uncooked

½ bunch broccoli, bottom 1 inch removed and discarded, chopped

1 quart milk

1 cup heavy cream

2 or 3 shakes Tabasco

Salt to taste

1 teaspoon black pepper

1. Melt the butter in a large uncovered pot. Add the onions, shallots, parsley, and thyme. Cover and cook over low heat, stirring frequently, for 15 minutes or until onions are tender. Add the carrots, celery, potato, wine, tomatoes, and zucchini. Bring to a boil over medium heat, uncovered. Lower the heat, stir in the rice, and simmer, stirring frequently about 1 hour until the rice is cooked.

2. Stir in the broccoli and continue cooking for 15 minutes. Stir in the milk, cream, Tabasco, salt, and pepper. Taste for seasoning.

Dandelion Soup

This soup is even more delicious the next day after it has had time for the flavors to meld.

Serves 6–8

2 tablespoons extra-virgin olive oil

2 tablespoons organic butter (or you may substitute 2 tablespoons extra-virgin olive oil)

2 organic scallions, white and green parts, coarsely chopped

1 large tomato, coarsely chopped (reserve juices)

½ organic jalapeño pepper, seeded and finely chopped

Sea salt and pepper, to taste

2 large bunches of organic dandelion greens, about 2 pounds, well washed, bottom 2 inches of stems cut off and discarded, leaves and remaining stems cut into 2-inch pieces

8 cups water

¼ pound whole wheat spaghetti, strands broken into quarters (hold a small bunch of spaghetti strands at a time in your hands and break into fourths)

3 organic eggs, beaten lightly

Grated Asiago or pecorino Romano cheese (optional)

1. Heat the oil and butter in a large, heavy pot over low-medium heat. Add the onions, tomato and its juices, jalapeño pepper, salt, and pepper. Cover and cook for about 10 minutes, stirring occasionally until the onions and tomatoes have softened and released some of their liquids.

2. Add the dandelion greens and sprinkle with additional salt. Using tongs, turn the greens to coat with the oil. Cover and cook for 10 minutes, stirring occasionally, until the greens are wilted and have released some of their liquids.

3. Stir in 8 cups of water, cover the pot, and raise the heat to high. Bring to a boil. (This will take about 5 minutes.) Reduce the heat to medium. Cover and cook at a low-medium boil, stirring occasionally, for about 20 minutes.

4. Add the broken spaghetti, cover, and cook for about 7 minutes, stirring occasionally until the spaghetti is barely tender.

5. Stir in the beaten eggs and cook, uncovered, stirring frequently for 1–2 minutes, until the eggs are just set. Taste for seasonings. Serve hot, with grated cheese on top, if desired.

Summer Vegetable Soup V GFO

I like to serve this healthful soup with a simple frittata (a baked Italian omelette) and good bread. It's a wonderful summer meal to enjoy outside on the porch.

Serves 8

3 tablespoons butter or trans fat–free and dairy-free buttery spread

2 tablespoons extra-virgin olive oil

2 large organic sweet onions, coarsely chopped

2 large cloves organic garlic, sliced

Sea salt and pepper, to taste

8 small organic carrots, cut into ¼-inch slices

4 large ribs organic celery, with leaves, cut into ¼-inch slices

3 large ripe organic heirloom tomatoes, chopped, including juices

3 quarts water

1 cup chopped organic Italian flat-leaf parsley

10 fresh organic basil leaves

2 bay leaves

2 large bunches organic Toscano kale, about 1½ pounds, cut into 1-inch slices

3 medium organic potatoes, diced

5 medium zucchini, cut into ½-inch pieces

²/₃ cup tiny pasta bits, pastina or acini de pepe

1. Heat the butter and oil in a large pot over medium low heat. Add the onions and garlic, then sprinkle with sea salt and pepper. Stir to coat. Cook, stirring occasionally, for 5 minutes, or until the onion is softened but not brown.

2. Add the carrots, celery, tomato, water, parsley, basil, and bay leaves. Raise the heat to high, cover, and bring to a boil. Lower the heat to medium-low and cook, covered, at a medium-low boil for abut 20 minutes, stirring occasionally. Add the kale, and stir well to combine. Cover and continue cooking, stirring occasionally, for another 30 minutes or until the celery is crisp-tender. Add the potatoes and zucchini. Cover and continue cooking, stirring frequently, for about 15 minutes, or until the potatoes are barely tender. Stir in the pasta bits, cover, and continue cooking, stirring frequently, for about 8 minutes or until the pasta is tender. Taste for seasonings.

Tip: Use gluten-free pasta to make this recipe gluten free.

Fall Renewal Soup V GF

This healthful and delicious soup is a great way to start the fall season and to boost your immune system before the cold and flu season starts. I think we can use a little renewal every season, so I make this soup often. It's loaded with protein, fiber, iron, and vitamin A, and the kale, cauliflower, and broccoli lend important cruciferous power that may protect us from many cancers. The drizzle of organic flax oil brings yet another powerful immune booster, from the omega-3 fatty acids.

Serves 8

1 pound green split peas, picked over for stones and rinsed

1 large sweet onion, coarsely chopped

4 cloves garlic, sliced

4 medium carrots, coarsely chopped

1 bunch Italian flat-leaf parsley, coarsely chopped

Sea salt

Pepper

1 bunch kale, thick stems and ribs removed, leaves torn into small pieces

4 tablespoons canola oil

1 head cauliflower, core removed and florets cut into small pieces

1 bunch broccoli, stems removed and saved for another dish, florets cut into small pieces

8 large basil leaves

Organic flax oil, if desired

1. Bring 4 quarts of water to a boil in a covered pot over high heat. When the water reaches a boil, add the split peas, onion, garlic, carrots, parsley, a little sea salt and pepper, the kale, and the canola oil. Reduce the heat to medium and cook at a medium boil, covered, for about 40 minutes, stirring frequently, until the peas have broken down.

2. Add the cauliflower and the broccoli. Tear the basil leaves into pieces and add to the soup. Stir well to combine. Cover and continue to cook at a medium boil (the soup will return to a boil after about 5–8 minutes), stirring frequently for about 15 minutes, until the cauliflower is tender to your preference. Taste for seasonings.

3. When serving, ladle into bowls, then drizzle each bowl with a teaspoon of organic flax oil.

Pasta, Potato, and Green Pea Soup V GFO

At first, our customers were a bit puzzled that we would combine pasta with potatoes, but really, it's a classic Italian combination, and something my beloved mother made frequently. And it's so beautiful and delicious that everyone's up for it.

Serves 6

3 quarts water

2 28-ounce cans whole peeled tomatoes, crushed with your hands

2 large yellow onions, sliced

6 cloves garlic, chopped

¼ cup chopped Italian flat-leaf parsley

5 large leaves fresh basil

¼ cup extra-virgin olive oil

Salt and pepper

6 medium potatoes, organic Russet or other, diced

1 10-ounce box frozen green peas

¼ pound cooked medium pasta shells

1. Bring the water to a boil in a large covered pot over high heat. Add the tomatoes, onions, garlic, and the parsley. Chop the basil and add to the pot along with the olive oil, salt, and pepper. Stir well to combine. Reduce the heat to medium and cook, uncovered, at a medium boil, stirring frequently for 30 minutes until it reduces slightly.

2. Add the potatoes and continue cooking for about 20 minutes, stirring occasionally, until the potatoes are soft. Add the peas and continue cooking for about 5 minutes, stirring once or twice until the peas are defrosted and heated through. Stir in the cooked pasta. Taste for seasonings.

Tip: Use gluten-free pasta to make this recipe gluten free.

Pumpkin and Sweet Potato Soup V GF

I spiced this beautiful soup with a little curry, turmeric, and nutmeg. The combination is loaded with vitamins A and C, fiber, iron, and protein, and it's antioxidant-rich, which can help boost your immune system. You cannot ask for much more than that—except maybe to share it with those you love.

Serves 6 plus

2 tablespoons extra-virgin olive oil, divided

1 large sweet local onion, coarsely chopped

4 large cloves local garlic, sliced

Sea salt and pepper

2 large organic sweet potatoes, peeled and cut into medium cubes

1 15-ounce can organic pumpkin

2 teaspoons organic curry powder

1 teaspoon organic turmeric

¼ teaspoon ground nutmeg

2 15-ounce cans organic chickpeas

1 large organic apple, Fuji or other

1. Heat 1 tablespoon of the oil in a heavy, 6-quart pot over medium heat. Add the onion and garlic. Sprinkle with sea salt and pepper. Cover and cook for about 7 minutes, stirring occasionally until the onions have softened and are just golden in color and have released some of their liquids.

2. Add the sweet potatoes, pumpkin, curry powder, turmeric, and nutmeg. Add 2 quarts of water. Stir well to combine. Raise the heat to high, and cover the pot. Bring to a boil, stirring occasionally. This should take about 12–15 minutes. Once the soup reaches a boil, reduce the heat to medium and continue cooking at a low-medium boil, stirring occasionally for about 20 minutes until the sweet potatoes are soft.

3. Using a potato masher, smash the sweet potatoes until they break down into little bits. Drain the cans of chickpeas into a colander set into the sink, then rinse them under cold water and drain them again. Add the drained chickpeas to the soup.

4. Core the apple, then chop it into small pieces. Add this to the soup. Stir well to combine. Cover and continue cooking for about 5 minutes, stirring occasionally until the chickpeas are heated through. Drizzle the remaining tablespoon of olive oil over the soup and stir to combine. Taste for seasonings.

Curried Carrot-Apple Soup V GF

My mom has a handy tip for a shortcut when preparing soups that require lots of cut vegetables—she cuts them a day in advance and covers them with water, then refrigerates them and uses the water that covers them in the recipe. (Vegetables that get cooked together can be stored together.)

Serves 8

2 tablespoons organic and trans fat–free margarine spread

2 tablespoons extra-virgin olive oil

1 large yellow organic onion, coarsely chopped

3 large cloves garlic, sliced

4 medium carrots, cut into medium dice

3 ribs organic celery, cut into ½-inch slices

1 large butternut squash, peeled, seeded, cut into medium dice

1 tablespoon garam masala powder, found in the spice section at the market

1 teaspoon turmeric

1 2-inch piece fresh ginger, peeled and finely chopped

Sea salt and pepper

1 bay leaf

1 35-ounce can Italian San Marzano whole peeled tomatoes in juice, crushed with your hands

1 13.5-ounce can light coconut milk

6 cups water

3 large organic Yukon Gold potatoes, cut into medium dice

2 organic apples, Gala or other, cored and cut into small dice

10 large fresh organic basil leaves

¼ cup chopped organic cilantro

2 cups cooked organic brown rice

1. Melt the margarine and olive oil in a large, heavy pot over medium-low heat. Add the onion, garlic, carrots, celery, butternut squash, garam masala, turmeric, ginger, a little salt and pepper, and the bay leaf. Cover and cook, stirring occasionally, for 20 minutes, or until the vegetables have released some of their moisture.

2. Add the tomatoes, coconut milk, and water. Stir well to combine. Raise the heat to high and bring to a boil. (This should take about 10 minutes.) Lower the heat to medium, cover, and cook at a medium boil, stirring occasionally, for 30 minutes.

3. Add the potatoes, apples, basil, cilantro, and rice. Stir to combine. Cover and continue cooking at a medium boil, stirring occasionally, for about 15 minutes, or until the potatoes are tender. Taste for seasonings.

Swiss Onion Soup

This soup should be called Connecticut Onion Soup, because I source almost every ingredient right here in this state, grown by local farmers. Top the soup with Garlic Croutons (page 43).

Serves 4–6

4 tablespoons organic butter, sliced into a few pats

6 large yellow onions (about 3 pounds), cut in half and then sliced into thin ribs

5 large cloves garlic, coarsely chopped

1 large bay leaf or 2 small leaves

1 cup chopped organic Italian flat-leaf parsley

Sea salt and pepper

½ cup organic unbleached all-purpose flour

4 cups water

4 cups organic 2 percent milk

¼ teaspoon ground nutmeg

¾ cup grated organic Parmesan cheese

4 ounces organic swiss cheese, coarsely grated, about 1 cup

1. Melt the butter in a heavy pot. Add the onions, garlic, bay leaf, parsley, and a little sea salt and pepper. Cover and cook over a low-medium heat for about 30 minutes, stirring occasionally until the onions are very soft but not brown.

2. Sprinkle the flour evenly over the onions, stirring well to combine. Raise the heat to medium and continue cooking, stirring frequently (you are making a roux), for about 3 minutes, until the mixture is blended and there is no visible uncooked flour remaining.

3. Stir in the water, milk, and nutmeg. Continue cooking, stirring frequently, for about 15 minutes, until the soup is slightly thickened and close to a simmer. Tiny bubbles will begin to form around the edges of the soup. Stir in the Parmesan and swiss cheeses and stir to combine for about a minute, until the cheeses have melted into the soup. Taste for seasonings.

Claire's Classic

My Mom's Onion Soup V GF

This is what my mom made for us at the first sign of a cold, and as they say, Mom always knows best. Besides, this medicine is not at all hard to swallow.

Serves 6

½ cup olive oil

10 large onions, chopped

½ cup chopped parsley

3 quarts water

Salt, to taste

1 teaspoon black pepper

1. Heat the olive oil in an uncovered large pot over low heat. Add the onions and parsley. Cover and cook over low heat, stirring frequently, for 30 minutes, until the onions are golden brown.

2. Add the water and raise the heat to medium. Cook covered, stirring frequently, for 30 minutes. Add the salt and pepper. Taste for seasoning.

Garlic Croutons V

Make a big batch of these crunchy croutons with leftover bread and use them to top a salad or soup, or just have them as a snack. (They're terrific dipped into a bean dip, too.) We like big croutons in our family, but if you prefer a smaller size, just cut the cubes into ½-inch squares. Store cooled croutons in a covered container in a cool, dry place for up to a week.

Makes about 10 cups

6 1-inch-thick slices good Italian or French bread, cut into 1-inch cubes (about 10 cups)

2 tablespoons extra-virgin olive oil

4 cloves organic garlic, finely chopped

1 teaspoon dried organic oregano

Sea salt and pepper

1. Preheat the oven to 375°F. Line a cookie sheet with parchment paper or spray it with olive oil spray.

2. Place the cut bread cubes in a shallow bowl. Drizzle the olive oil evenly over the top, then toss well to coat, using your hands or two wooden spoons. Scatter the garlic over the top, sprinkle the oregano or Italian herb mix evenly over the top, then sprinkle the cubes lightly with sea salt and pepper. Toss well to coat. Taste for seasoning.

3. Turn the coated cubes onto the prepared cookie sheet, arranging the cubes in a single layer. Bake for 35–40 minutes, until the cubes are firm and dry.

Fresh Corn Soup V GF

This creamy soup is so simple to prepare and is the essence of summer's end. We make it with freshly harvested corn and potatoes, both grown by local farmers.

Serves 8 (2-cup servings)

Sea salt

9 ears locally grown corn, yellow, white, or a combination

1 tablespoon organic buttery spread

4 medium locally grown organic potatoes, peeled and diced

Pepper, to taste

1 large locally grown organic red, yellow, or orange bell pepper, seeded and finely chopped

6 tablespoons organic low-fat sour cream (optional)

1. Bring 18 cups of lightly salted water to a boil in an 8-quart covered pot over high heat.

2. Meanwhile, shuck the corn and, using a sharp knife, remove the kernels from the cobs, reserving the cobs and the kernels. You should have about 6 cups of kernels. When the water reaches a boil, add the buttery spread and the corncobs to the water. Cover and cook at a rapid boil, stirring occasionally for 30 minutes, until the water turns a pale yellow and is fragrant. Place a large plate by the stove, and using tongs, carefully remove the corncobs from the water, then discard them. Add the reserved corn kernels and the diced potatoes. Add a little pepper. Stir to combine. Cover and continue boiling for another 30 minutes, stirring occasionally, until the potatoes have broken down into small pieces.

3. Taste for seasoning. Remove from heat. Carefully ladle the soup into a blender cup to fill it only half full. (Do not fill the blender cup all the way because hot liquids expand as you blend them and you'll get burned.) Set an empty pot by the blender. Put an oven mitt on the hand that you'll use to cover the blender cup to protect yourself from burning your hand should any hot soup splatter the cover. Cover the blender, keeping one hand on top to hold down the cover, and blend the soup first on low speed for about 10 seconds, then on high speed for about 30 seconds until it is smooth and creamy.

4. Pour the blended soup into the empty pot. Continue blending the rest of the soup. Serve the soup hot, topped with a little of the chopped bell pepper and with a spoonful of sour cream swirled in if you desire. Sprinkle with additional black pepper, if desired.

Celery Velvet Soup with Pine Nuts

If you love celery, as I do, you'll love this soup. Be sure to use the leaves from the celery, because the flavor from the leaves is even more intense than the stalks.

Makes about 5 cups, can be doubled

2 tablespoons organic dairy-free buttery spread

1 large bunch organic celery, cut into ½-inch slices (leaves included), about 6 cups

1 large clove garlic, finely chopped

1 bay leaf

Sea salt and pepper

1 teaspoon herbes de Provence

1 teaspoon dried dill or 1 tablespoon fresh dill, finely chopped

4 cups water

¼ cup lightly toasted pine nuts (optional)

1. Melt the buttery spread in a heavy 4-quart pot over medium-high heat. Add the celery, garlic, and bay leaf. Sprinkle with a little sea salt and pepper. Stir to coat. Cover and cook for about 15 minutes, stirring occasionally, until the celery has released some of its liquids. Add the herbes de Provence, the dill, and the water. Stir to combine. Raise the heat to high, cover, and bring to a boil. This should take about 10 minutes.

2. When the mixture reaches a boil, reduce the heat to medium and cook, covered, at a medium boil for about 20 minutes, stirring occasionally until the celery is soft. Taste for seasonings. Transfer about a cup of the soup to a blender. Put the cover on the blender cup then cover the top with a kitchen towel. Wearing oven mitts to protect your hands, pulse several times until blended smooth. Pour this into a clean pot, and repeat to blend the remaining soup. Taste for seasonings. Serve topped with a tablespoon or so of toasted pine nuts, if using.

3. To toast the pine nuts: Arrange the pine nuts in a small skillet and place over medium-high heat. Cook, moving the pan, rotating it to shake the pine nuts and turn them, for about 2–3 minutes until they are golden brown, but not burned. It's always tempting to pop a pine nut right into your mouth, but wait a minute or two before tasting because they will be really hot.

Caution: Hot liquids expand when blending, so whenever blending hot liquids, always protect yourself from a burn by filling the blender cup less than one-third full, covering the lid with a kitchen towel, and wearing oven mitts. Also, keep your face away from the blender top just in case the hot liquid leaps up over the lid.

Luxurious, Creamy Soups without the Cream

While a nice bowl of hot soup is always a welcome sight during the winter months, soup really has no season for us in our family. Instead, it's a staple for lunch or as a first course to supper. It always has been. From the time I was a little girl, I can remember my mother serving my brothers and me soup—and us eating it—nearly every single day (even during scorching hot weather!). Well, her persistence stuck. My brothers and I continue to be "good soup eaters" thanks to her example. And this is a good thing. Soup is a great way to eat your vegetables, beans, and grains. And because it's eaten by the spoonful, we tend to take our time eating it, thereby giving our bodies time to realize we're full and making us less apt to overeat.

Although I love most soups, creamy soups were never particularly attractive to me. I never liked it that the cream often masked the flavor of the vegetables (I really love vegetables), and I don't care for that creamy feel that hot soup leaves on my palate. Besides, I'd rather save my saturated fats for ice cream!

But all of that changed a couple of weeks ago. It was one of those days when I was sure that I didn't have anything at home to eat—you know that feeling—but then I saw that I had a big bunch of beautiful organic celery. That started the idea for my creamy Celery Velvet Soup (page 45). I made it with the basic staples I always have on hand. Frank and I really enjoyed it, which lead to the Broccoli Velvet Soup (page 47). Both are delicious, healthful, quick and easy to prepare, and low in calories. And, I love the crunchy contrast of toasted pine nuts, oyster crackers, or Garlic Croutons (page 43) in the smooth soup. I hope you'll enjoy these soups, as well.

Broccoli Velvet Soup V GF

This "creamy" and rich soup is luscious yet really low in fat. And it's incredibly healthful, with the potential for cancer prevention from the broccoli, the cruciferous vegetable sweetheart of the plant kingdom.

Makes about 7 ½ cups

2 tablespoons organic dairy-free buttery spread

1 tablespoon extra-virgin olive oil

1 large organic red or yellow onion, coarsely chopped

1 large bunch broccoli, tough bottom stems trimmed and discarded, coarsely chopped

Sea salt and pepper

6 cups water

½ teaspoon curry powder

½ teaspoon turmeric

1 cup oyster crackers or Garlic Croutons (optional)

1. Melt the spread and the olive oil in a heavy 8-quart pot over medium-high heat. Add the onion, broccoli, and a little sea salt and pepper. Stir to coat the vegetables with the oil. Cover and cook for about 10–12 minutes, stirring occasionally until the broccoli and onions have softened. Add the 6 cups of water, the curry powder, and the turmeric. Stir to combine. Cover and raise the heat to high. Bring to a boil. This should take about 12 minutes.

2. When the soup reaches a boil, reduce the heat to medium and cook at a medium boil for about 15 minutes, stirring occasionally until the broccoli is soft. Taste for seasonings. Transfer about a cup of the soup to a blender. Put the cover on the blender cup, then cover the top with a kitchen towel. While wearing oven mitts to protect your hands, pulse several times until blended smooth. Pour this into a clean pot and repeat to blend the remaining soup. Taste for seasonings.

3. Serve topped with oyster crackers or Garlic Croutons (page 43), if desired.

Cream of Tomato and Asparagus Soup GF

We are lucky to have the largest asparagus grower in New England right here in Connecticut, and we take full advantage of the season by cooking with asparagus every day during the late spring and summer months.

Serves 8

3 tablespoons organic butter

2 medium spring onions, coarsely chopped

4 cloves organic garlic, coarsely chopped

2 organic shallots, thinly sliced

1 large bunch local asparagus, tough stems trimmed, remaining stems and tips cut into ¼-inch slices

Sea salt and pepper

1 35-ounce can San Marzano tomatoes in juice, squeezed with your hands

4 cups water

2 bay leaves

1 quart organic half-and-half or organic whole milk

1 tablespoon chopped fresh tarragon

Pinch of nutmeg

1. Place the butter, onions, garlic, shallots, and asparagus in a 6-quart pot over medium heat. Sprinkle with sea salt and pepper. Cook, stirring occasionally, for about 7–10 minutes, until the vegetables are softened.

2. Add the tomatoes, water, and bay leaves. Cover, raise the heat to high, and bring to a boil. When the mixture reaches a boil, reduce the heat to medium and cook, covered, at a medium boil for about 30 minutes, stirring occasionally until the asparagus is tender-soft.

3. Gradually stir in the half-and-half, tarragon, and nutmeg. Continue cooking for about 5 minutes, stirring frequently until heated through. Taste for seasonings.

Fresh Tomato Soup with Garlic and Fresh Cheese Toasts

Make this soup when the tomatoes are ripe and in season.

Serves 4

2 tablespoons extra-virgin olive oil

1 medium yellow onion, coarsely chopped

1 large clove garlic, finely chopped

10 large, ripe plum tomatoes, coarsely chopped, including juices

¼ cup coarsely chopped Italian flat-leaf parsley

Sea salt and pepper

6 cups water

1 tablespoon chopped fresh dill

   Garlic and Fresh Cheese Toasts:

1 tablespoon extra-virgin olive oil

1 large clove garlic, finely chopped

Sea salt and freshly ground black pepper

4 ½-inch-thick slices Italian bread

3 tablespoons fresh cheese, such as local goat's cheese

1. Heat the oil in a medium pot over medium-low heat. Add the onion, garlic, tomatoes, and parsley. Sprinkle lightly with salt and pepper. Stir to mix. Cover and cook, stirring occasionally, for 15 minutes, or until the tomatoes are soft and have released their juices.

2. Add the water. Raise the heat to high, cover, and bring to a boil. Remove the cover and lower the heat to medium. Cook, uncovered, at a medium boil, stirring occasionally for about 45 minutes, or until the soup is reduced slightly. Stir in the dill. Taste for seasonings.

3. While the soup is cooking, prepare the toasts.

4. Preheat the oven to 350°F. Measure the olive oil into a small bowl. Add the garlic and a little salt and pepper. Arrange the slices of Italian bread, cut side down, on a cookie sheet. Bake the bread for about 10 minutes, then turn the slices over and bake the other side for about 10 minutes or until just firm to the touch.

5. Remove from the oven and, using a small metal spatula, spread a couple of teaspoons of the cheese on one side of each toast, then spoon a little of the garlic and oil mixture evenly over each. Sprinkle a little pepper onto each toast if desired.

6. Serve the toasts with the soup, or place a toast in each soup bowl and ladle the soup over the toasts.

Claire's Classic

Tomato-Barley Soup

This ever-popular soup is quick, easy to prepare, and delicious, and it remains a favorite at Claire's even after thirty-five years.

Serves 6

2 quarts water

2 28-ounce cans whole tomatoes, crushed with your hands

¼ cup chopped parsley

2 large onions, chopped

5 cloves garlic, chopped

¼ cup olive oil

¼ teaspoon dried dill weed

¼ teaspoon dried basil

½ pound barley

Salt, to taste

1 teaspoon black pepper

Bring the water to a boil in a large covered pot. Add the remaining ingredients and cook, uncovered, over medium heat, stirring frequently, for 1¼ hours or until the barley is soft and the soup is thick. Taste for seasoning.

Chilled Heirloom Tomato Soup with Ricotta, Basil Pesto, and Pine Nuts GF

During the summer, I grow most of our organic heirloom tomatoes for Claire's. And every year I expand the gardens because of recipes like this one, where the quality of the tomatoes is integral to the flavor. This year I hope to exceed my record of producing 3,000 pounds of tomatoes!

Make this pretty and absolutely delicious soup straight from the garden or the farm and enjoy the glorious bounty of the season.

Serves 6

2 tablespoons extra-virgin olive oil

1 large shallot, chopped

10 large, assorted locally grown heirloom tomatoes, cut into wedges

1 large orange bell pepper, seeded and chopped

4 large leaves basil

Salt and pepper, to taste

½ cup ricotta cheese, preferably hand-packed

¾ cup basil pesto, fresh or a good store-bought variety

¼ cup toasted Pine Nuts

1. Heat the olive oil in a large pot over medium-high heat. Add the shallot and cook for about 1 minute, stirring frequently until softened. Add the tomatoes, bell pepper, basil leaves, salt, and pepper. Cover and cook for about 15 minutes, stirring occasionally until the tomatoes are soft and have given off much of their liquid. Remove from the heat.

2. Turn into the bowl of a food processor fitted with a metal blade. Cover and process for about 20 seconds until blended. Taste for seasonings. Pour into a bowl and set aside until the mixture reaches room temperature, then refrigerate for a couple of hours until chilled; you may refrigerate overnight if desired.

3. To serve, ladle 1 cup of soup into each of six shallow rimmed bowls. Spoon a heaping tablespoon of ricotta in the center of each bowl. Spoon 2 tablespoons of pesto on top of the ricotta in each bowl. Scatter several toasted Pine Nuts (page 46) evenly over the soup.

Wilted Spinach, Crunchy Broccoli, Pickled Red Onion, and Wasabi Wraps VO GFO

I love these wraps! They have lots of textures from the crunchy vegetables and wilted spinach. And the pickled onions and wasabi mayonnaise add a terrific burst of flavors, sweet and sour and with just enough heat to get your attention.

Serves 6–8

1 medium red onion, cut Into thin rings, separated

1 cup white vinegar

¼ cup sugar

Sea salt and pepper

1½ cups steamed broccoli florets

½ each, small red, yellow, and green bell peppers, seeded and diced

2 teaspoons flax oil with lemon, or canola oil

2 teaspoons extra-virgin olive oil

2 medium shallots, finely chopped

1½ pounds baby spinach, rinsed and drained

6 10-inch spinach or wheat tortillas

⅓ cup wasabi mayonnaise

1. To prepare pickled red onions, combine the onion, vinegar, sugar, and a little salt and pepper in a bowl. Toss well to combine. Set aside.

2. In a bowl, combine the steamed broccoli florets and the diced bell peppers. Drizzle the oil evenly over the top. Sprinkle lightly with salt and pepper. Toss to coat. Taste for seasonings. Set aside.

3. To wilt the spinach, heat the olive oil in a large, deep skillet over low-medium heat. Add the shallots and a little salt and pepper. Stir to coat. Cook for a minute, stirring frequently until softened and golden. Add the spinach and sprinkle with a little salt and pepper. Using two wooden spoons, toss to coat with the oil. Cook for a minute, tossing frequently until the spinach wilts to your preference. Taste for seasonings.

4. To assemble the wraps, lay one tortilla on a cutting board. Using a rubber spatula, spread 2 teaspoons of the wasabi mayonnaise evenly over the tortilla. Scatter one-sixth of the wilted spinach evenly over the tortilla, then scatter one-sixth of the steamed broccoli florets and peppers evenly over the spinach. Using tongs or a fork, lift out one-sixth of the pickled onions from the liquid, shaking off as much liquid as possible and leaving it behind in the bowl, and scatter the onions evenly over the vegetables. Starting at one end, roll the tortilla jelly-roll fashion. Cut in half diagonally. Transfer to a large platter to serve. Assemble the remaining sandwiches.

Tips: Use vegan mayonnaise to make this recipe vegan. Use gluten-free tortillas to make this recipe gluten free.

Monte Cristo

Who doesn't love French toast? And when you turn it into a delicious, spinach-packed sandwich, it's a real treat for everyone. Try it for your next brunch. (Note: Recipe can be doubled.)

Serves 2

2 teaspoons extra-virgin olive oil

1 10-ounce bag organic baby spinach

Salt and pepper

4 slices multigrain bread

¼ cup good ricotta cheese, hand-packed or other

12 sweet grape tomatoes, cut in half lengthwise

¼ pound fresh mozzarella cheese, diced, or ½ cup shredded mozzarella

2 organic eggs

2 tablespoons water

2 tablespoons organic butter

Powdered sugar for dusting sandwiches

¼ cup raspberry preserves

1. Heat the olive oil in a large skillet over medium heat. Add the spinach, sprinkle with salt and pepper. Cook for about 1 minute, using tongs to turn the spinach until it wilts. Transfer the spinach to a plate. Carefully wipe out the skillet for later in the recipe.

2. Lay 2 slices of bread on a plate. Arrange the spinach evenly on the 2 slices of bread. Using a teaspoon, dollop the ricotta cheese evenly over the spinach. Arrange 12 of the grape tomato halves over the spinach. Scatter the mozzarella over the top. Top with the other 2 slices of bread. Lightly press the sandwich together using your hand.

3. Crack the eggs into a shallow bowl. Add the water and whisk to blend. Season with salt and pepper. Dip the sandwiches into the eggs to coat evenly.

4. Melt the butter in the skillet over low-medium heat. Arrange the sandwiches in the skillet and cook for 2–3 minutes, until the egg on the underside is cooked and golden brown, then using two spatulas, carefully turn the sandwich to cook the other side for about 2 minutes until the egg is cooked and golden brown. Transfer to a clean plate. Cut each sandwich in half on the diagonal. Dust with powdered sugar and serve with raspberry preserves for dipping.

Claire's Classic

Eggplant Parmigiana Sandwich

This standby sells quickly whenever we offer it at Claire's. I sometimes eat the fried eggplant cutlets, without marinara sauce and cheese, in a sandwich with just a squeeze of lemon. It's a delicious change and travels well.

Makes 4 sandwiches

---

1 medium eggplant, peeled and sliced into
   ¼-inch rounds

1 cup flour for dredging the eggplant

6 eggs, slightly beaten

¼ cup chopped parsley

Salt, to taste

½ teaspoon black pepper

½ cup soybean or vegetable oil for frying

1 loaf Italian or French bread, cut into
   4 pieces and then split lengthwise

1 cup heated marinara sauce or any
   good tomato sauce

¼ cup grated Parmesan

4 ounces shredded mozzarella

1. Preheat the oven to 350°F. Stack the eggplant slices on a plate and set aside. Measure the flour into a shallow bowl and set aside. Beat the eggs in a bowl, stir in the parsley, and sprinkle with salt and pepper. Beat together lightly. Heat the oil in a large nonstick skillet over low heat. After 2 minutes, test the oil by sprinkling in a pinch of flour, which will sizzle if the oil is hot. Using a fork, dredge a slice of eggplant in the flour, coating both sides in the egg mixture. Lightly shake off the excess and place in the heated oil. Cook each side until golden brown, 1 or 2 minutes per side. Drain on a plate lined with a double thickness of paper towels.

2. Spread each piece of bread with a little marinara sauce. Divide the eggplant slices among the bottom slices of bread, topping each with a little marinara sauce, grated Parmesan, and shredded mozzarella. Cover each sandwich with a top slice of bread. Arrange the sandwiches on a cookie sheet and bake for 10 to 15 minutes, until the cheese melts

The Club Sandwich VO

This is one of my favorite "go-to" foods to take to the beach because it can be made ahead and because all of my non-vegetarian family and friends love it, too. It's that yummy!

Serves 4

3–4 tablespoons good mayonnaise

8 slices good whole grain bread, toasted

4 large leaves local organic romaine leaves, torn in half

8 strips meatless bacon, cooked according to package directions

1 large or 2 medium local organic heirloom tomatoes, sliced

1 small local red onion, sliced into rings

1 medium ripe avocado, pitted and sliced

1 12-ounce bag frozen meatless chicken tenders, cooked according to package directions

1. Spread mayonnaise on one side of each slice of toasted bread. Arrange the romaine leaves on 4 slices of the toast. Arrange 2 slices of cooked meatless bacon on the romaine leaves. Then place 1–2 slices of tomato over the bacon, add a slice of onion, and place 1–2 slices of avocado on top. Divide the cooked meatless chicken evenly on top of each sandwich. Cover each sandwich with the remaining slices of toast, mayonnaise side down.

2. Using your hand, press the sandwiches just enough so they hold together, but don't worry if some of the ingredients slide a bit; just push them back into place. Insert two little wooden or other skewers into each sandwich, about an inch from the end, to hold it together. Then use a large, sharp knife to cut each sandwich in half on the diagonal. Enjoy it.

Tip: Use vegan mayonnaise to make this recipe vegan.

Grilled Cheese Florentine

This is a most-popular sandwich at Claire's. It's not grilled, but it bakes in a really hot oven, and this makes for a nice toasty sandwich without the added butter but with plenty of flavor. It's rich in vitamins A and C, iron, fiber, and lycopene, too. Make one for yourself, or multiply the ingredients and make several for a big group—either way, it's a delicious and easy way to help reach your goal of seven to nine fruits and vegetables a day.

Makes 1 sandwich

1 cup packed organic baby spinach, well washed and drained

¼ medium red onion, cut in half, then into thin slices

½ ripe tomato, cut into medium dice, juices reserved

½ small clove garlic, minced

½ cup shredded mozzarella

1 teaspoon extra-virgin olive oil

Sea salt and pepper

2 slices multigrain bread

1. Preheat the oven to 425°F. Combine the spinach, onion, tomato and juices, garlic, and mozzarella into a bowl. Toss to combine, using your hands or tongs. Drizzle with the olive oil, and sprinkle with salt and pepper. Toss again to combine. Spray a cookie sheet with olive oil spray or line it with parchment paper. Place one slice of bread on the prepared cookie sheet. Pile the spinach mix on the bread, and don't worry about it overflowing. Place the second slice of bread on the pile of spinach.

2. Bake for 7–9 minutes or until the spinach is wilted and the bread is toasted. If desired, you can flip the bread over using a spatula and bake the other side for 3–4 minutes until toasted, but we like the bottom slice soft so we serve it right from the oven with only one side toasted. Transfer to a plate, and include all the filling ingredients that have fallen out. Serve with a fork and knife for eating.

appetizers, salads, dressings, dips & salsas

This is a big section because we love little plates, bountiful salads, homemade dressings, dips, and salsas. It's how we eat both at Claire's and at home—a little plate of Squash Blossom Pancakes, some Marinated Olives, and Creamy Yogurt Dip with some crostini or pitas, and you have a great meal. Put together Onion-Gruyere Puffs, and serve them with Pickled Eggplant and Ricotta di Natale, and you have a party. Serve a Salad of Baby Spinach, Caramelized Onions, and Roasted Eggplant with Bruschetta of Beets with Goat Cheese and Truffle Oil for a wonderful summer supper on the back porch. Take along Fancy Pants Pasta Salad to your next cookout. So many of these recipes are great as leftovers, which gives you the opportunity to mix and match for the next day or two for delicious variety. Have fun, use the finest and freshest ingredients you can access, and cook for those you love. You absolutely count, too.

Black Bean and Sweet Corn Quesadillas GFO

Black beans are so healthy and they've become the sweetheart of the bean world, something we're thrilled about because we love to include them in soups, salads, and Mexican dishes.

Serves 6

1 tablespoon extra-virgin olive oil or organic corn oil

3 scallions, white part and most of green part cut into ¼-inch pieces

3 cups sweet locally grown corn, from about 3 large ears

Salt and pepper

1 teaspoon ground cumin

1 teaspoon oregano

1 12-ounce can organic black beans, drained, rinsed, and drained again

3 large organic heirloom tomatoes, diced

3 tablespoons chopped cilantro

4 ounces feta cheese, crumbled

6 10-inch whole-wheat tortillas

4 ounces fresh mozzarella, drained and cut into tiny cubes

1½ cups salsa, homemade or store bought

¾ cup fat-free sour cream

1. Preheat the oven to 350°F.

2. Heat the oil in a large skillet over low-medium heat. Add the scallions, corn, salt and pepper, the cumin, and oregano. Stir to coat. Cover and cook for about 6 minutes, stirring frequently until the corn is tender. Add the beans, tomatoes, cilantro, and feta cheese. Stir to combine. Cover and cook for 2 minutes, stirring frequently, until just heated through. Taste for seasonings.

3. Remove the skillet from the heat. Line two cookie sheets with parchment paper or spray them with olive oil spray. Arrange 3 tortillas on each prepared cookie sheet. Spoon one-sixth of the filling onto each tortilla. Scatter the cubes of mozzarella evenly over the filling. Fold each tortilla over the filling and gently press to seal. Bake for about 12 minutes, until the tortillas are soft-crisp. Remove from the oven and serve with salsa and fat-free sour cream.

Tip: Use gluten-free tortillas to make this recipe gluten free.

Crispy Baked Onion Rings

We all say that we don't like to eat fried foods, but we really do love crunchy, crispy foods, and these oven-baked onion rings are a delicious and healthful compromise.

Serves 6

Onion rings:

2 cups unbleached flour

Sea salt

$1/8$ teaspoon cayenne pepper

1 organic egg

2 cups buttermilk

2 cups bread crumbs

1 cup cornmeal

3 medium yellow onions, peeled, cut into ¼-inch rings, separated

Dip:

¼ cup ketchup

1 teaspoon ground fresh chili paste, more if you want a hotter dip (I use Sambal Oelek brand)

1. To prepare the onion rings, center the oven racks. Preheat the oven to 500°F. Place two sheet pans in the oven to preheat them while you prepare the onion rings for baking. Measure the flour into a deep bowl. Add a pinch of salt and the cayenne, then whisk to combine.

2. Into another deep bowl, place the egg, buttermilk, and pinch of salt, then whisk to combine this egg wash.

3. Into a third deep bowl, measure the bread crumbs, cornmeal, and pinch of salt, then whisk to combine. Set a platter or a flat pan by the bowls of flour mix, egg wash, and bread crumb mix. Take a handful of onions and drop them into the flour mix, then toss to completely coat them. Lift out the floured rings and shake off excess, then place them in the egg wash, pushing them into the liquid to coat them. Lift out the rings and shake off excess. Place the coated rings in the bread crumb mix and toss to thoroughly coat them. Lift them out and shake off excess.

4. Arrange the breaded rings on the platter. Continue coating the remaining rings and mounding them onto the platter. Using oven mitts, remove one preheated sheet pan and set it on the stove. Line the pan with parchment paper, then spray with olive oil spray. Arrange a single layer of the breaded onion rings on the pan. Place in the preheated oven. Repeat with the second sheet pan. Bake the rings until the underside is browned and crisp, about 10 minutes. Then, using tongs, turn the rings over and bake till the other side is browned and crisp, about 10 minutes. Transfer to a serving platter. Spray the pans again, and bake another batch. Continue until you've baked all the onion rings.

5. To prepare the dip, whisk together the ketchup and the chili paste until combined.

Deviled Eggs GF

Once again, my mother was right—everything old will become new again. Deviled eggs have returned as the quintessential picnic or party food, with an updated ingredient or two like the newer Dijon mayonnaises and the crunchy texture from omega-3-rich ground flax seeds.

Makes 24, perfect for a party

12 organic eggs

¼ cup finely minced orange bell pepper

1 tablespoon finely chopped scallion (about 1 scallion, using the white part and 2 inches of the green)

3 tablespoons Dijon mayonnaise

1 tablespoon ground flax seeds (optional)

Salt and pepper, to taste

1. Cook the eggs in boiling water for 9–10 minutes. Drain and peel the eggs. Cut the eggs in half lengthwise. Using a little spoon, scoop out the yolks and place them in a bowl. Add the remaining ingredients. Stir to combine. Taste for seasonings.

2. Arrange the egg whites on a serving platter. Using a small spoon, fill the cavity in each egg white with the filling, mounding it slightly. Serve immediately or cover and refrigerate for up to 2 days.

Edamame Martini V GF

I like to serve this lovely and elegant appetizer in stemmed martini glasses for a stunning presentation of a most-healthful combination.

Serves 6

1 10-ounce package frozen organic edamame (found in the frozen vegetable section at the supermarket)

3 small organic bell peppers (1 red, 1 yellow, and 1 orange)

½ small organic red onion

1 medium organic carrot

2 tablespoons snipped organic dill

Coarsely grated zest from 1 organic orange

Freshly squeezed juice from 1 organic orange (about ½ cup)

1 tablespoon extra-virgin olive oil (a Tuscan, "grassy" olive oil would be nice)

Sea salt and pepper, to taste

1. Bring a small covered pot of water to a boil over high heat. Stir in the edamame and cook for about a minute, then drain. Run under cold water, gently tossing while the cold water runs over the edamame to cool them down. Drain again, then turn them into a bowl.

2. Seed and coarsely dice the bell peppers, then add them to the bowl. Finely chop the red onion and add it to the bowl. Cut the carrot into matchstick-size julienne pieces and add them to the bowl. Add the dill and the orange zest; then, using two spoons or your hands, toss gently but thoroughly to combine. Drizzle the orange juice and the olive oil evenly over the top. Toss gently but thoroughly to coat the vegetables. Sprinkle with sea salt and pepper, then toss to combine. Taste for seasonings. Spoon into martini glasses or other pretty stemware.

Fresh Cheese GF

I love the inquisitive look on the faces of passersby when we have our fresh cheese hanging in the front window. And, of course, I love serving it, spread on toast or paired with grapes and a glass of wine.

Makes a heaping half-cup

1 quart organic low-fat milk

Juice from 2 organic lemons
(about 6 tablespoons)

Sea salt (optional)

1. Prepare a double boiler. Pour the milk into the top pot, then attach a thermometer inside the pot.

2. Set the double boiler over high heat and heat the milk to 170°F. Meanwhile, set a mesh strainer or a colander over a bowl big enough to hold a quart of liquid. Line the strainer with a double thickness of cheesecloth, overlapping the sides by about 4 inches all around.

3. Place a long wooden spoon across a second large bowl. Set the bowl aside on the counter by the stove until later—you'll need it to drain the cheese.

4. When the milk reaches 170°F, carefully remove the top pot from the bottom one. Set the top pot on the stove over an unlit burner. Remove the thermometer. Stir in the lemon juice, stirring well to combine. Set aside for about 10–15 minutes, until you see the milk turn a yellow-green. Using a slotted spoon, gently stir the milk; when there are small curds (little lumps), it's ready.

5. Carefully turn the liquid into the cheesecloth-lined strainer, being careful to keep the overlapping cheesecloth in place. Lift the cheesecloth by the edges, then tie the ends into a loose knot (the bundle will be dripping). Slip the knot over the spoon and hang the cheesecloth over the pot to collect the liquid as it drains. Reserve the whey (the liquid left behind after you collected the curds in the cheesecloth) and use it when making bread or a soup, as you would buttermilk. Drain the cheese for about 15 minutes or until it stops dripping. Turn the cheese out of the cheesecloth onto a plate and sprinkle lightly with sea salt if desired. Enjoy it warm or chilled. Refrigerate any leftovers for up to a day.

Marinated Olives V GF

These are a must for every party at my house. I serve them from a stemmed martini glass.

Serves 10–12 for appetizers

1 pound assorted olives (kalamata, Cerignola, Sicilian, and Niçoise are some of my favorites)

1 tablespoon extra-virgin olive oil

2 teaspoons fennel seeds

¼ teaspoon crushed red pepper flakes

2 teaspoons grated lemon zest

2 teaspoons grated orange zest

Freshly cracked black pepper

Sea salt, if needed

Drain the olives and turn them into a bowl. Add all the remaining ingredients except the sea salt. Toss to combine. Taste for seasonings before adding any sea salt, as olives can be salty.

Onion-Gruyere Puffs

Makes 40 appetizer-size puffs

1 cup water

½ cup salted butter (1 stick),
   cut into 6 slices

⅓ cup finely chopped yellow onion,
   about ½ medium onion

Sea salt and pepper

1 cup unbleached all-purpose flour

½ cup shredded Gruyere cheese,
   about 2 ounces

4 large or 3 extra-large eggs

1. Center two oven racks. Preheat the oven to 400°F. Line two cookie sheets with parchment paper or spray them with nonstick cooking spray.

2. Measure the water, butter, and onion in a heavy pot. Sprinkle lightly with sea salt and pepper. Bring to a boil over high heat, stirring occasionally until the butter melts.

3. Add the flour all at once. With a wooden spoon, immediately stir the mixture and beat it for about 2 minutes until it is smooth and thick and it pulls away from the sides of the pan. Stir in the cheese until it melts into the mixture.

4. Remove the pot from the stove and continue beating for about a minute to cool down the mixture slightly.

5. Add 1 egg and beat vigorously for about 1 minute, or until the mixture is smooth. Add the remaining eggs, one at a time, beating for 1 minute after each addition, until the mixture is smooth.

6. Drop the mixture by rounded teaspoons onto the prepared cookie sheets, leaving about an inch between each. Bake the cookie sheets on separate racks in the preheated oven for 20 minutes, then rotate the sheets from top to bottom rack and continue baking for about another 5 minutes, or until the puffs are a medium golden brown.

Pan-Grilled Vegetable Fattoush V

Fattoush is a Lebanese bread salad made with pita bread. Just cut the pita into 6–8 pie-shaped triangles and lightly toast them. If your pita bread is leftover and hard, just break the pitas into pieces and add them to the salad. You can grill the vegetables in a grill pan or a vegetable basket on the outdoor grill.

Serves 4

3 wheat pita bread rounds, each cut into 6–8 triangles and then lightly toasted until just crisp

Sea salt and pepper

1 medium white eggplant (local when available), cut into ½-inch-thick slices

2 medium zucchini (local when available), cut into diagonal ¼-inch-thick slices

1 large Vidalia onion, cut into large ribs

2 medium organic bell peppers (1 red and 1 yellow; local when available) cut in half, seeded, then cut into thick ribs

5 tablespoons extra-virgin olive oil, divided

Pepper

Juice from 1 fresh lemon, about ¼ cup

8–10 fresh mint leaves, torn

1. Place the toasted pita triangles in a large bowl. Sprinkle salt and pepper on the eggplant and zucchini slices, then place them into another bowl. Add the onion ribs and bell peppers. Toss to combine. Drizzle 1 tablespoon of olive oil evenly over the vegetables; then, using two wooden spoons or your hands, toss to coat with the oil.

2. Heat a large grill pan over medium-high heat. Brush the grill pan with a teaspoon of the olive oil, then arrange as many of the vegetable slices as you can in a single layer on the heated pan. Cook for about 3–4 minutes, or until the vegetables are medium brown but not burned. Turn to cook the other sides for 2–3 minutes, until fork-tender.

3. Transfer the cooked vegetables to the bowl with the pita. Grill the remaining vegetables and add to the bowl. Using two wooden spoons, toss the vegetables with the pita to combine. Drizzle the remaining olive oil (about 3 tablespoons) and the lemon juice evenly over the salad, then toss to coat. Scatter the mint leaves over the top and toss to combine. Taste for seasonings. Serve warm or chilled for up to 8 hours, tossing again just before serving.

Pan-Seared Romaine with "Bacon" and Gorgonzola

This is a lovely and delicious change from a tossed salad and it's fancy enough for a dinner party, too.

Serves 4

2 small heads romaine

2 tablespoons extra-virgin olive oil

2 tablespoons freshly squeezed lemon juice, about ½ lemon

Sea salt and pepper

2 strips meatless bacon, cooked until crisp, crumbled

4 ounces Gorgonzola cheese, crumbled

1. Leaving the romaine heads intact, rinse the leaves well under cold water, spreading the leaves open to allow any grit to wash away. Turn the heads upside-down and, holding the head by the stem, shake lightly to remove excess water. Transfer to a plate. In a shallow bowl, combine the oil, lemon juice, salt, and pepper. Taste for seasonings.

2. Using your fingers, coat the outside of the romaine heads with some of the oil mixture, then return to the plate. Heat a large skillet over medium heat. Add the oiled romaine heads in a single layer and cook for about 20 seconds, until the underside wilts but doesn't burn. Using tongs, turn the heads and cook evenly for about 20–30 seconds per side until romaine is evenly wilted and lightly browned on all sides. Transfer to a serving plate.

3. Using a sharp knife, cut each head in half lengthwise and arrange them with the cut side up. Drizzle the remaining oil mixture evenly over the romaine and scatter the crumbled meatless bacon and the Gorgonzola evenly over the top. Serve immediately.

Panzanella V

This delicious recipe for panzanella calls for biscotti, which are crispy oven-baked savory biscuits. They're often found in the bread section at the supermarket. I'm so lucky that a local bakery, Apicella's, makes them right here in New Haven.

Serves 6–8

1 7-ounce pack biscotti

3 tablespoons hot water

4 large ripe tomatoes

1 large red onion

1 large red, green, or yellow bell pepper

1 medium cucumber

12 fresh basil leaves

12 small leaves arugula

2 tablespoons fresh oregano leaves, from about 2 sprigs

¼ cup plus 2 tablespoons extra-virgin olive oil

¼ cup red wine vinegar

½ teaspoon dried oregano

Sea salt and pepper, to taste

1. Using your hands, break up the biscotti, one at a time, into a big bowl, breaking each biscuit into about 6 pieces. Sprinkle the hot water evenly over the biscotti. Cut the tomatoes into wedges, then scatter evenly over the biscotti, including all the juices, too. Peel the onion, cut it in half, then cut each half into thin slices. Scatter the slices evenly over the tomatoes. Seed and chop the bell pepper and scatter the pieces over the salad. Cut the cucumber in half lengthwise, scoop out the seeds and soft pulp, and cut each half into slices. Scatter the slices over the salad. Tear the basil and arugula leaves into pieces; scatter these and the fresh oregano leaves evenly over the salad.

2. Using two spoons or your clean hands, toss the salad to combine the ingredients. Drizzle the olive oil evenly over the salad, then drizzle the vinegar. Sprinkle the dried oregano, sea salt, and pepper evenly over the top. Toss well to combine. Taste for seasonings.

Pickled Eggplant V GF

I save empty glass jars to store Pickled Eggplant, Strawberry-Mint Vinegar (page 135), and other foods that I make. Glass is clean, non-porous, and safe, and I prefer it to plastic.

Makes five 8-ounce jars

8 cups organic white vinegar

8 cups water

3 medium-large eggplants, about 3 pounds

Sea salt

$1/3$ cup extra-virgin olive oil, plus additional for topping off the jars of pickled eggplant

8 cloves organic garlic, coarsely chopped

1 tablespoon minced hot cherry peppers, jalapeño peppers, or other hot peppers

½ teaspoon dried oregano

Freshly ground black pepper

1. Clean and dry five 8-ounce glass jars. Set aside.

2. Pour the white vinegar and the water into an 8-quart pot. Cover and bring to a simmer over high heat. Lower the heat to the warm setting and keep warm while you proceed with the recipe.

3. Peel the eggplants and trim the ends. Cut each eggplant in half lengthwise. Slice one half into ¼-inch slices, then stack and slice widthwise into $1/8$-inch strips. Place the strips in a bowl and sprinkle with a generous amount of salt and toss well to mix. Repeat the process of slicing, salting, and tossing until all the eggplant has been sliced. It will seem like you're using a lot of salt, and you are, but you need it for the eggplant to release its moisture, and the vinegar bath will remove any overly salty taste.

4. By the time you finish slicing the eggplant, it will have released a lot of dark liquid. Set a colander in the sink. Raise the heat under the pot of vinegar to medium and bring it to a simmer. You'll be working quickly for the next few minutes, so avoid any distractions or you'll overcook the eggplant and make it mushy. Remove the cover from the pot and pick up a handful of the eggplant. Using both hands, squeeze as much liquid out of the eggplant as you can, letting the dark juices fall back into the bowl. Carefully lower the eggplant into the simmering vinegar. Continue quickly squeezing handfuls of the eggplant, then adding them to the vinegar. Stir the eggplant with a slotted spoon. Immediately after adding the last of the eggplant, carefully drain the eggplant into the colander you've set in the sink. Squeeze out as much liquid as you can. I place a cover from a small pot on the eggplant, then use my hands to press on it to squeeze out the excess vinegar bath.

5. Turn the eggplant into a bowl. Add $^1/_3$ cup of olive oil and the garlic, peppers, oregano, and a little black pepper. Toss well to combine. Taste for seasonings. Pack the eggplant mixture into the clean glass jars, stopping 1 inch from the top. Add olive oil to fill the jars completely. Cover and tighten the lids on the jars. Label the jars and add the date. Set aside in a cool, dry place (unrefrigerated) for 5 days.

6. Open the jars every day and add olive oil as needed to fill the jars as the eggplant absorbs some of the oil. Cover tightly after checking each day. After 5 days, store in the refrigerator for up to 5 months.

7. Serve at room temperature.

Ricotta di Natale   GF

Locally produced, hand-packed ricotta cheese has a wonderfully creamy texture and is loaded with calcium and vitamin D. Pair it with organic apples or local berries, then drizzle it with local honey and sprinkle it with sliced almonds or other antioxidant-rich nuts—you'll have a delicious and healthful appetizer or after-school snack. Serve it with toasted slices of good Italian wheat bread (crostini) or trans fat–free whole grain crackers. It even makes a delicious sandwich filling on whole wheat sliced bread. And wait until you see how beautiful this dish is. The name of the dish is translated as "Ricotta for Christmas," but you'll be missing out if you don't enjoy it year-round.

Serves 6

1 pound locally produced, hand-packed ricotta cheese

3 organic apples, Gala or other, cored and sliced

1 cup organic and local blueberries, raspberries, blackberries, and/or small strawberries

¼ cup sliced almonds

2 tablespoons local honey

Mound the ricotta cheese in the center of a large, round plate. Arrange the apple slices around the ricotta cheese in a circular pattern, overlapping as needed. Scatter the almonds and berries evenly over the ricotta cheese. Drizzle the honey over the cheese and fruit.

Party Season

It's impossible to get through the holidays without overeating and drinking at a party here or there. What's a girl (or guy) to do? This year I've adopted a strategy that my brother Billy has forever preached to me. For any holiday event where you know there will be plenty of wonderful temptations, before you leave the house, eat some fresh vegetables and fruits and have a big glass of water. Then when you're faced with the cookies, the candies, the crispy fried foods, the over-the-top martinis, and the glorious cheeses, you'll still enjoy them, but you'll eat and drink much less.

For me, Crunchy Broccoli Salad (page 121) is something I love, and I can eat lots of it, which fills me up both hunger-wise and with a great big dose of vitamins A and C and antioxidants galore. It's easy to keep a bowl of blanched broccoli in the refrigerator for convenience. Then you can toss what you want with a little olive oil, fresh lemon juice, and garlic for a nice pre-party snack. Another good choice is Citrus Salad (page 98). It's made with slices of fresh oranges, grapefruits, tangerines, thin slices of red onion, and capers. Drizzle this vitamin C–rich salad with a little citrus honey for a healthful snack.

Another tip from my brother Billy is to bring something to the party that's both delicious and healthful. This is where our Roasted Chestnuts recipe (page 76) comes in handy. Chestnuts are rich in flavor, low in sodium, and low in calories, with less than thirty calories per nut. They are in prime season during the winter holidays, grown in California and also imported from Italy. Their flavor is deep and earthy, with a natural sweetness. Choose big chestnuts with smooth, glossy shells. Boil or roast them, then peel the tough outer shell and bitter skin before eating. They are lovely eaten alone, as part of a stuffing, in a dessert (especially with chocolate), or tossed with whole wheat pasta, mushrooms, and a good olive oil for a great and speedy supper before you rush off for holiday shopping.

Store chestnuts in a cool, dry place for no more than a week or they will dry out. If you shake a chestnut and it rattles, it has dried out, so it's good to shake them before buying.

Roasted Chestnuts V GF

It's fun to serve warm chestnuts to your guests and let them each peel their own. Just provide little bowls for the shells.

Serves 6

18 chestnuts, rinsed

1. Center the oven rack. Preheat the oven to 425°F.

2. Using a sharp paring knife, carefully cut a 1-inch X shape into the flat side of each chestnut, deep enough to cut through the shell and into the flesh. Arrange the chestnuts cut side up in a baking dish. Bake in the preheated oven for 30–35 minutes, or until the X cut into the shells opens to expose the chestnut flesh.

3. Set aside for a few minutes until cool enough to handle. Then, using your fingertips, peel off the shell from one chestnut, starting at the X. The inside flesh should be tender-soft; if not, pop the chestnuts back in the oven for another 5 minutes.

4. Peel the shells from the remaining chestnuts. Using the paring knife, remove the bitter skin. Serve warm or at room temperature.

Spinach-and-Pecan-Stuffed Mushroom Caps

These make great appetizers for a cocktail party, but they are also yummy for supper. Pair them with a salad made with the tender inner leaves of escarole (reserve the tougher outer leaves for a soup or a sauté), and a handful of white beans, tossed with a little extra-virgin olive oil and fresh lemon juice and a sprinkle of sea salt and black pepper.

Makes 12 pieces; allow 2–3 per person for appetizers or 3–4 per person as an entree

12 stuffing mushrooms, button or cremini, stems removed (reserve for soup or a sauce)

1 7-ounce package (about 3 packed cups) organic baby spinach, rinsed and drained

1 tablespoon Dijon mustard

1 tablespoon white wine

2 tablespoons low-fat mayonnaise or dairy-free mayonnaise

4 ounces (about 1 cup) shredded cheddar cheese or dairy-free cheddar substitute

¼ cup coarsely chopped pecans

2 tablespoons plain bread crumbs

½ teaspoon black pepper

1. Preheat the oven to 400°F. Wash and drain the mushroom caps. In a bowl, measure the spinach, mustard, wine, mayonnaise, cheddar, pecans, bread crumbs, and pepper. Toss well, using your hands to combine. Taste for seasonings. Mound the stuffing in the mushroom caps.

2. Arrange in a single layer in a glass baking dish. Pour in water to ¼ inch deep, around but not over the mushrooms. Spray a sheet of foil with olive oil spray, then cover the baking dish and try to tent the foil so that it doesn't touch the mushroom stuffing. (If it does touch during baking, the cooking spray will prevent it from sticking.)

3. Bake, covered, for about 20 minutes, then uncover and continue cooking for 5 minutes or until the mushrooms are tender and the stuffing has crisped somewhat.

Squash Blossoms

I wait all year for the zucchini plants to blossom, but really I'm mostly looking forward to the squash blossoms, those tender flowers from the zucchini, that I need to make my grand-mother's recipe for Squash Blossom Pancakes (page 79).

My grandmother, Assunta Maria Lucibello Bigio, was from Amalfi, Italy, and she always referred to the squash blossoms as "shoo-deel." My mother and I use this reference, as well, but I cannot find a dictionary definition that can give me the correct spelling in Italian, so if anyone out there can help me, I'd be ever so grateful.

"Wool-ee" was the word used in my house when you had a desire for something, and my "wool-ee" was mostly for "shoo-deel," but the translation and pronunciation of the Italian

words that were spoken in our house were different from the original words in Italian, I'm sure. Today I find it easier to just say, "I'm making squash blossom pancakes." But, between you and me, I do like to follow that with the word "shoo-deel" because I like to keep my grandmother's voice in my ear.

Squash blossoms don't have much of a shelf life; they must be cooked within a day of picking, or else they wilt and rot. If you plan to store your squash blossoms, place them, single-layer, in a covered glass container and store them in the refrigerator—but for only 1 day, so you'll want to plan accordingly. Growing zucchini in your garden or visiting farm stands and markets really comes in handy for this specialty.

I've never found a substitute for freshly picked squash blossoms from zucchini, not even those from pumpkin or cantaloupe. I've tried those, and they don't taste the same. Only the flower, the blossom from the zucchini, will do. And so I wait all year—honestly, it's worth it. These pancakes are tender, light, and delicious, and the subtle yet distinct flavor of the "shoo-deel" is exactly what I wait for. I hope you develop a "wool-ee" for these as well.

Squash Blossom Pancakes

I like to serve these pancakes alone, or with warm or chilled Marinara Sauce (page 183), or with a few drops of fresh lemon juice on top.

Makes about 24 pancakes

3 cups unbleached all-purpose flour

1 tablespoon baking powder

5 eggs

1 cup milk

¾ cup water

15 squash blossoms, piston removed, rinsed and coarsely chopped

¼ cup chopped Italian flat-leaf parsley

Sea salt and pepper

½–¾ cup grapeseed oil, olive oil, or canola oil for frying

1. Measure the flour and baking powder into a bowl. Whisk to combine. In a separate bowl, measure the eggs, milk, and water, then whisk to combine. Pour the liquid ingredients evenly over the dry ingredients and stir to combine. Add the chopped blossoms and the parsley, and sprinkle with a little sea salt and pepper. Stir to mix well.

2. Place a cookie sheet near the stove, and line it with a double layer of paper towels or a paper bag. Heat ½ cup of the oil in a large skillet over medium heat. Carefully drop ¼ cup of batter into the heated oil, leaving space in between to allow for turning. (Do not overcrowd the skillet or the temperature will drop and you'll have greasy pancakes.) Cook for about 2 minutes, or until the underside is a medium golden brown. Turn the pancakes and cook about a minute, or until the underside is a medium golden brown. Transfer the cooked pancakes to the paper towel–lined cookie sheet. Continue frying the remaining batter, heating additional oil as needed. Serve hot, at room temperature, or chilled.

Tostones ⅤGF

When you're looking for an unusual appetizer for your next party, try *tostones*. They are twice-fried slices of green plantains (fruits that hail from the Puerto Rican and Cuban communities). Although I don't often fry foods, when I do want that crispy and rich outer crust that comes only when you fry in hot oil, I always choose the right oil—one that can withstand high temperatures without dangerous smoking. I hope that you'll choose wisely as well. I use almond oil for this recipe, but a refined avocado, sunflower, grapeseed, or safflower oil is also a good choice for high-heat cooking.

Serves 8 as an appetizer

Sea salt

3 green plantains

¾ cup almond oil

1. Pour 4 cups of warm water into each of two separate bowls. Stir 1 teaspoon of sea salt into each bowl and stir to dissolve. Set aside.

2. Peel the plantains: Cut off and discard the tips and cut each plantain in half lengthwise, then cut a lengthwise slit just through the peel, and peel back and remove the entire peel. Slice each plantain into 1-inch rounds, placing the rounds into one bowl of the salted water as you cut them. This process helps to keep your *tostones* moist. Place an absorbent kitchen towel or a double layer of paper towels on your countertop.

3. Using your hands, lift the plantains from the salted water, shake off excess water, and lay the slices in a single layer on half of the kitchen towel. Using the other half of the towel, cover and blot dry the plantain slices. You'll be using the kitchen towel twice, so leave it on the counter while your proceed. Line a cookie sheet with a double layer of paper towels (or with a brown paper bag) and set it by the stove. This will be for draining excess oil from the fried plantains.

4. Heat the oil in a large skillet over high heat. Arrange the plantains in a single layer, without crowding, in the hot skillet. Fry them for about 6 minutes, until the underside is golden brown; using tongs, turn and fry the other side for about 4 minutes, until golden brown. Transfer the fried plantains onto the paper-lined cookie sheet. Turn off the heat but leave the skillet on the stove.

5. Using the bottom of a heavy coffee mug, press each fried plantain to flatten to about ¼-inch thickness and about 50 percent larger circumference. One at a time, dip each fried plantain into the second bowl of salted water, lift out, and shake off excess water. Set the plantains in a single layer on half of the kitchen towel. Lift the other half of the towel, cover and blot dry the plantains.

6. Reheat the almond oil over high heat and fry the plantains for about 2 minutes per side, until deep golden brown. Unless you're using a huge skillet, you'll have to do this second frying in two batches because the slices are now wider. Drain them on the paper-lined cookie sheets. Sprinkle with salt. Repeat until all the plantains are fried. Serve warm.

Spanish Tomato Bread V

Lori "Sav," a former (and favorite) employee of mine at Claire's, beamed as she shared with me what she'd found to be the most seemingly ordinary, yet sublime, snack she enjoyed in outdoor cafes in Spain. This is where a rich, fruity extra-virgin olive oil, perfect tomatoes, and a particularly wonderful sea salt come into their own.

Serves 4

8 ¼-inch slices whole wheat Italian bread or baguette, toasted

2 ripe tomatoes, cut into thin slices

1½–2 tablespoons of your finest and favorite extra-virgin olive oil

Coarse sea salt

Each person at the table should get the opportunity to prepare his or her own portion, so just set out the ingredients. Guests should take a slice of toasted bread and place a slice of tomato on it. They should use the flat side of a butter knife to spread the tomato over the bread, as one would butter, allowing it to "melt" into the bread. Have them repeat with a second slice of tomato, then drizzle a little extra-virgin olive oil evenly over the tomato and sprinkle some coarse sea salt. Enjoy it!

Parmesan-Herb Garlic Bread

How can you go wrong with fresh garlic and herbs and Parmesan cheese? I serve this bread with just about any soup or salad and we love it in our house and at Claire's Corner Copia, too.

Serves 6

2 tablespoons organic butter or organic cholesterol-free buttery spread, softened

1 tablespoon extra-virgin olive oil

3 large cloves organic garlic, finely chopped

1 tablespoon each finely chopped organic chives, basil, and parsley

3 tablespoons grated Parmesan cheese

Sea salt and pepper

6 1-inch slices whole wheat Italian or French bread

1. Arrange the oven rack on the second rung from the top. Preheat the broiler to high. In a bowl, combine the softened butter with the olive oil, garlic, herbs, and Parmesan cheese. Sprinkle lightly with sea salt (the Parmesan cheese is a bit salty) and pepper. Using a spoon, mix to combine. Taste for seasonings.

2. Spread about a heaping teaspoon of the butter spread on one cut side of each slice of bread. Arrange the bread slices, spread side up, in a single layer on a cookie sheet. Broil for about 3 minutes, until the butter has melted and the bread slices are golden brown around the edges.

Bruschetta of Beets with Goat Cheese and Truffle Oil

Serve this beautiful and absolutely scrumptious appetizer to your guests, then sit back and enjoy the compliments. Try golden and red beets together for dramatic color contrast.

Makes 8

2 medium beets, unpeeled, well-washed, and with 1 inch of stem attached

8 ½-inch slices of whole wheat Italian bread, or a baguette

8 ounces goat cheese, soft or semi-firm

2 leaves basil, torn

2 4-inch chives, snipped into ½-inch pieces

2 tablespoons whole milk or heavy cream

Freshly ground black pepper

1 tablespoon extra-virgin olive oil

1 tablespoon freshly squeezed lemon juice

Sea salt

1 tablespoon white truffle oil

1. Bring a medium pot of water to a boil, covered, over high heat. When the water reaches a boil, add the beets, cover, and cook for about 30–45 minutes, depending on size, until fork-tender. Drain and set aside until cool enough to handle. After the beets have cooled, peel the skin from them using your fingers or a peeler. Slice the beets into about ½-inch slices, then cut the slices into about ½-inch cubes so you'll have small to medium dice. Turn the cubed beets into a bowl. Set aside. You can refrigerate them for a day in advance.

2. Arrange the oven rack on the top rung, closest to the broiler. Preheat the broiler to high. Arrange the slices of bread, cut side down in a single layer on a cookie sheet. Broil the bread to toast each side, about 1 minute per side, until medium brown but not burned. Set aside. If not using immediately, cool to room temperature, then store in a container in a dry place for up to a few days. Place the goat cheese in the bowl of a food processor fitted with a metal blade. Add the torn basil leaves, the snipped chives, and the milk or cream. Grind a little black pepper over the top. Cover and process for about 30 seconds or until smooth and creamy and well blended, stopping once to scrape down the sides of the bowl with a rubber spatula. Taste for seasoning. Turn this mixture into a small bowl and set aside, or refrigerate for up to a day.

3. When ready to assemble the bruschetti, drizzle the olive oil and lemon juice over the cubed beets. Sprinkle lightly with sea salt and freshly ground black pepper. Toss to coat. Taste for seasoning.

4. Spread the goat cheese mixture over the toasted bread, dividing the cheese among the 8 slices. Spoon the beets evenly over the cheese. Drizzle each with a little truffle oil. Serve immediately.

Peach Puree and Ricotta Bruschetta

My mother always kept crostini in a basket on the refrigerator, and this is the combination I most remember and adored during the summer months. It continues to hold a special place in my heart—for breakfast or with a glass of wine after a long day at work.

Makes 16 bruschetta

8 large ripe peaches

¼ cup freshly squeezed orange juice, from about ½ small orange

½ teaspoon pure almond extract

½ loaf whole wheat Italian or French bread

1 16-ounce container ricotta cheese, locally produced if possible

2 tablespoons pure maple syrup, local if available

1. Peel and pit the peaches over a small, heavy pot so the juices drip into the pot. Slice the peaches and add them to the pot. Add the orange juice. Cover the pot and cook over low heat for about 15–20 minutes, stirring occasionally, until the peaches are tender to soft.

2. Using a potato masher, mash the peaches into a slightly chunky consistency. Stir in the almond extract. Taste for sweetness. If the peaches are not sweet enough for your taste, stir in a teaspoon or two of sugar or agave until they're sweet enough for your preference. Set the puree aside to cool to room temperature.

3. Meanwhile, place the cooking rack on the highest shelf in your oven. Preheat the broiler to high. Slice the bread into ¼-inch slices. Arrange in a single layer on a cookie sheet. Toast under the broiler for about 1 minute until golden brown. Remove from the oven and, using tongs, carefully turn over each slice of bread, or crostini. Return to the broiler and toast the bread for about 1 minute more, until golden brown. Remove from the broiler and cool to room temperature.

4. While the puree and crostini are cooling, measure the ricotta cheese into a small bowl. Add the maple syrup. Using a spoon, beat until combined.

5. To assemble the bruschetta, place the crostini on a plate. Spoon about 2 tablespoons of sweetened ricotta onto each toast, using the back of the spoon to spread it. Spoon about 2–3 tablespoons of peach puree on top. Enjoy it.

Cajun Grilled Tofu over Tri-Color Bell Pepper Salad V GFO

This recipe combines the heat from Cajun spices, a slight salty hit from the capers, and the brightness of lemon into a really delicious salad. Serve it with good bread and add fresh fruit for dessert and you'll have one satisfying meal.

Serves 4

1 14-ounce package organic extra-firm tofu, drained

3 medium bell peppers (1 red, 1 orange, and 1 yellow), seeded and cut into thin ribs

1 small red onion, cut into thin rings

1 clove garlic, finely chopped

1 7-ounce bag organic baby spinach

2 tablespoons extra-virgin olive oil

2 tablespoons freshly squeezed lemon juice (about ½ lemon)

1 tablespoon capers, drained

Sea salt and pepper, to taste

Cajun blend seasoning mix

Grapeseed oil spray

1. Line a cookie sheet with a double layer of paper towels. Cut the tofu cake in half lengthwise, to form two thin slices, then cut each piece in half on the diagonal, to form four triangles. Arrange the triangles on the paper towels to drain while you prepare the salad.

2. Place the thin ribs of peppers in a bowl. Add the onion rings, garlic, and baby spinach. Using two wooden spoons, toss to combine. Drizzle the olive oil and the lemon juice evenly over the salad. Toss to coat the vegetables. Add the capers and toss again. Sprinkle a little salt (don't overdo; capers tend to be salty) and pepper evenly over the salad and toss to combine. Taste for seasonings. Arrange the salad on a serving platter.

3. Set a plate next to the tofu. Lifting one triangle at a time, sprinkle the Cajun seasoning evenly over both sides of each triangle, then set on the plate. Spray a grill pan or skillet with grapeseed oil and heat over medium-high heat, or spray the grill rack with grapeseed oil then light grill to medium heat. Arrange the coated tofu triangles evenly on the prepared skillet, grill pan, or grill rack in a single layer. Cook for 1–2 minutes until the spices are blackened; then, using a spatula, carefully turn and cook the other side for about a minute until the spices blacken.

4. Arrange the blackened tofu over the salad, overlapping slightly in a decorative arrangement. Serve immediately.

   Tip: Use a gluten-free seasoning mix to make this recipe gluten free.

Roasted Asparagus with Sauces for Dipping GF

After tulips, asparagus is the first sign that spring has arrived in Connecticut, where I live. In fact, we are home to the largest asparagus farm in New England, so once these gorgeous, deep green and purple-tinged stalks start to grow, we take the opportunity to enjoy them in many dishes. Roasted asparagus makes a lovely first coarse to any spring meal. It's rich in vitamins A and C and fiber. Look for deep green stalks with tight, purple tinged tips. The thickness of the asparagus has to do with the age of the plant and has no bearing on the tenderness. Big, thick asparagus stalks are from mature plants and thin ones are from younger plants, so let your personal taste dictate.

As soon as you get home, wrap a moistened paper towel around the cut ends of the stalks. Place a paper bag over the tops. Refrigerate the asparagus. Proper storage and cooking within a few days will help to preserve the asparagus spears' natural sugars and prevent the dryness that leads to toughness. Before cooking, rinse the spears well, especially the tight tips because asparagus is grown in sandy soil.

Serves 4–6

Roasted Asparagus:

1 pound asparagus, thick or thin (my favorite is thick)

1 teaspoon Italian extra-virgin olive oil

Sea salt and freshly ground organic black pepper, to taste

2 teaspoons organic butter

Sauces:

½ cup low-fat organic plain yogurt or organic mayonnaise, divided

1 tablespoon finely grated organic lemon, orange, or lime zest

1 teaspoon tamari or organic balsamic vinegar

1 tablespoon organic black olive spread, tapenade, or finely minced organic black olives

1 tablespoon minced organic sun-dried tomatoes—if using oil-packed, drain well

1. To make the asparagus, preheat oven to 400°F. Thoroughly rinse the asparagus, then drain. Cut or snap off the tough bottom 2 inches of the stalks; discard or save for making stock. Spray a cookie sheet with nonstick organic olive oil spray.

2. Arrange the trimmed asparagus in a single layer in the prepared pan. Drizzle the olive oil evenly over the asparagus, then sprinkle sea salt and pepper to taste. Using your hands, roll the spears to coat with the oil. Dollop little bits of the butter evenly over the asparagus.

3. Roast in the preheated oven for about 5 minutes, then carefully shake the pan back and forth to distribute the melted butter. Continue roasting for another 10 minutes or until just tender when tested with a fork. Meanwhile, prepare the sauces.

4. To make the sauces, divide the yogurt or mayonnaise into four bowls. Stir the zest into one of the bowls, the tamari into another, the olive spread into the third, and the sun-dried tomatoes into the remaining bowl.

5. To serve, arrange the asparagus on a serving platter. Place the sauces at the table with the asparagus, allowing everyone to choose which sauce (or combination of sauces) they would like to drizzle atop their asparagus.

No Peanuts, No Problem

A little over 1 percent of Americans have peanut allergies. This may not sound like a significant number, but for those million-plus people with allergies, it can be a very big deal. For some, even a little exposure can produce serious consequences that could result in hospitalization, or far worse. Rather than take a chance, many institutions have opted to go peanut-free. Most school systems have a policy regarding allergies, ranging from being

completely peanut-free, as is the case in most pre-K and daycare centers, to having a peanut-free table in the school cafeteria.

Peanut allergies can be a logistical nightmare when you're traveling and also when eating out because you really have to trust the people who are delivering the service to you. And, of course, mistakes can happen.

Wanting to empathize, I imagined what our house would be like without Frank's beloved peanut butter (he's a huge fan of the stuff). What could he spread onto his toast or crackers? There would be no more of those yummy Thai peanut noodles. Could he even eat his Pasta e Fagioli (page 26) without a coat of peanut butter spread onto a slice of whole wheat bread to dip in? What would be the alternative to that beloved stand-by, the ubiquitous PB&J? I headed to the supermarket to find an alternative. There I picked up a jar of sunflower seed butter, made from sunflower seeds rather than from peanuts.

It tasted, well, just like sunflower seeds, which is a good thing if you like them (which I do). So I decided to try out sunflower seed butter in some recipes that I usually make with peanut butter. And I discovered that it's a nice change from peanut butter, even if allergies aren't an issue for you. Sunflower seed butter has a rich, nutty (well, seedy) flavor; it has about the same rich source of protein as peanut butter; it has more fiber than peanut butter; and it contains a healthy dose of vitamin E, zinc, and iron. Now we use sunflower seed butter regularly in our recipes.

You can buy sunflower seed butter under various brand labels at all major supermarkets and specialty gourmet shops.

Spicy Thai Sunflower Noodles V GFO

We went peanut-free at Claire's several years ago because we had several children who were highly allergic, and honestly, I was just too worried. Today, we use sunflower seed butter and it's delicious, too.

Serves 6–8

Sea salt

1 13-ounce package organic brown rice spaghetti or other rice noodles

1 teaspoon organic toasted sesame oil

2 medium cloves garlic

1-inch piece fresh ginger, peeled and sliced

1 medium jalapeño pepper, sliced

1 lime

1 tablespoon organic grapeseed oil or extra-virgin olive oil

1 shallot, coarsely chopped

½ teaspoon crushed red pepper flakes

3 tablespoons brown sugar, packed

1 cup sunflower seed butter (I like Sunbutter brand, available in most supermarkets)

¼ cup organic tamari sauce

2 tablespoons organic apple cider vinegar

1 cup water

White pepper, to taste

Cayenne pepper (optional)

1 medium organic carrot, cut into julienne pieces

2 tablespoons fresh cilantro leaves

1. Bring a large covered pot of lightly salted water to a boil over high heat. When the water reaches a boil, add the brown rice noodles and cook according to package directions. When the pasta is cooked to your preference, drain it, rinse the noodles under cold water, then drain again. Turn into a bowl. Drizzle the sesame oil evenly over the top and toss to coat. Set aside. Place the garlic, ginger, and jalapeño pepper into the bowl of a food processor fitted with a metal blade. Finely grate the lime and add the zest to the food processor bowl, then squeeze the juice from the lime and add it to the bowl. Cover and process for about 20 seconds, until the vegetables are finely minced and well blended.

2. Heat the grapeseed oil in a medium pot over medium heat. Add the shallot and cook for about 2 minutes, stirring frequently until softened. Add the crushed red pepper flakes and the brown sugar, then stir to blend. Stir in the processed garlic mixture. Cook for about 10 seconds, stirring continuously until the sugar melts. Add the sunflower seed butter and stir well, then stir in the tamari, vinegar, and the water. Whisk well to blend, then continue cooking for about 5 minutes, whisking frequently until the sauce becomes first smooth and then, toward the end of the 5 minutes, slightly thickened.

3. Sprinkle with a little white pepper, then stir well to combine. Add the drained noodles. Using two spoons, toss well to coat. Taste for seasonings, and if you want it a little spicier, add just a sprinkle of cayenne, toss the noodles until well blended, then taste again for seasonings.

4. Turn onto a serving platter. Scatter the julienne strips of carrot and the cilantro leaves evenly over the top. Serve warm, at room temperature, or chilled.

Tip: Use gluten-free tamari to make this recipe gluten free.

Fancy Pants Pasta Salad   V GFO

A favorite manager of ours, Kathleen, always comes up with fun names for her dishes, such as "Top Notch" and "Fancy Pants." Whenever a recipe has "fancy" ingredients she refers to the dish as Fancy Pants. Saffron is expensive, incredibly flavorful, and indeed fancy.

Serves 8

Salt

1 pound organic Italian pasta (I like to use Bionaturae gobetti)

2 cups fresh green peas or defrosted frozen green peas

1 12-ounce can organic chickpeas, drained

4 local plum tomatoes, cut into wedges

¼ pound local baby arugula

Pinch of saffron

¼ cup hot water

1 clove garlic

1 small red bell pepper, seeded and coarsely chopped

2 tablespoons fresh tarragon

6 grape or cherry tomatoes

¼ cup extra-virgin olive oil

2 tablespoons freshly squeezed lemon juice (from about ½ lemon)

Sea salt and pepper, to taste

1. Bring 8 quarts of lightly salted water to a boil in a large covered pot over high heat. Cook the pasta according to package directions until al dente or to your preference. If using fresh peas, add the peas to the pasta during the last 2 minutes of cooking. Drain the pasta (and the fresh peas, if using). Rinse under cold water to stop the cooking, then drain again. Turn the drained pasta into a large bowl. If using defrosted peas, add to the pasta. Add the chickpeas, plum tomatoes, and arugula. Using two wooden spoons, toss to combine. Set aside.

2. Place the pinch of saffron in a small bowl. Add the hot water and set aside. Place the garlic clove in the bowl of a food processor fitted with a metal blade. Add the bell pepper, tarragon, and grape tomatoes. Cover and process for about 20 seconds until finely minced. Add the saffron with the hot water, using a rubber spatula to scrape every expensive drop; then, with the motor running, add the olive oil, lemon juice, sea salt, and pepper to taste. Process for about 10 seconds until well blended. Taste for seasonings.

3. Turn this mixture over the pasta salad, using a rubber spatula to scrape the processor bowl. Using two wooden spoons, toss to coat the salad and to combine. Taste for seasonings. Serve at room temperature or refrigerate for up to 2 days. Toss again just before serving.

Tip: Use gluten-free pasta to make this recipe gluten free.

Pasta Salad with Summer Vegetables and Basil-Parsley Dressing V GFO

We serve a side salad with every sandwich and veggie burger at Claire's. This one is our favorite combination during the summer, when our farmers bring us fresh ears of sweet corn and other vegetables straight from the soil.

Serves 4

Sea salt

6 tablespoons extra-virgin olive oil, divided

2 small shallots, coarsely chopped

½ pound of organic penne or other pasta

1 basket of green and yellow wax beans, about ¼ pound, trimmed and cut into thirds

4 ears of sweet corn, kernels cut, about 4 cups corn kernels

15 each Sun Gold and red cherry tomatoes

½ cup coarsely chopped Italian flat-leaf parsley

24 fresh basil leaves

2 cloves fresh garlic, sliced

Pepper

1. Bring a covered pot of lightly salted water to a boil over high heat. Meanwhile, heat a teaspoon of the olive oil in a skillet over medium heat. Add the shallots and sprinkle with a little sea salt. Cook, for about a minute, stirring frequently until the shallots have softened and are just golden. Set aside. Add the pasta to the water and cook according to package directions. Three minutes before the pasta should be done, stir in the green beans. About 2 minutes later, add the corn and cook until the pasta and the green beans are tender. Drain the pasta and the vegetables into a colander, then turn into a bowl.

2. Add the cooked shallots. Using two wooden spoons, toss to combine and to cool down the pasta and vegetables a bit. Quarter the cherry tomatoes, add them to the pasta, and toss to combine. Into a blender cup, place the parsley, basil, garlic, and the remaining 5 tablespoons and 2 teaspoons of olive oil. Add 2 tablespoons of cold water. Add a little sea salt and pepper. Cover and blend for about 30 seconds, or until somewhat smooth. Taste for seasoning. Pour over the pasta salad, using a spatula to scrape the blender cup. Toss to coat the salad. Taste for seasonings. Serve at room temperature or chilled for up to 1 day. Toss again just before serving.

Tip: Use gluten-free pasta to make this recipe gluten free.

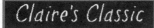

Greek Pasta Salad

We've been making this salad ever since we opened our doors, and it's as popular as ever. It's beautiful, too, with the vibrant colors from the healthful ingredients.

Serves 8

1 pound rigatoni pasta

2 large bell peppers (1 red and 1 yellow), seeded and cut into large dice

1 medium red onion, cut into thin rings

1 pint sweet grape tomatoes, cut in half

1 7-ounce bag organic baby spinach

3 sun-dried tomatoes, cut into thin strips

16 kalamata olives, pitted and cut in half

2 tablespoons capers, drained

1 broccoli crown, florets cut into small pieces

¼ cup extra-virgin olive oil

3 tablespoons red wine vinegar

2 tablespoons freshly squeezed lemon juice (from about ½ lemon)

2 teaspoons dried oregano

3 tablespoons chopped fresh mint leaves

Salt and pepper, to taste

4 ounces feta cheese, crumbled

1. Cook the pasta according to package directions. Drain, rinse under cold water, and drain again. Turn the pasta into a large bowl. Add the peppers, onion, tomatoes, spinach, sun-dried tomatoes, olives, capers, and broccoli. Using two wooden spoons, toss gently to combine. Drizzle the olive oil evenly over the salad and toss to coat. Drizzle the vinegar and the lemon juice evenly over the salad and toss gently to combine.

2. Add the oregano and the mint; add just a little salt and pepper, as the sun-dried tomatoes, olive, and capers tend to be salty. Toss to combine. Taste for seasonings. Turn the salad onto a serving platter. Distribute the crumbled feta evenly over the top.

Connecticut Cole Slaw GF VO

This crunchy slaw makes a delicious and nutritious side dish for any entree, but also try it in a sandwich with slices of soy turkey on whole grain bread. It's really delightful.

Serves 4

3 small heads of locally grown green cabbage, cored and shredded or sliced into thin strips, about 2 packed cups

1 medium local apple, Gala or other, cored and cut into matchstick pieces

¼ cup organic raisins (golden, Thompson, or other variety)

Sea salt and pepper

1 tablespoon apple cider vinegar

1 tablespoon Dijon mustard

1 tablespoon extra-virgin olive oil

1 teaspoon local honey

Combine the cabbage, apple, and raisins in a bowl. Sprinkle lightly with sea salt and pepper. Using two spoons, toss to combine. In a separate bowl, combine the vinegar, mustard, olive oil, and honey. Whisk to blend. Pour the dressing evenly over the salad, using a rubber spatula to scrape the bowl of the dressing. Using two spoons, toss well to coat evenly. Taste for seasonings.

Tip: Use agave instead of honey to make this recipe vegan.

Summer Potato and Vegetable Salad V GF

Why make potato salad with just potatoes when you can add lots of other healthful vegetables? We couldn't think of a reason either.

Serves 6

Salt, to taste

4 medium red-skin potatoes

2 medium carrots, cut on the diagonal into fairly thin slices

3 stalks asparagus, tough 2 inches of the bottom stalk removed, remaining stalk cut on the diagonal into ½-inch slices

1 broccoli crown, florets separated

1 scallion, white part and 3 inches green, cut into thin slices

½ small red onion, sliced into thin ribs, separated

3 tablespoons extra-virgin olive oil

3 tablespoons freshly squeezed orange juice (from about ½ orange)

1 tablespoon apple cider vinegar

2 tablespoons snipped fresh dill or 6 fresh basil leaves, sliced into strips right before using

Pepper, to taste

1. Bring a large covered pot of lightly salted water to a boil over high heat. Add the potatoes and cook for about 18 minutes, until barely fork-tender. Add the carrots, asparagus, and broccoli and continue cooking for about 3 minutes until the potatoes are fork-tender. Drain the vegetables.

2. When the potatoes are cool enough to handle, peel the skins. They should easily slip off as you rub them with your fingers. Slice the potatoes into ¼-inch rounds and turn them into a bowl. Add the remaining ingredients and toss well, using your hands to combine. Taste for seasonings. Serve warm or at room temperature.

Summer Potato Salad with Fresh Peas

You can enjoy this delicious salad for lunch or a light supper as it contains good protein and iron from the peas and the soy chicken, along with plenty of carbohydrates, vitamins, and minerals. Serve it over tender local organic greens like baby spinach for a wonderful summer meal.

Serves 6

Sea salt

6 medium organic potatoes, red skin, purple, or other

2 medium carrots, diced

1 pound fresh peas, shelled, about 1 cup

1 small organic zucchini, diced

1 6- or 8-ounce package meatless chicken strips

2 tablespoons chopped fresh organic chives

¼ cup low-fat mayonnaise

¼ cup low-fat organic sour cream

3 tablespoons organic milk

Pepper, to taste

¾ pound organic baby spinach or other organic local greens

1. Bring a large covered pot of lightly salted water to a boil over high heat. Add the potatoes. Cook for about 20 minutes, until barely tender when tested with a fork. Add the carrots, peas, zucchini, and the soy chicken strips. Continue to cook for about 2 minutes, stirring once to combine, until the potatoes are tender. Drain. Turn onto a large platter.

2. Using two wooden spoons, toss gently to cool the vegetables. When the potatoes are cool enough to handle, lift them out onto a separate plate. Peel the potatoes, then cut them into large dice.

3. Turn the diced potatoes and the other vegetables into a large bowl. Add the chives, mayonnaise, sour cream, milk, and a little salt and pepper. Toss well to combine. Taste for seasonings. Serve warm or chill for up to a day. When ready to serve, arrange the organic spinach on a large platter and spoon the potato salad over the greens.

Claire's Classic

Tabouli Salad V

Tabouli is a healthful salad of bulgur (cracked wheat). You can find bulgur in health food stores and in the gourmet section of most supermarkets. Bulgur is a delicious way to add more fiber to your diet. It's been popular on our menu for thirty-five years, and one of the "foodie" magazines listed it as a "hot food trend" a couple of years ago!

Serves 8

1 pound bulgur

1 bunch parsley, leaves chopped, stems discarded

1 small red onion, coarsely chopped

¼ cup olive oil

Juice of 2 lemons

2 teaspoons dried mint

Salt, to taste

½ teaspoon black pepper

Romaine leaves, torn, for serving

1 tomato, cut into wedges, for serving

1 lemon, cut into wedges, for serving

Place the bulgur in a large bowl. Pour over it enough hot water to cover by ¼ inch. Let stand for 1 hour. Add the parsley, red onion, olive oil, lemon juice, and mint, toss well, and taste for seasoning. Serve over torn romaine leaves with tomato and lemon wedges. Drizzle with additional olive oil, if desired.

Fruit Salad, Amalfi Style   V GF

Fruit salad, or *macedonia di frutta* in Italian, is available in every restaurant and snack bar throughout Amalfi. It's made using a variety of the best and freshest fruits.

Serves 6

2 apples, cored and cut into bite-size pieces

2 ripe peaches, pitted and cut into bite-size pieces

2 ripe plums, pitted and cut into bite-size pieces

30 cherries, pitted and cut in half

2 tablespoons granulated raw sugar

4 tablespoons freshly squeezed lemon juice (from about 1 lemon)

6 small fresh mint leaves, cut in half lengthwise

Place the cut fruit in a bowl and toss gently to combine. Sprinkle the sugar and lemon juice evenly over the top and scatter the mint leaves over the top. Toss gently to combine. Serve immediately.

Citrus Salad GF VO

This refreshing salad is loaded with vitamin C, something we can all use more of during cold and flu season. And studies consistently show that eating local honey each day can help build your resistance to pollen-related allergies. Besides, it tastes so delicious.

Serves 4–6

2 organic red grapefruits, peeled, seeded, and cut into small sections

2 large navel oranges, peeled and cut into thin slices

2 tangerines, peeled and cut into thin slices

1 small red onion, peeled and cut into thin rings, separated

1 tablespoon capers, rinsed, drained, then squeezed by hand to remove as much moisture as possible

12 small leaves fresh mint, apple mint or other variety

Freshly squeezed juice from 1 lemon, about 3 tablespoons

3 tablespoons local honey

1. Arrange the grapefruit sections in a circular pattern around a pretty plate. Arrange the oranges and tangerines overlapping in a circular pattern over the grapefruits. Scatter the onion rings, capers, and mint evenly over the oranges.

2. In a small bowl, whisk together the lemon juice and the honey. Drizzle this over evenly over the salad.

Tip: Use agave instead of honey to make this recipe vegan.

Summer Strawberry Salad with Ricotta Salata Cheese GF

This salad celebrates the glories of summer gardening. And, if you don't grow your own greens or strawberries, there are plenty for sale at farm stands and farmers' markets. For the freshest flavor, buy only the amount you plan to eat within 2 days. Store strawberries on a plate, lightly covered with a kitchen towel, in the refrigerator for up to 2 days. Or, freeze them to use after the local season. To freeze, rinse the strawberries, remove the stems, and drain them on kitchen towels. Arrange the dried berries in a single layer on a cookie sheet, then freeze until solid. Turn the berries into freezer bags and freeze them for up to 3 months.

Serves 4

8–10 cups mixed organic and local greens, about 8 ounces

12–16 local organic strawberries, cut in half or left whole if small

12 walnut halves, lightly toasted and quartered

3–4 ounces ricotta salata cheese, cut into small cubes

2 tablespoons extra-virgin olive oil

1 tablespoon red wine vinegar

Sea salt and pepper

Place the washed and drained greens in a large salad bowl. Scatter the strawberries, walnut quarters, and cubes of ricotta salata cheese over the top. Drizzle the olive oil and the vinegar evenly over the top. Sprinkle with sea salt and pepper. Using two wooden spoons, toss gently enough to coat the salad and avoid bruising the berries. Serve immediately.

Avocado Stuffed with Waldorf Tofu Salad GF

We're all for combining delicious combinations of healthy fruits and vegetables for our customers, and this salad is spot-on for flavor and for variety, too.

Serves 4

1 14-ounce pack organic firm tofu, drained and cut into small cubes

1 medium apple, cut into small cubes

4 small local Italian prune plums, pitted and cut into quarters

¼ cup raisins

12 seedless grapes, cut in half

¼ cup chopped pecans

¼ cup low-fat mayonnaise

¼ cup buttermilk

1 tablespoon snipped chives

Sea salt

Pepper

1 small head romaine, leaves torn in half

2 medium-ripe heirloom tomatoes, sliced

2 ripe avocados

1. Place the tofu cubes in a bowl. Add the apple, plums, raisins, grapes, and pecan pieces. Toss gently using your hands or two wooden spoons. Into a separate bowl, measure the mayonnaise, buttermilk, and chives. Sprinkle lightly with sea salt and pepper. Whisk to combine, then taste for seasonings. Drizzle about two-thirds of the dressing over the tofu salad, saving the remaining dressing for the tomatoes and romaine. Gently toss the tofu salad to coat it thoroughly.

2. Arrange the romaine leaves on a serving platter. Arrange the slices of tomatoes in a circular pattern over the romaine leaves. Drizzle the remaining dressing evenly over the top. Cut each avocado in half, remove the seed, then, using a spoon, scoop out each half, leaving the peel behind. Arrange the peeled and seeded avocado halves cut side up over the salad. Fill each avocado half with tofu salad. Enjoy it.

Turkish Vegetable Salad

We recently had the honor to serve lunch to a group of international leaders, many of whom were from Turkey, and we made this salad for them. They enjoyed it, and now we often make it for our deli case, too.

Serves 10–12 as appetizers

1 English cucumber, peeled and diced

2 small bell peppers (1 yellow and 1 green), cored, seeded and diced

1 small red onion, diced

1 small bunch Italian flat-leaf parsley, finely chopped, including tender stems

2 vine-ripened tomatoes, cut into medium dice

2 tablespoons extra-virgin olive oil

2 tablespoons snipped fresh dill

Sea salt, to taste

Place the diced cucumber, peppers, and onion in a bowl. Add the chopped parsley and the diced tomatoes with their juices. Using your hands or two wooden spoons, gently toss the ingredients to combine. Drizzle the olive oil evenly over the top, then gently toss to coat. Scatter the dill over the top and sprinkle with sea salt. Toss gently but thoroughly to combine. Taste for seasonings. Serve at room temperature.

Whole Grains

Diet fads, it seems, come and go with the ages. Back when the "fat police" were in vogue, their disciples came in claiming to eschew all fats. My response was always, "What about essential fatty acids?" Oddly enough, the diet rages that followed the fat-free diet obsession were the high-protein fad and incredibly high-fat diet fad that also encouraged an extremely low consumption of carbohydrates. It was impossible for me to understand how cholesterol levels wouldn't jump through the sky if you followed a high-fat/low-carb diet. Furthermore, I think it's a boring way to go through life. The only way

I'd ever give up eating carbohydrates is perhaps as a sacrifice for Lent.

The truth is that we need carbohydrates—make that *good* carbohydrates—for energy and as part of a healthful and interesting diet each and every day. By "good carbohydrates," I'm referring to whole grains such as wheat, corn, rice, oats, barley, quinoa, and rye, rather than highly processed grains. Whole grains are a good source of B vitamins, vitamin E, fiber, protein, important minerals such as iron and magnesium, and healthful fats—all important nutrients for good health. Studies show that diets that include whole grains can reduce the risk of heart disease, stroke, some cancers, diabetes, and obesity.

Whole grains contain all three parts of the entire seed: the bran, the germ, and the endosperm. Each part has value. The bran, or the outer layer, contains rich antioxidants,

B vitamins, and fiber and protects the kernel from disease. The germ is the embryo and also contains B vitamins, a little protein, minerals, and healthful fats, and, when fertilized by pollen, it will sprout another plant. And the endosperm contains carbohydrates, protein, vitamins, minerals, and fiber, and it provides the germ with its food supply.

Unfortunately, since the nineteenth century, many manufacturers have "refined" the whole grain, removing the outer bran and germ layers to make the grain cook in less time, make it more tender, and give it a milder flavor. This is how we ended up with white rice, white bread, bleached white flour, and other unfortunate ingredients that we now know are best to avoid or at least not rely on entirely for our carbohydrate needs. Brown rice, wheat bread, unbleached and whole wheat flour, whole oats, and other whole grains taste much more interesting and are a better choice for a balanced diet. And pasta made from semolina flour, which in turn is made from durum wheat, is a good source of carbohydrates, too.

Health professionals recommend that we eat three to five servings (about 300 grams) of whole grains a day. A serving size is a ½ cup of oatmeal, quinoa, or brown rice, or 1 cup of pasta. To break down how important whole grains are, 45 to 60 percent of your daily calories should be from carbohydrates, with 25 to 30 percent coming from fats and 15 to 20 percent from protein.

Again, look for good sources of these important basics. Choose fresh fruits and vegetables, whole grains, and beans, along with low-fat dairy products, including yogurt. These all contribute to a diet that's rich in vitamins, fiber, minerals, and the protein and carbohydrates a body needs for good health. Remember that sodas and candy, cakes, and other desserts have empty calories, with little, if any, nutritional value, so don't waste too many calories on them. Look for 100 percent whole wheat, barley, or other grain when reading ingredients listed on package labels, or else you're not getting the whole grain.

Chimichurri Quinoa and Bean Salad V GF

Quinoa and beans are staples in our house and in our restaurant, and for good reason: They're incredibly nutritious, providing fiber, protein, vitamins, and minerals. Quinoa is a complete protein and one of the oldest grains known. It's gluten-free and has an interesting nutty flavor. This special grain originated in the Andes, and thanks to the Incas it has been shared with much of the world. This favorite recipe, based on the traditional Argentinian sauce *chimichurri,* is generally served alongside meats. Serve it as an entree or as a side to a veggie burger for a delicious meal.

Serves 6

Salt

1 cup quinoa

2 cloves garlic

1 bunch cilantro

1 bunch Italian flat-leaf parsley

3 tablespoons fresh oregano, or
   1 tablespoon dried

¼–½ teaspoon crushed red pepper flakes

1 small jalapeño pepper, coarsely chopped

1 tablespoon white vinegar

2 tablespoons freshly squeezed lemon juice
   (from about ½ lemon)

3 tablespoons freshly squeezed orange juice
   (from about ½ orange)

1 cup grapeseed oil, dairy-free mayonnaise,
   or other mayonnaise

Pepper, to taste

1 12-ounce can organic black beans,
   drained

1 medium carrot, peeled and diced

1 small sweet organic onion, diced

12 sweet grape tomatoes, halved

1 large broccoli crown, florets separated
   into small pieces

1 tablespoon organic flax oil with lemon
   (optional; available at natural food
   stores)

1. Bring 2 cups of lightly salted water to a boil in a medium covered pot over high heat. Reduce the heat to low-medium and add the quinoa. Cover and cook at a simmer for about 25 minutes, until the water is absorbed and the quinoa is just tender.

2. Turn the quinoa into a large bowl, and using two forks, toss the quinoa to fluff it and to separate the grains. Set aside to cool, occasionally tossing the quinoa to facilitate cooling.

3. Meanwhile, prepare the chimichurri. Place the garlic, cilantro, parsley, oregano, pepper flakes, jalapeño, vinegar, lemon and orange juices, oil or mayonnaise, salt, and pepper in the bowl of a food processor fitted with a metal blade. Cover and process for about 30 seconds until well blended. Taste for seasonings.

4. When the quinoa is cooled to room temperature, add the beans, carrot, onion, tomatoes, and broccoli; add the flax oil, if using. Using two wooden spoons, toss to combine. Add the chimichurri and toss well to coat. Taste for seasonings. Serve at room temperature or refrigerate for up to 2 days. Toss again before serving.

Curried Brown Rice Salad V GF

Use traditional brown rice or, for a nice change, try basmati brown rice, an aromatic rice with a rich, nutty flavor.

Serves 6

1 cup organic apple juice

1 cup water

Salt and pepper, to taste

½ teaspoon turmeric

1 tablespoon curry powder

¼ teaspoon cinnamon

1 cup organic brown rice

2 cups corn kernels (cut from about 2 ears of corn)

2 cloves garlic

1-inch piece peeled fresh ginger, coarsely chopped

¼ cup freshly squeezed orange juice (from about ½ orange)

3 tablespoons peanut oil or pumpkin seed oil

1 teaspoon curry powder

Pinch of cayenne pepper

Salt and pepper, to taste

¼ cup organic raisins

1 small red onion, cut into thin rings, separated

2 small organic bell peppers, seeded and diced

1. Measure the apple juice, water, salt, pepper, turmeric, 1 tablespoon curry powder, cinnamon, and brown rice into a medium-size pot. Cover and bring to a boil over high heat. As soon as it reaches a boil, reduce the heat to low-medium and simmer for about 18 minutes, until the liquid is nearly absorbed, then stir in the corn kernels. Cover and continue cooking for about 3 minutes, until the rice and the corn are tender. Remove from the heat and turn into a large bowl.

2. Using two wooden spoons, toss to cool down a bit. Set aside to cool for about 15 minutes, occasionally tossing to facilitate cooling.

3. Meanwhile, measure the garlic, ginger, and orange juice into the bowl of a food processor fitted with a metal blade. Cover and process for about 20 seconds, until smooth and creamy-looking. With the motor running, add the oil, curry powder, cayenne, salt, and pepper to taste. Set aside this dressing.

4. Add the raisins, onion, and bell peppers to the cooled rice and corn. Using two wooden spoons, toss to combine. Add the dressing and toss well to coat the salad. Taste for seasonings. Serve at room temperature or refrigerate for up to 2 days. Toss again just before serving.

French Lentil Salad V GF

French lentils are smaller and more round than the traditional disc-shaped "green" lentils, and they're a dark green-black color. They have a strong and delicious lentil flavor. Like green lentils, they're loaded with protein and contain respectable amounts of calcium and iron.

Serves 4–6

4 quarts water

12 ounces organic French lentils, sorted for stones, rinsed

Sea salt

3 tablespoons extra-virgin olive oil

2 tablespoons organic apple cider vinegar

3 tablespoons freshly squeezed lemon juice (from about 1 lemon)

1 small organic shallot, quartered

2 cloves local organic garlic, cut in half

3–4 sprigs fresh local organic tarragon

Pepper

2 cups thinly sliced local organic Toscano kale

1. Bring the water to a boil in a covered pot over high heat. Add the lentils and a little salt. Reduce the heat to low-medium, cover, and cook the lentils at a low-medium boil, stirring occasionally, for about 20 minutes or until just tender. Drain the lentils, then turn them onto a platter to cool while you prepare the dressing.

2. Measure the olive oil into the bowl of a food processor fitted with a metal blade. Add the vinegar, lemon juice, shallot, and garlic. Strip the leaves of tarragon from the sprigs and add the leaves to the processor bowl. Discard the stems. Add a little sea salt and pepper. Cover and process until smooth, about 30 seconds. Taste for seasonings.

3. Turn the lentils into a bowl. Add the sliced kale. Using two wooden spoons, toss gently but thoroughly to combine ingredients. Add the dressing, using a rubber spatula to scrape the bowl of the contents. Toss again gently and thoroughly to combine. Taste for seasonings. Serve at room temperature or chilled.

Black Bean and Wheat Berry Salad V

This delicious salad with dressing offers an abundance of protein, fiber, vitamins and minerals and makes a wonderful lunch or side to any supper.

Serves 6

3 cups water

¾ cup wheat berries

Sea salt

1 15.5-ounce can black beans, drained, rinsed, and drained again

2 ripe peaches, pitted and diced

1 large ripe local tomato, diced

2 medium carrots, diced

½ small red onion, diced

1 clove garlic, sliced

1 small bunch cilantro, coarsely chopped

1 medium jalapeño pepper, sliced

Juice from 1 lime, about ¼ cup

¼ cup extra-virgin olive oil

Pepper, to taste

1. Measure the water and the wheat berries into a heavy pot. Sprinkle lightly with sea salt and bring to a boil over high heat. After it reaches a boil, reduce the heat to low-medium, cover the pot, and cook at a low boil for about 45 minutes until the wheat berries are just tender to your preference. Drain the wheat berries and turn them into a bowl. Using two wooden spoons, toss to cool slightly. Add the drained black beans, diced peaches, tomato, carrots, and onion, and sprinkle lightly with sea salt and pepper.

2. Using the two wooden spoons, toss to combine.

3. Place the garlic, cilantro, jalapeño, lime juice, and olive oil into a blender cup. Sprinkle lightly with sea salt and pepper. Cover and blend for several seconds until smooth. Taste for seasonings. Pour this dressing evenly over the salad, using a rubber spatula to scrape the remaining dressing from the blender cup. Toss the salad thoroughly to coat with the dressing. Taste for seasonings. Serve immediately, or refrigerate for up to 1 day and toss again just before serving.

Black-Eyed Pea and Spinach Salad V GF

I think black-eyed peas are woefully underused in much of the country. At Claire's, we're trying to change this. They are rich in fiber and protein, and they're a tremendous part of Southern history, all reasons to enjoy these lovely beans.

Serves 4

1 12-ounce can organic black-eyed peas

½ medium organic red onion, coarsely chopped

1 7-ounce bag organic baby spinach or arugula

1 tablespoon extra-virgin olive oil

2 tablespoons organic apple cider vinegar

1 tablespoon organic agave syrup or local honey

1 teaspoon dried organic thyme

½ teaspoon organic cumin

Sea salt and pepper

Drain the black-eyed peas, rinse them under cold water, and drain again. Turn the peas into a bowl. Add the onion and spinach, and using two wooden spoons, toss to combine. Drizzle the olive oil, vinegar, and agave syrup or local honey evenly over the top, then sprinkle the thyme, cumin, sea salt, and pepper evenly over the top. Toss well to coat. Taste for seasonings. Serve at room temperature or refrigerate for up to a day. Toss again before serving.

Warm Bean Salad V GF

This lovely side dish becomes a good entree if you serve it over cooked noodles.

Serves 4

1 tablespoon extra-virgin olive oil

1 small sweet onion, cut into thin rings, separated

½ small red cabbage, finely chopped

8 cremini mushrooms, cut in half

Salt and pepper

2 tablespoons fresh lemon juice, from about ½ lemon

1 tablespoon small fresh mint leaves, or ½ teaspoon dried

1 11-ounce can chickpeas, drained

Heat the oil in a large skillet over medium heat. Add the onion, cabbage, and mushrooms. Sprinkle with salt and pepper. Cover and cook for about 15 minutes, stirring occasionally, until the cabbage is wilted. Add the lemon juice, mint, and chickpeas. Stir to mix. Cook for about 3 minutes, stirring occasionally, until heated through. Taste for seasonings.

Green Bean Salad V GF

Enjoy the best flavor and nutrients by buying fresh from your local farmers.

Serves 4

Salad:

Sea salt

¾ pound string beans, trimmed and cut into thirds

2 ears fresh sweet corn, shucked and kernels removed, about 2 cups kernels

3 heirloom tomatoes, cut into wedges then into thirds, juices reserved

1 small red onion, cut into thin rings, separated

Dressing:

¾ cup organic soy or dairy milk

3 medium-size cloves garlic, sliced

1/3 cup each chopped Italian flat-leaf parsley, basil, and mint

½ cup organic mayonnaise, regular or dairy-free

Sea salt and pepper

1. Bring 2 quarts of lightly salted water to a boil in a covered pot over high heat. Add the string beans, cover, and cook for 2 minutes. Add the corn, cover, and continue cooking for another minute. Test the string beans; they should be crisp-tender, but if you prefer them more tender, cook for another minute. Drain the string beans and corn, then turn onto a platter to cool the vegetables to room temperature.

2. Meanwhile, place the dressing ingredients in a blender cup. Cover and blend for about 30–60 seconds, until well blended, stopping once to scrape down the sides of the blender cup with a rubber spatula. Taste the dressing for seasoning.

3. After the vegetables have cooled slightly, turn into a bowl. Add the tomatoes and their juices, and the onion. Toss gently to combine, using two wooden spoons. Pour the dressing evenly over the vegetables, using a rubber spatula to scrape the blender cup. Using two wooden spoons, toss the salad gently but thoroughly until well coated. Taste for seasonings.

Coconut and Chile-Marinated Tofu Salad V GF

I've always loved combining fruits with vegetables for our salads, and this particular combination is lovely. The combination of coconut milk, ginger, and lemongrass is sublime.

Serves 4

Marinated Tofu:

1 14-ounce package organic extra firm tofu, drained, cut into small dice

1 clove garlic

1-inch piece ginger, peeled, sliced

1 stalk lemongrass, soft inner part sliced, or grated zest from ½ lemon and ½ lime

¼ teaspoon crushed red pepper flakes

1/3 cup coconut milk

Salad and Dressing:

1 7-ounce package organic baby greens

1 ripe mango, peeled and cubed, or 12 cubes frozen mango, defrosted

1 teaspoon extra-virgin olive oil

1 teaspoon toasted sesame oil

2 tablespoons freshly squeezed orange juice (from about ½ orange)

Salt and pepper, to taste

2 tablespoons sliced almonds

1 Granny Smith apple, cored and cut into small cubes

1. To prepare the marinated tofu, cover a cookie sheet with a double layer of paper towels. Arrange the drained and diced tofu on the paper towels in a single layer to drain again while you prepare the marinade.

2. Place the garlic clove in the bowl of a food processor fitted with a metal blade. Cover and process for about 5 seconds until minced. Add the ginger, lemongrass, and pepper flakes. Cover and process for about 15 seconds until minced to a fine blend, nearly a paste. Using a rubber spatula, scrape down the sides of the processor bowl. Add the coconut milk. Cover and process for about 20 seconds until smooth.

3. Place the drained tofu into a bowl. Add the coconut milk marinade, using a rubber spatula to scrape the bowl. Toss gently using your hands or two wooden spoons to coat the tofu with the marinade.

4. To prepare the salad and dressing, arrange the greens and the mango on a platter. Drizzle the olive oil, sesame oil, and orange juice evenly over the top. Using tongs, toss gently to coat. Sprinkle with salt and pepper and toss again. Taste for seasoning. Scatter the almonds and apple cubes over the top. Using a slotted spoon, lift the tofu cubes from the bowl, leaving behind any juices. Scatter the tofu cubes evenly over the salad. Serve immediately.

Golden Beet Salad `GF`

Beautiful, delicious, and rich in antioxidants—really, this lovely salad has it all. I like to serve it over organic mixed greens.

Serves 4

Sea salt

4 medium organic golden beets, unpeeled and with 1 inch of stem remaining

2 medium organic oranges (I like to use Valencia)

1 medium red onion, cut in half, then sliced into thin ribs, separated

3 ounces feta cheese, crumbled

12 pecan or walnut halves, chopped

1 tablespoon extra-virgin olive oil

1 tablespoon red wine vinegar

Black pepper

1. Bring a covered pot of lightly salted water to a boil over high heat. Meanwhile, wash the beets well to remove the sand. When the water reaches a boil, add the beets. Cover the pot and cook the beets at a high boil for about 20–40 minutes, depending on size, until they are just fork-tender.

2. Using a slotted spoon, transfer the cooked beets to a colander. Any remaining sand from the beets will be left behind in the water, so just drain it into the sink. Set the beets aside until they are cool enough to handle, then remove the skin using your fingertips. The skin should slip off easily, and you can use a paring knife to remove any skin that remains. Cut the beets into medium-thick slices and arrange them in a row on a platter.

3. Using a sharp paring knife, remove the skin and the white pith from the oranges; do this over a bowl so that you can collect any juices. Cut the oranges into thin rounds. Arrange the orange rounds in between the slices of beets. Scatter the onion ribs evenly over the beets and oranges. Scatter the cheese and the chopped nuts evenly over the top. Drizzle the salad first with olive oil and then with vinegar. Sprinkle lightly and evenly with sea salt and pepper. Serve immediately.

Golden Beet Salad over Beet Greens with Sherry Wine Vinegar Syrup V GF

Golden beets are at their peak from July through mid October, and you should take advantage of their freshness and flavor during those months. These root vegetables have a sweet, mild flavor and a silky, smooth texture. And they're rich in iron and vitamins A and C.

Serves 4

Sea salt

2 large golden beets (each about the size of a large orange)

6–12 beet leaves with tender stems

¼ cup sherry wine vinegar

2 tablespoons grapeseed oil

Salt and pepper, to taste

1 small red onion, cut into thin rings, separated

1. Bring a large pot of lightly salted water to a boil over high heat. Wash the beets and greens under cold water to remove the sand and any grit. Trim the beets to 2 inches above the stems. Trim away and discard any brown leaves and the tough stems from the beet greens; reserve the remaining leaves and tender stems. Wash the beets again, using your hands to rub off any remaining sand. Cook in the boiling water for 20–45 minutes, depending on the size, until they are just fork-tender.

2. Meanwhile, bring a small pot of lightly salted water to a boil over high heat. Fill a bowl or the sink with cold water, scatter the beet greens in the water, and thoroughly wash the greens to remove any sand. Lift the greens out of the water, and if there is any sand remaining in the bowl or sink, drain the water and repeat until all the sand is removed. This second washing will assure removal of all sand. Drain and coarsely chop the leaves and stems. When the water in the small pot reaches a boil, add the chopped greens and stir to coat the greens with the boiling water. Cook for a minute until they wilt. Drain and turn into a small bowl.

3. Heat the sherry wine vinegar in a heavy pot over low-medium heat and cook at just below a simmer, swirling the pot every now and again, for about 7 minutes or until thickened and reduced to 1 tablespoon. Transfer vinegar to a small bowl and combine with grapeseed oil, salt, and pepper, whisking to mix. Taste this dressing for seasoning.

4. When the beets are tender, drain them and set aside until they are cool enough to handle. Remove the skin using your fingers; it should peel off easily. Cut the beets into ¼-inch slices. Drizzle a tablespoon of the dressing over the wilted greens and toss to coat, using your hands or tongs.

5. Arrange the greens on a platter. Arrange the sliced beets in the center of the platter, overlapping to form an attractive design. Scatter the onion rings evenly over the beets. Drizzle the remaining 2 tablespoons of dressing evenly over the beets.

Arugula Salad V GF

If you don't grow your own arugula, try to buy produce with small leaves for a more tender salad.

Serves 6

12–14 cups arugula, about ¾ pound, well rinsed and drained

12 sweet grape or cherry tomatoes, cut in half

1 small sweet onion (local, Vidalia, or other), sliced into thin rings, separated

1 small bulb fennel, dark green, feathery top cut off and discarded, bottom bulb trimmed and cut in half, and each half cut into thin slices, separated

2 tablespoons extra-virgin olive oil

3 tablespoons freshly squeezed lemon juice, from about 1 lemon

Salt and pepper, to taste

Combine the arugula, tomatoes, onion, and fennel in a bowl. Using two wooden spoons, toss to combine. Drizzle the olive oil evenly over the salad and toss well to coat the leaves with the oil. Drizzle the lemon juice evenly over the salad and toss well to combine. Sprinkle with salt and pepper, then toss well to combine. Taste for seasonings.

A self-proclaimed Claire's Corner Copia fanatic, I order lunch from Claire's at least three days a week. Their healthy, delicious, and filling salads make it easy to get protein—from beans, legumes, nuts, and seeds. I love the smoothies, too. But Claire's is so much more than just a restaurant. For so many of us, it's a home away from home. When you walk into Claire's, you feel the love that goes into every single meal. That's why I keep going back.

—Anne P. Worcester, tournament director, New Haven Open at Yale; and chief marketing officer, Market New Haven

Arugula Salad with Lemon, Honey, and Goat Cheese GF

I never tire of locally grown organic arugula; maybe because it's only available here in Connecticut for less than five months a year. Arugula is loaded with iron, calcium, and vitamin A, nutrients we all need for good health.

Serves 6

1 pound organic arugula, well washed because it's gritty, and drained

1 pint organic Sun Gold cherry tomatoes, cut in half

1 garlic scape, cut into ½-inch pieces, or 1 small organic scallion, cut into thin rings, separated

2 tablespoons organic raisins

2 tablespoons chopped walnuts

2 teaspoons walnut oil

2 teaspoons extra-virgin olive oil

2 tablespoons freshly squeezed lemon juice, from about ½ lemon

1 teaspoon local honey

Sea salt and pepper, to taste

4–6 ounces local goat's milk cheese

1. Place the well-washed and drained arugula in a large bowl. Add the tomato halves, garlic scape or onion, raisins, and walnuts. Drizzle the walnut oil and the olive oil evenly over the top. Using two wooden spoons or tongs, toss to coat. Drizzle the lemon juice and the honey over the top. Toss to coat. Sprinkle with salt and pepper. Toss to combine. Taste for seasonings.

2. Turn the salad out onto a platter. If using aged cheese, crumble it over the top of the salad. If the cheese is young and soft, then use a small spoon to scoop out bits of cheese and arrange over the salad. Serve immediately.

Heirloom Tomato Salad with Fresh Herb Pesto Drizzle V GF

I grow organic heirloom tomatoes (about 3,000 pounds a season!) and herbs for Claire's in my backyard. While I adore my time in the garden, it's a ton of work. Salads as luscious as the one below remind me of why the work is totally worth it!

Serves 6

3 large locally grown heirloom tomatoes
(I like to use 1 each of Brandywine, Black Prince, and Juliet), cut into thick slices

½ cup packed assorted fresh herbs
(chives, basil, oregano, mint, or others)

3 tablespoons extra-virgin olive oil

1 lemon

Salt and pepper, to taste

Arrange the tomato slices in a circular pattern on a platter. Place the herbs in the bowl of a food processor fitted with a metal blade. Drizzle the olive oil over the herbs. Using a citrus zester or paring knife, peel thin strips from the skin of the lemon and set aside. Cut the lemon in half and squeeze the juice from half into a bowl. Measure out 2 tablespoons of the juice and add it to the processor. Add salt and pepper. Cover and process for about 20 seconds, stopping once to scrape the sides of the processor bowl with a rubber spatula, until the herbs are finely minced. Taste for seasonings. Using a small spoon, drizzle the herb pesto evenly over the tomatoes. Scatter the lemon strips evenly over the salad. Top with additional pepper, if desired.

Claire's Classic

Greek Salad GF

You can enjoy this salad year-round. It also makes a tasty filling for a pita pocket.

Serves 4

Salad:

3 bell peppers, 1 each red, yellow, and green, seeded and sliced

1 small red onion, sliced into rings

1 English (seedless) cucumber, peeled and sliced into ¼-inch rounds

1 bunch broccoli, 1 inch trimmed from ends of stems and then discarded, remainder chopped into small pieces

8–12 Greek olives, drained

2 tomatoes, cut in half and then sliced

8 ounces feta cheese

Dressing:

⅓ cup olive oil

2 tablespoons lemon juice

1 tablespoon red wine vinegar

½ teaspoon dried oregano

½ teaspoon dried mint

Salt and black pepper, to taste

Toss the peppers, onion, cucumber, broccoli, and olives in a bowl. Arrange the tomatoes and feta in a separate bowl or platter, then add the tossed vegetables. In a separate bowl, whisk together the dressing ingredients. Taste for seasoning. Pour the dressing over the salad and toss well.

Barley, Greek-Salad Style

This salad makes a complete meal in less than an hour. Pair it with good Greek pita bread and a juicy blood orange for dessert and you'll have a perfect weeknight supper.

For this recipe, I like to use meatless chicken-style strips made by Lightlife®, found in the produce section of the supermarket, or strips made by Morningstar Farms®, found with the frozen veggie burgers and other frozen veggie meats.

Serves 4

6 cups water

2 cups barley

1 broccoli crown, florets cut into small pieces

2 small organic bell peppers (1 red and 1 yellow), seeded and diced

2 scallions, white part and 3 inches green, sliced thin

1 pint cherry tomatoes, cut in half

12 pitted kalamata olives, cut in half

1 6-ounce package soy chicken strips

2 tablespoons chopped fresh mint leaves, or ½ teaspoon dried mint

3 tablespoons snipped fresh dill, or 2 teaspoons dried dill

½ teaspoon dried oregano

3 tablespoons lightly toasted pine nuts

¼ cup extra-virgin olive oil

3 tablespoons freshly squeezed lemon juice, from about 1 lemon

1 tablespoon red wine vinegar

3 ounces feta cheese, cut into tiny cubes

Salt and pepper, to taste

Bring the water to a boil in a covered pot over high heat. Add the barley, then lower the heat to low-medium. Cover and cook at a low boil for about 40–45 minutes until the water has absorbed and the barley is tender. Turn the cooked barley into a bowl. Add the remaining ingredients except the salt, and, using two wooden spoons, toss to combine. Taste for seasonings before adding the salt as some soy chicken strips are a bit salty.

Broccoli Rabe Salad V GF

Broccoli rabe is a classic Italian bitter green and it's a favorite in our family. It's so rich in fiber, iron, and vitamins A and C that we try to serve it at least once a week.

Serves 4–6

Sea salt

2 bunches broccoli rabe, local if available, about a pound

Pepper

3 tablespoons extra-virgin olive oil

3 cloves organic garlic, sliced

¼ teaspoon crushed red pepper flakes

1 organic lemon

1. Bring 2 quarts of lightly salted water to a boil in a covered pot over high heat. Trim and discard the bottom inch or so of tough stems from the broccoli rabe. Thoroughly rinse the broccoli rabe, then drain it. Add the broccoli rabe to the boiling water, and using tongs, turn it to coat with the boiling water. Cover and cook for about 4 minutes, using the tongs to occasionally turn the broccoli rabe, until it's cooked to your preference. Drain the broccoli rabe, then transfer it to a large serving platter. Set aside to cool slightly, then cover and refrigerate for about 15 minutes to chill; if you prefer to serve it warm, skip this step.

2. Sprinkle a little sea salt and pepper on top, then drizzle the olive oil evenly over the top. Using the tongs, turn the broccoli rabe to coat with the oil. Scatter the garlic and crushed red pepper flakes over the top. Taste for seasonings.

3. Cut the lemon into wedges. Arrange the wedges around the platter and instruct your guests to squeeze a little lemon over their broccoli rabe. Refrigerate any leftovers and serve chilled.

Carrot Salad GF

This salad is colorful, healthy, and delicious—three reasons to enjoy a second helping!

Serves 4–6

8 locally grown organic carrots, grated

1 small head locally grown red cabbage, shredded

1 cup locally grown blueberries

1 tablespoon caraway seeds

¼ cup raspberry vinegar

½ cup low-fat organic plain yogurt

Sea salt and pepper, to taste

Combine the ingredients in a bowl. Using your hands or two spoons, toss well to combine. Taste for seasonings.

Carrot-Raspberry Salad V GF

Carrots are so rich in color, flavor, and beta-carotene, and they're available and affordable year-round. And who doesn't like carrots?

Serves 4

8 medium carrots, shredded

½ pint raspberries

2 medium Valencia or other oranges

4 large or 8 small mint leaves, apple mint or other, cut in half lengthwise

¼ cup raspberry vinegar

Sea salt and pepper

1. Place the shredded carrots and raspberries in a bowl. Grate a teaspoon of the orange zest from one orange and add it to the bowl. Peel the oranges, cut in half, then cut each half into thin slices. Add to the bowl, including any juices. Add the mint leaves.

2. Using your hands or two wooden spoons, toss gently to combine. Drizzle the vinegar evenly over the salad, then sprinkle with sea salt and pepper. Toss gently but thoroughly to coat. Taste for seasoning.

Crunchy Broccoli Salad V GF

Broccoli is one of the healthiest vegetables around, and I'm so glad that our customers love it. This is the classic preparation that my mother made several times a week when I was growing up. I still love it.

Serves 4–6

Sea salt

3 large bunches broccoli crowns

1 large clove garlic, cut into thin slices

1 tablespoon extra-virgin olive oil

Freshly squeezed juice from 1 lemon (about 3 tablespoons)

1. Bring 4 cups of lightly salted water to a boil in a covered pot over high heat. Meanwhile, trim about ¼ inch from the bottoms of the broccoli crowns, then cut into small bunches of florets.

2. When the water reaches a boil, add the broccoli. Stir to coat with the water. Cook for 1½–2 minutes, stirring frequently until the broccoli is crisp-tender to your preference. Drain and turn into a bowl. Scatter the garlic slices over the top, then drizzle the olive oil evenly over the top. Using two wooden spoons, toss to coat. Drizzle the lemon juice evenly over the top. Sprinkle lightly with sea salt.

3. Toss to coat. Taste for seasonings. Serve warm or refrigerate for up to 2 days. Toss again before serving.

Dandelion Salad V GF

Look for smaller greens for this simple yet flavorful salad—they are more tender than the older, larger ones. Most bitter greens need a bit more salt for balance, so be prepared. Drizzle a little organic flax oil over your salad for a brightly flavored dose of your omega-3s.

Serves 4–6

1 large bunch (about 1 pound) organic dandelion greens, well washed

8–10 thin chives

4–5 young garlic shoots or garlic chives, snipped into ½-inch pieces

2 tablespoons extra-virgin olive oil

Freshly squeezed lemon juice from ½ lemon (about 2 tablespoons)

Organic flax oil with lemon, to taste (optional; available at natural food stores)

Sea salt and fresh pepper, to taste

Combine the dandelion greens, chives, and garlic shoots in a serving bowl. Using tongs or two wooden spoons, toss to combine. Drizzle the olive oil evenly over the greens, and toss to coat. Drizzle the lemon juice evenly over the greens, then drizzle flax oil evenly over the top, sprinkle with sea salt and pepper, and toss to combine. Taste for seasonings.

Salad of Baby Spinach, Caramelized Onions, and Roasted Eggplant GF

This salad is a whole meal and perfect for any time of the year, especially during the season when your garden-fresh spinach is young and tender.

Serves 6

Salad:

2 small white or Sicilian eggplants, or other small eggplants

Salt

1 large sweet onion, sliced into thin rings, separated

3 tablespoons extra-virgin olive oil, divided

Pepper

12 ounces baby spinach leaves, well washed to remove any grit, drained well

12 oil-cured black olives

4 ounces ricotta salata cheese, coarsely grated

Vinaigrette:

1½ cups extra-virgin olive oil

3 large plum tomatoes, coarsely chopped, with juice

1 small bunch basil, coarsely chopped

¼ cup chopped Italian flat-leaf parsley

Salt and pepper

1. To begin preparing the salad, preheat the oven to 400°F. Cut the eggplants into ½-inch rounds. Separate the rounds and place them in a bowl. Sprinkle generously with salt—about 2 tablespoons—using your hands to toss and coat the eggplant rounds. Set aside for about 20 minutes, tossing occasionally until the liquids begin to leach from the eggplant.

2. Meanwhile, in another bowl, toss the sliced onion rings with 1 tablespoon of the olive oil. Sprinkle with salt and pepper to taste. Turn onto a jelly roll pan, using a rubber spatula to scrape the bowl and to spread the onions evenly in the pan. Bake in the preheated oven for about 30 minutes, stirring occasionally until the onions are golden brown and a little crisp around the edges. Remove from the oven and set aside to cool.

3. Brush or spray another jelly roll pan with olive oil. Pour ¼ cup of water into the pan. Using your hands, squeeze the excess liquid from the eggplant rounds and place the rounds in a single layer on the prepared pan. Drizzle lightly and evenly with the remaining 2 tablespoons of olive oil. Sprinkle lightly with salt and pepper. Cover the pan tightly with foil. Bake in the preheated oven for about 30 minutes or until the eggplants are tender-soft when tested with a fork. Remove from the oven to cool.

4. Meanwhile, prepare the vinaigrette. Combine the oil, tomatoes, basil, parsley, salt, and pepper in the bowl of a food processor. Cover and blend for about 30 seconds, until nearly smooth. Taste for seasonings.

5. To assemble the salad, arrange the spinach leaves on a large serving platter. Scatter the caramelized onions, roasted eggplant, and olives over the spinach. Toss with about ¼ cup vinaigrette. Scatter the grated ricotta salata evenly over the top. Enjoy it.

Salad of Oranges, Avocado, and Red Onion V GF

I'm so glad that we all now know that avocados are so healthy. They are rich in heart-healthy omega-3 fatty acids, and they're lovely and delicious, too. Customers enjoy them in this and many other dishes at Claire's.

Serves 4–6

2 large organic oranges (I like to use Valencia oranges)

1 large organic red onion

2 large organic ripe avocados

Sea salt and pepper

1 teaspoon extra-virgin olive oil

Freshly squeezed juice from 1 organic lime, about 2 tablespoons

1 tablespoon finely chopped organic cilantro

1. Peel the oranges, then cut them into ¼-inch slices, picking out and discarding any seeds. Arrange them in a circular patter on a large round plate. Peel the onion, cut it into thin rings, and arrange the rings over and around the oranges. Peel, pit, and slice the avocados into ¼-inch slices. Arrange them over the onions and oranges in a circular patter closer to the center of the dish, or in any other pattern you like. Sprinkle lightly with sea salt and pepper.

2. In a small bowl, combine the olive oil, lime juice, cilantro, and a little sea salt and pepper. Taste for seasonings. Spoon the mixture evenly over the salad.

Grilled Asparagus and Arugula Salad with Strawberry Vinaigrette GF

This is the perfect salad to welcome early summer, when the local asparagus and the first harvest of strawberries are at their best.

Serves 6

1 large bunch asparagus, bottom inch of stem trimmed

1 teaspoon extra-virgin olive oil

Sea salt and freshly ground black pepper

6 cups organic baby arugula

6–8 fresh mint leaves (optional)

1 pint fresh strawberries

3 tablespoons brown rice vinegar

1 tablespoon walnut oil

3 tablespoons grapeseed or other mild oil

Sea salt and freshly ground black pepper

3 ounces feta cheese, crumbled

1. Arrange the asparagus on a plate. Drizzle the olive oil over the asparagus, then sprinkle with the sea salt and pepper. Using your hands, coat the asparagus with the oil. Heat the grill, or use a grill pan on the stove over medium-high heat. (If you're using the grill, use a vegetable holder to keep the asparagus from falling through the grill rack.) Cook the asparagus in a single layer for about 3 minutes, using tongs to turn the stalks so they cook evenly.

2. Transfer the cooked asparagus to a plate. Arrange the arugula on a large serving platter. Scatter the mint leaves over the arugula. Arrange the asparagus over the arugula. Rinse and then remove the green caps from the strawberries. Scatter half the berries (the smaller ones) evenly over the salad.

3. To prepare the dressing, place the remaining strawberries in a blender cup. Add the vinegar and oils. Blend on high speed for about 20 seconds until well blended. Taste for seasonings.

4. Pour the dressing evenly over the salad. Scatter the crumbled feta cheese evenly over the top.

Springtime Eats

When it comes to the first day of spring, particularly after a long winter, I can't think of a better way to celebrate than to enjoy spring fennel, English peas, and asparagus. Fennel, also known as *finocchio* in the Italian community, has a pale cream-colored bulbous base with pale green stems and bright green feathery, dill-like foliage. The flavor is like anise, or like a mild, somewhat sweet licorice. You can eat it raw as a snack, toss it in a salad, or enjoy the base and stems braised, stewed, roasted, or grilled. Snip the feathery foliage and toss it with your salads. You can use the whole thing. When buying fennel, look for crisp, firm bulbs, without any brown or soft spots, and with deep green foliage. Once you get it home, store it in the fridge, wrapped in a kitchen towel, for up to 5 days. Fennel is a wonderful source of vitamin A and contains good amounts of calcium and potassium.

English peas start to appear on the supermarket shelves in early spring in all parts of the country, and by July they're available from local farmers in many areas. Freshly picked peas, much like corn, begin to convert their sugars to starch right after they're picked, so fresher is better, which means you'll need to plan to use the peas within a day or two or buying them. Be sure to store them in their pods in a paper bag in the fridge and to shell them right before cooking. A pound of pods will yield anywhere from ½ cup to 1 cup of peas, depending on the size of the pods. You can cook the shelled peas in lightly salted boiling water for a couple of minutes and enjoy them with just a drizzle of extra-virgin olive oil on top and a sprinkle of sea salt. The peas are a good source of protein, vitamin A, niacin, and iron.

Asparagus is a member of the lily family. It starts to become available across the country in the spring. Whether you prefer the thicker stalks, which are from older, more established plants, or the thinner ones, which are cut from younger plants, they are a rich source of iron and vitamins A, B, and C. Look for firm, deep green stalks, with tightly closed tips. Store them wrapped in a kitchen towel in the fridge for up to 3 days. Before cooking, trim off the tough bottom inch or two of the stems. Enjoy the stalks steamed, roasted, grilled, or braised. They are also lovely in an omelet or a frittata.

Spring Asparagus Salad GF

This is the quintessential spring and summer salad for me, particularly because Connecticut is home to the largest asparagus grower in New England and also because my friend Rose has chickens and gives me fresh eggs! You can't get better than this.

Serves 6

Sea salt

1 large bunch asparagus, bottom 2 inches removed and discarded (or saved for making stock), remaining spears cut on the diagonal into 1-inch pieces

1 tablespoon organic extra-virgin olive oil

2 hard-cooked eggs, finely chopped

1. Fill a medium pot halfway with water. Cover and bring to a boil over high heat, then add a little sea salt. Set a colander over the pot of boiling water and add the asparagus. Cover and steam the asparagus for about 2 minutes, until it turns bright green.

2. Remove from the colander and arrange on a platter. Drizzle the olive oil evenly over the top, then sprinkle lightly with sea salt. Scatter the hard-cooked eggs evenly over the top.

Spring Salad GF

There's something special about the flavors of fennel paired with tangerine, and the combination always reminds me of spring—hence the name.

Serves 4

Dressing:

2 tablespoons extra-virgin olive oil

Fresh juice from ½ lemon, about 2 tablespoons

1 tablespoon local honey

Sea salt and pepper

Salad:

8 cups organic mixed greens

½ small bulb fennel

1 organic tangerine

½ small organic spring onion

¼ cup sliced almonds

1 organic apple (I like to use Gala)

4 ounces fresh local sheep's milk cheese

1. To prepare the dressing, measure the ingredients into a small bowl. Whisk to combine. Taste for seasoning. Set aside.

2. To prepare the salad, place the mixed greens in a bowl. Cut the fennel into thin half-circles and add to the bowl. Peel the tangerine and separate the segments, then add to the bowl. Cut the spring onion into thin half-circles, separate them, and add to the salad. Drizzle the salad dressing over the top and toss well to coat.

3. Turn the salad onto a platter. Scatter the almonds evenly over the top. Core the apple, cut it in half, then slice each half into thin wedges. Arrange them around the salad. Break off little pieces of the cheese and scatter over the top. Serve immediately.

Spring Salad with Local Cheeses GF

Early season greens are so tender that you'll look forward to a bountiful and healthful salad every day. This beautiful salad was inspired by my talented friend Stewart London, the chef from Sankow's Beaver Brook Farm in Lyme, Connecticut.

Serves 4–6

Salad:

¾ pound assorted local organic greens

8–10 assorted local organic edible flowers (I like to use nasturtium and pansies)

2 tablespoons snipped local organic chives

4–5 leaves local organic basil, stacked, rolled, and cut into strips

5–6 local organic tarragon leaves

1 teaspoon grated organic lemon zest

Dressing:

2 tablespoons extra-virgin olive oil

1 clove organic garlic, finely chopped

2 tablespoons SABA Biodynamic Traditional Grape Syrup, or good balsamic vinegar aged 12 years or more

1 tablespoon local maple syrup

1 tablespoon freshly squeezed organic lemon juice (squeezed from ½ lemon)

Sea salt and pepper

Topping:

4 ounces local cheese (I like Pleasant Son Aged Cheese from Sankow's Beaver Brook Farm or feta), cut into small cubes (optional)

1. To prepare the salad, combine the greens, flowers, herbs, and zest in a salad bowl. Using your hands, gently toss to combine.

2. To prepare the dressing, combine the oil, garlic, SABA, maple syrup, lemon juice, salt, and pepper in a bowl. Taste for seasoning.

3. Just before serving, scatter the cheese cubes, if using, over the salad, then pour the dressing evenly over the salad. Using two wooden spoons or your hands, gently toss to coat. Taste for seasoning.

Summer Salad with Corn and Avocado V GF

This salad is so delicious and healthful and if you add a little shredded Monterey Jack cheese, it makes a terrific filling for grilled quesadillas.

Serves 4

8 ears fresh, local corn

2 ripe avocados

8 medium cremini mushrooms, quartered

4 freshly picked squash blossoms, piston removed and blossoms cut into strips (optional)

20 local cherry tomatoes, cut in half

1 small red onion, coarsely chopped

1 clove garlic, finely chopped

¼ cup chopped cilantro

½ small jalapeño pepper, finely chopped

2 tablespoons extra-virgin olive oil

2 tablespoons freshly squeezed lime juice, from about 1 lime

Sea salt and black pepper, to taste

1. Bring a covered pot of water to a boil over high heat. Meanwhile, shuck the corn and cut the kernels from the cobs; you should have about 4 heaping cups. When the water reaches a boil, add the corn and cook for about 3 minutes, then drain. Turn the cooked corn into a bowl. Using two wooden spoons, toss to help cool it.

2. Cut the avocados in half and remove the pits. Using a spoon, scoop the pulp out of the skin. Cut the avocado halves into cubes and add them to the corn. Add the mushrooms, squash blossoms, halved cherry tomatoes, onion, garlic, cilantro, and jalapeño pepper. Using the two wooden spoons, toss gently but thoroughly to mix. Drizzle the olive oil and the lime juice evenly over the top, sprinkle with sea salt and pepper, then toss to coat. Taste for seasonings.

Fall Harvest Salad GF

Serve this colorful salad for a bounty of healthful and delicious ingredients.

Serves 4

3 medium local golden or red beets, peeled and each cut into 6 wedges

1 head red leaf lettuce (organic if possible), rinsed and drained, torn into pieces

1 small local onion, cut into thin rings and separated

1 small organic local carrot, shredded

3 tablespoons dried cranberries

1 clove local garlic, finely minced

1 tablespoon fresh oregano leaves, or 1 teaspoon dried oregano

1 tablespoon walnut oil

2 tablespoons extra-virgin olive oil

3 tablespoons red wine vinegar

2 teaspoons local honey

Sea salt and pepper

4 ounces feta cheese, crumbled

3 tablespoons chopped pecans

1. Bring a covered medium pot of water to a boil over high heat. Add the beets and cook, uncovered, at a medium boil for about 20 minutes until fork-tender. Drain and set aside.

2. Place the lettuce, onion, carrot, cranberries, garlic, and oregano in a salad bowl.

3. Using two wooden spoons, toss to combine. Drizzle the walnut and olive oils evenly over the salad, then toss gently to coat. Drizzle the vinegar and the honey evenly over the salad, sprinkle with salt and pepper, then toss to combine. Taste for seasonings. Scatter the crumbled feta and the pecans evenly over the top. Serve immediately.

Winter Salad with Arugula and Persimmons V GF

Persimmons are in season during the winter months. The Hachiya variety, which is readily available in supermarkets, is large and round, with a slightly elongated bottom. The fruit absolutely must be soft and ripe before you eat it or it will be bitter, so plan ahead to allow firm fruit to ripen on the counter for a few days. When ripe, the red-orange flesh is creamy and juicy and the flavor is tart-sweet and unlike anything else—well worth waiting for or planning ahead. And it's a wonderful source of vitamins A and C. Atop any salad it's sure to dazzle you, but do try it with this super-healthful combination of calcium-, iron-, and vitamin A–rich organic arugula. Add thin slices of anise-flavored fennel and enjoy the combination of the peppery, mustardlike flavor of the arugula and the sweetness of the persimmon. It will make you do the "food dance."

Serves 4

1 7-ounce container of organic arugula, rinsed and drained well

½ small fennel bulb, cut in half, then cut into thin half-rings, separated

1 clove garlic, thinly sliced

1½ tablespoons extra-virgin olive oil

2 tablespoons freshly squeezed lemon juice (from about ½ lemon)

Sea salt and pepper

1 large persimmon, soft and ripe

1. Place the arugula, sliced fennel, and garlic in a bowl. Drizzle with the olive oil and lemon juice. Sprinkle with sea salt and pepper. Using two wooden spoons, toss well to coat. Taste for seasoning.

2. Arrange the arugula mixture on a platter. Rinse the persimmon and, using a sharp paring knife, cut off the top stem. Cut the persimmon in half lengthwise, then cut each half into 3 or 4 wedges. Arrange the wedges over the salad. Serve immediately.

Jalapeño-Chive Ranch Dressing GF

This flavorful dressing is one of the newest additions to our menu. It's popular on our salads and as a dip for raw vegetables.

Makes a little over 2 cups

¼ medium jalapeño pepper

¼ cup snipped chives

3 small cloves garlic

1¼ cups sour cream

¼ teaspoon salt, to taste

¼ teaspoon black pepper, to taste

½ cup buttermilk

Place the jalapeño, chives, and garlic into the bowl of a food processor fitted with a metal blade. Cover and process for about 10 seconds until finely minced. Add the sour cream, salt, pepper, and the buttermilk. Cover and process for about 15 seconds until fully blended. Taste for seasonings. Store in a covered jar in the refrigerator for up to 3 days.

Claire's Classic

Mustard-Tarragon Dressing GF

I love this dressing on a vegetable salad, tossed with a pasta salad, as a sandwich spread, and as a dip for vegetables. It's so good that some of our customers ask for an extra serving to spread on their bread in place of butter.

Makes about 1 pint

1 cup mayonnaise

½ cup Dijon mustard

2 teaspoons dried tarragon

2 teaspoons white vinegar

½ cup buttermilk

Salt and black pepper, to taste

Combine all ingredients in a bowl. Whisk well. Taste for seasoning.

Claire's Classic

Herbal Vinaigrette Dressing V GF

This dressing is perfect for tossed green salads, pasta salads, and potato or other vegetable salads. It remains ever-popular at Claire's, thirty-five years later!

Makes about 1 pint

1 cup olive oil

1/3 cup red wine vinegar

Juice of 2 lemons

Salt, to taste

1 teaspoon black pepper

2 teaspoons each dried basil, oregano, and tarragon

1 tablespoon Dijon mustard

1 tablespoon soy sauce

Combine all ingredients in a bowl. Whisk well. Taste for seasoning.

Claire's Classic

Salt-Free Yogurt Dressing GF

We make this dressing with our homemade yogurt and it has a delicious, fresh taste. It's among our oldest and most popular dressings. Try it as the dressing for a potato salad or as a dip for carrot sticks, too.

Makes about 1 pint

1 pint plain non-fat yogurt

2 teaspoons freshly grated lime zest

Juice of 1 lime

1/4 teaspoon ground ginger

1 teaspoon dried dill weed

Black pepper, to taste

Combine all ingredients in a bowl. Whisk well. Taste for seasoning.

Claire's Classic

Creamy Romano-Dill Dressing GF

This is another luscious salad dressing, rich and creamy and immensely popular at Claire's.

Makes about 1 pint

1 cup low-fat mayonnaise

²/₃ cup buttermilk

½ cup grated pecorino Romano cheese

4 large cloves garlic, minced

1 tablespoon dried dill weed

1 teaspoon black pepper

Salt, to taste

Measure all the ingredients into a bowl and whisk well. Taste for seasoning.

Strawberry-Mint Vinegar V GF

I love to make big batches of this vinegar and give it to friends or take it to a party as a hostess gift.

Makes 3 cups

3 cups organic white wine vinegar

6 large frozen organic strawberries

20 mint leaves, from about 2 stems of mint

1. Measure the vinegar into a clean glass jar. Defrost the strawberries on a glass plate in the microwave for about a minute, or just set on the counter until they defrost and release some of their juices. Using your fingers, crush the strawberries and add them and any juices to the vinegar. Rub the mint leaves with your fingers to bruise them and release some of their fragrant oils, then add them to the vinegar, pushing them down into the jar.

2. Cover the jar and label it with the content and date. Set it on the counter by a sunny window for 1 to 2 weeks, shaking it daily. After a week, taste it. If you like the intensity of the strawberry and mint flavor, it's ready, or if you prefer a stronger flavor, let it stand for another week.

3. When the mixture has steeped to your liking, use a fine mesh strainer to drain the vinegar into a bowl. Use the back of a wooden spoon or your fingers to press out as much juice from the berries and mint as you can. Discard the berries and mint, or puree them in the blender with a little olive oil, sea salt, and pepper and use on your tossed salad later in the day.

4. Pour the strained vinegar into a clean bottle. Cover and label it with the recipe name and date.

Tip: When bottling food for a gift, attach a pretty label with the name, the date it was made, a message, and maybe some suggestions for use. Here is a sample of what I might write on mine: "Strawberry-Mint Vinegar, made using organic vinegar and strawberries, and fresh mint grown in my garden, especially for you, with love from Claire. Store it in your refrigerator for up to 3 months. It's great mixed with walnut oil and extra-virgin olive oil for a salad of organic potatoes and green beans, with sliced red onions and a little sea salt and pepper. Also, I like to combine it with extra-virgin olive oil, a little mustard, sea salt and pepper, and a little fresh tarragon for a salad dressing. Have fun and enjoy it."

Pineapple-Lime Dipping Sauce V GF

This delicious sauce is perfect for dipping your Vietnamese Spring Rolls (page 200), or as a dressing for an Asian-inspired salad, maybe of tender greens, broccoli sprouts, and thinly sliced mushrooms.

Makes about ¾ cup

¾ cup finely chopped fresh pineapple, plus any juices

1 teaspoon freshly grated zest from 1 organic lime

Freshly squeezed juice from 1 lime, about 2 tablespoons

1 teaspoon organic flax oil with lemon

2 teaspoons organic brown sugar

1 teaspoon organic brown rice vinegar

Combine the ingredients in a bowl. Stir to combine. Taste for seasoning, adding additional brown sugar if needed.

Peanut-Tamari Dip V GFO

Serve this lively dressing with Vietnamese Spring Rolls (page 200) or on a salad of thin slices of mixed cabbages.

Makes about ¾ cup

¼ cup organic crunchy peanut butter

¼ cup warm water

1 tablespoon organic tamari

2 tablespoons plain organic soy milk

1 tablespoon unsweetened organic shredded coconut

½ teaspoon crushed red pepper flakes

½ teaspoon organic brown sugar

Sea salt and pepper, to taste

Combine the ingredients in a bowl. Whisk well to combine. Taste for seasoning.

Tip: Use gluten-free soy milk to make this recipe gluten free.

Queso Blanco Dip GF

This is a great dip for toasted pita triangles and a lovely spread for crostini or crackers. It can also be enjoyed as a sandwich spread.

Makes about 2 cups

1 clove garlic, sliced

8 ounces cream cheese

8 ounces feta cheese, crumbled

2/3 cup buttermilk

Black pepper, to taste

Measure the ingredients into the bowl of a food processor fitted with a metal blade. Process for about 25 seconds or until smooth, stopping once to scrape down the sides of the bowl using a rubber spatula. Taste for seasonings. Store unused dip in the refrigerator for up to 3 days.

Claire's Classic

Guacamole V GF

This recipe for guacamole is delicious and simple to make. Just remember the basics: Start with perfectly ripened avocados, and prepare the guacamole just before you plan to serve it. Once an avocado is cut open, it will not continue to ripen and cannot be saved. Test an avocado for ripeness by gently pressing its skin in several places. If it feels uniformly soft, the avocado is ready to be cut open and enjoyed. Guacamole makes a great dip for corn chips, and we love it in a pita bread sandwich, topped with lettuce, tomatoes, and red onion. We use at least a case of avocados a day at Claire's, mostly by spooning dollops of guacamole onto enchiladas, veggie burgers, salads, and sandwiches and with so many of our Mexican dishes. Surprise your family with chips and guacamole before dinner.

Serves 8

5 ripe avocados, peeled and pitted

½ small yellow onion, chopped

2 tablespoons olive oil

Juice of 1 lemon

Salt and black pepper, to taste

Place the avocado pulp and the remaining ingredients in a bowl. Mash together, using a potato masher, until soft but still chunky. Taste for seasoning. Serve immediately.

Claire's Classic

Salsa V GF

Our customers like our salsa so much that we sell it for take-home. At the restaurant, we serve it with chips and on our enchiladas, burritos, Eggplant Veracruz (page 271), and other Mexican dishes. It's delicious stirred into sour cream and served as a dip with chips. Make a double batch for the weekend.

Makes about 1 quart

¼ cup olive oil

2 small onions, chopped

6 cloves garlic, minced

2 teaspoons chili powder

2 teaspoons cumin

1 teaspoon dried oregano

¼ teaspoon crushed red pepper flakes, or more, to taste

2 green bell peppers, seeded and coarsely chopped

1 28-ounce can whole tomatoes in juice, crushed by hand

½ cup chopped parsley

Salt and black pepper, to taste

Heat the oil in a large pot over low heat. Add the onions, garlic, chili powder, cumin, oregano, red pepper flakes, and peppers. Cook, uncovered, over low heat for 15 minutes, stirring occasionally, until the onions are soft. Add the tomatoes, parsley, salt, and pepper. Simmer for 30 minutes, stirring frequently. Taste for seasoning.

Grilled Pineapple-Jalapeño Salsa V GF

This is a great salsa to pair with corn tortillas or corn fritters, or any time you want an interesting and yummy salsa.

Serves 6

½ large pineapple, peeled and cut into 5 ½-inch round slices

½ medium organic red onion, finely chopped

½ large jalapeño pepper, seeded and finely minced

1 tablespoon freshly squeezed lime juice, from about ½ lime

1. Heat the grill to medium-high (which means you can safely hold your hand about 4 inches from the grill rack for about 4 seconds). Place the pineapple slices in a single layer on the heated grill rack. Cover and cook for about 3 minutes, until there are golden brown grill marks on the underside and the bottoms look caramelized. Using a metal spatula (two make it easier), turn the pineapple, cover, and grill for about 3 minutes until golden.

2. Transfer the grilled pineapple to a cutting board. Cut each slice into small dice, and place them and their juices in a small bowl. Add the remaining ingredients. Gently stir to combine. Serve warm or chilled.

3. Refrigerate any leftovers for up to 2 days, stirring again to combine just before serving.

Tomatillo Salsa V GF

Serve this fresh salsa with baked corn tortilla chips for a great appetizer.

Makes about 3 cups

1 small organic zucchini, cut into small dice

3 small organic tomatillos, husk removed and discarded, fruit rinsed and cut into small dice

8–10 organic cherry tomatoes, quartered

1 ripe avocado, seeded and diced

1 tablespoon organic extra-virgin olive oil

Juice from ½ organic lemon (about 2 tablespoons)

Sea salt and pepper

Combine the ingredients in a bowl. Using either your hands or two spoons, toss gently to combine. Taste for seasonings.

Garden Salsa V GF

Salsa made with vegetables picked fresh from your garden is a delight for the senses and something you'll want to make all summer long. Share a batch with your friends and neighbors and spread the joy.

Makes about 1 quart

3 tablespoons extra-virgin olive oil

2 small organic onions, coarsely chopped

6 cloves garlic, coarsely chopped

1 teaspoon chili powder

½ teaspoon cumin

2 tablespoons fresh organic oregano leaves

1 small organic jalapeño pepper, finely chopped

2 small organic bell peppers, seeded and finely chopped

8 large, ripe organic tomatoes, heirloom or other, coarsely chopped and juices reserved

Sea salt and pepper

½ cup coarsely chopped cilantro

Heat the oil in a large, deep sauté pan over medium heat. Add the onions, garlic, chili powder, cumin, oregano, jalapeño, bell peppers, and tomatoes. Sprinkle with salt and pepper. Stir to combine. Cover and bring to a low boil (in about 10 minutes), then cook at a medium boil, stirring occasionally, for about 10 minutes longer, until the tomatoes are soft. Stir in the cilantro. Taste for seasonings.

Fruit Salsa V GF

This is a delicious dip for children and adults and it's a wonderful way to add more fruit to your diet. Serve it with Honey-Cinnamon Tortilla Snacks (page 362) or atop your tacos or burritos.

Serves 6

4 ripe local peaches, pitted and cut into small dice

4 ripe plums, pitted and cut into small dice

½ small pineapple, peeled, cored, and diced

2 tablespoons fresh lime juice (from about ½ lime)

2 tablespoons minced cilantro

Combine the ingredients in a bowl. Toss gently but thoroughly to combine. Serve with Honey-Cinnamon Tortilla Snacks (page 362).

Creamy Salsa Dip GF

This dip is a natural for organic tortilla chips or sweet local carrots, or as a topping for a soy meat loaf before baking.

Makes about 2 cups

1 cup store-bought smoky mango salsa, or other good salsa

½ cup plain organic yogurt

½ cup low-fat sour cream

1 small orange organic bell pepper, seeded and finely chopped

2 tablespoons finely chopped organic cilantro

Sea salt, if needed

Combine the ingredients in a bowl. Stir well to combine the ingredients. Taste for seasoning, adding a little sea salt if needed.

Creamy Yogurt Dip `GF`

Serve this yummy dip with toasted pita wedges or your favorite vegetables.

Makes 3 cups, enough for 10–12 appetizers

1½ cups organic sour cream, not low-fat

1½ cups whole-milk plain organic yogurt

1 clove garlic, finely minced

1 teaspoon extra-virgin olive oil

Combine the sour cream and yogurt in a bowl. Whisk to combine. Cover and set aside unrefrigerated for about an hour to thicken. Stir in the garlic and olive oil.

Tzatziki `GF`

Tzatziki is a classic Greek dip. I was lucky to grow up next door to a Greek family, who gave me an early exposure to some of the wonderful flavors of their traditional cuisine. This dip is terrific with toasted pita triangles, potato chips, cucumber slices, or slices of boiled potato.

Makes about 2½ cups

16 ounces (2 cups) plain organic yogurt, Greek or other

4 cloves garlic, minced

½ small cucumber, peeled, minced, and drained

2 teaspoons organic flax oil with lemon (available at natural food stores)

Salt and pepper, to taste

1. Line a colander with a double layer of cheesecloth and set it in a bowl. Spoon the yogurt into the lined colander. Cover with plastic wrap and refrigerate for 1–2 hours, until slightly thickened.

2. Turn into a bowl. Stir in the garlic, cucumber, flax oil, salt, and pepper. Mix to combine well. Taste for seasonings.

Smoked Paprika Butter Spread V GF

Serve this delicious butter spread with bread sticks, crackers, or toasted bread slices, or try a bit on your corn on the cob.

Makes 4 tablespoons

4 tablespoons organic butter or organic dairy-free buttery spread, cut into 4 slices

¾ teaspoon smoked sweet paprika

Sea salt, to taste

1. Measure the butter into a small glass bowl. Heat the butter in the microwave oven for about 7–8 seconds or until nearly melted, or carefully melt it in a small skillet over a low heat until just melted but not browned. Whisk in the smoked paprika, mixing until completely blended.

2. Taste before adding salt; if you used salted butter, you may not need much additional salt. Turn the butter into a small bowl, using a rubber spatula to scrape the bowl or the skillet. Serve soft or chill until firm. You can store the butter in the refrigerator for up to 3 days.

Toasted Sesame and Garlic Dip VO GFO

The next time you want a delicious and incredibly easy to prepare dip, try this one. It's great with raw baby carrots, steamed green beans or edamame, grilled artichokes, asparagus, or other vegetables. We love it at Claire's Corner Copia, and I think you will, too.

Makes about 2¹/₂ cups

1 cup store-bought garlic mayonnaise

1 cup organic deli mustard or plain yellow mustard

2 tablespoons toasted sesame oil

Salt and pepper, to taste

Measure the mayonnaise, mustard, and sesame oil into a bowl. Whisk to combine. Taste for seasonings before adding salt and pepper. Serve immediately or refrigerate for up to 2 days.

Tip: Use a vegan mayonnaise to make this recipe vegan. Use a gluten-free mayonnaise to make this recipe gluten free.

Claire's Classic

Hummus V GF

We love hummus at Claire's. It's great for dipping or in a sandwich. This version has cayenne pepper and Tabasco to give it a little more zip than our hummus sandwich filling. Either way, it's cholesterol-free and delicious.

Serves 8–10

1 pound dried chickpeas

1 cup tahini (sesame paste, found in health food stores)

¼ cup olive oil

Juice of 2 lemons

3 tablespoons water

Large pinch of cayenne pepper

Dash Tabasco

4 cloves garlic, chopped

Salt, to taste

½ cup chopped parsley

¼ teaspoon paprika

1. Soak the chickpeas overnight in a large pot with 10 cups of water. Add fresh water to cover by 2 inches, then boil for about an hour or until soft, adding water as necessary. Drain.

2. Place all the ingredients except the parsley and paprika in the bowl of a food processor. Puree until smooth. Taste for seasoning. Turn into a bowl and sprinkle with parsley and paprika. Serve with pita triangles for dipping.

Roasted Red Pepper Hummus V GF

We use dried chickpeas at Claire's, but when I'm at home and need a last-minute dip for myself or for guests, I'm grateful for a can of chickpeas that I always have in the cupboard.

Serves 10–12 for appetizers

1 organic red bell pepper, halved and seeded

3 tablespoons plus 1 teaspoon extra-virgin olive oil, divided

4 cloves garlic, sliced

1 13-ounce can organic chickpeas, drained

½ teaspoon ground cumin

½ cup sesame tahini

2 tablespoons freshly squeezed lemon juice (from about ½ lemon)

2 tablespoons water

Sea salt, to taste

¼ teaspoon black pepper

Paprika

1. Preheat the oven broiler to the high setting and raise the oven rack to the highest rung. Line a sheet pan with parchment paper or spray it with nonstick olive oil spray. Arrange the pepper halves cut side down on the prepared sheet. Broil for about 10–12 minutes, until the pepper halves are charred and the skin shriveled. Remove from the broiler, set the halves in a bowl, and cover the bowl with an inverted plate. Let stand for about 20 minutes, until the peppers "steam" and are cool enough to handle. Using your fingers, remove most of the charred skin, but leave a little behind for good flavor.

2. Meanwhile, heat the 3 tablespoons of olive oil in a small skillet over low-medium heat. Add the garlic slices and cook for about 7 minutes, stirring frequently, until golden but not brown. Set aside to cool a bit.

3. Place the drained chickpeas in the bowl of a food processor fitted with a metal blade. Add the peeled roasted pepper halves. Add the cooked garlic and the remaining olive oil, using a rubber spatula to scrape the skillet. Add the cumin, tahini, lemon juice, water, salt, and pepper. Cover and process for about 30 seconds, stopping once or twice to scrape down the sides of the bowl, until nearly smooth. Taste for seasoning. Turn into a shallow rimmed bowl.

4. Just before serving, use the back of a teaspoon to make a well in the center of the hummus, then pour the remaining teaspoon of olive oil into the well. Sprinkle the hummus lightly with paprika.

Braised Red Bell Pepper and Tomato Dip V GF

Serve this fresh and luscious dip with toasted slices of Italian or French bread, crackers, or toasted pita triangles for a healthful and delicious appetizer or snack.

Serves 6

2 tablespoons extra-virgin olive oil

1 medium sweet locally grown organic onion, cut into thick ribs, separated

3 cloves locally grown organic garlic, cut into thin slices

4 medium locally grown organic red bell peppers, seeded and cut into thick ribs

2 locally grown organic plum tomatoes, cut into wedges

Sea salt and pepper

1 tablespoon chopped fresh organic oregano

Sea salt and pepper

1. Heat the olive oil in a large skillet over medium heat. Add the remaining ingredients. Stir well to mix. Cook, stirring occasionally, for about 20 minutes until the peppers are just tender. Taste for seasonings.

2. Remove from the heat and transfer to the bowl of a food processor fitted with a metal blade. Cover and process for about 20 seconds until the mixture is blended—a little chunky, but mainly blended. Serve warm or cool to room temperature then refrigerate for up to 3 days. Serve chilled or at room temperature.

Cranberry-Horseradish Sour Cream GF

Cranberries are so good for you—they're rich in vitamin C and bioflavonoids. They add a nice tartness to the sweet-tart flavor of sour cream, which pairs wonderfully with any vegetable pancakes, especially Butternut Squash Pancakes (page 238). But don't stop there; serve this lovely dip with raw vegetables at your next party.

Makes about 2 cups

8 ounces (about 2½ cups) organic cranberries

½ cup fresh clementine juice (from about 1½ clementines)

2 tablespoons natural cane sugar

1–2 tablespoons prepared horseradish

¾ cup reduced-fat sour cream

1. Place the cranberries, clementine juice, and sugar in a small pot and place on stove over high heat. Bring to a boil, then reduce heat to medium-high and cook at a medium boil for about 5 minutes, stirring frequently until the cranberries burst. Remove from heat and set aside to cool slightly, until mixture thickens.

2. Turn into a bowl. Stir in the horseradish and the sour cream, and mix to combine. Serve at room temperature or chilled.

Lemon-Ginger Crème Fraîche GF

You can buy crème fraîche at the supermarket, but it's so easy to prepare at home. And, as with everything homemade, the from-scratch version tastes fresher and better, so maybe you'll give it a try if you have the time. If not, just stir the lemon zest, lemon juice, and minced candied ginger into your store-bought crème fraîche for a delicious accompaniment to your latkes, fresh fruit, or angel food cake. Either way, it's rich and decadent—but then again, it's an indulgence, and I think there's room for a little indulgence in a healthy diet.

Makes about 1 cup

½ cup organic sour cream

½ cup organic heavy cream

Finely grated zest from 1 organic lemon

2 teaspoons freshly squeezed lemon juice from about ½ organic lemon

1 tablespoon finely minced organic candied ginger (oil your knife before mincing the candied ginger to prevent sticking)

Measure the sour cream and the heavy cream into a small glass bowl. Whisk to combine, then cover the bowl with plastic wrap. Set on the counter for about 8 hours or until it has thickened. Stir in the lemon zest, the juice, and the minced candied ginger. Refrigerate until ready to use, for up to 3 days.

pasta & sauces

Who doesn't like pasta and sauce? Sauces offer endless opportunities for creativity. Because it seems we can never make too many pasta-and-sauce dishes at Claire's, we get to have fun, add healthful ingredients, and keep things interesting. If anyone doesn't like pasta and sauce, we'd never know it, given that we make sauces every single day. Have for thirty-five-plus years! We like to try different pasta shapes for variety, and our preference is for organic semolina pastas for their quality and flavor, but we also keep gluten-free pastas on hand for our customers who are sensitive to gluten. Many organic rice pastas taste good and if you're careful to cook them just enough to give that al dente bite, the texture is excellent, too. If you cook for someone who is sensitive to gluten, they'll be so appreciative if you make them a gluten-free pasta dish. And that feels good for everyone.

We are very fussy about our ingredients, and that includes our canned tomatoes for our tomato sauces and salsas. The majority of the time, we use certified San Marzano tomatoes in juice, imported from the Campania region of Italy, for their flavor, quality, and texture. Lately, though, we're been mixing it up a bit by making some recipes using organic tomatoes from Italy and from California, and while I don't expect we'll ever stop using San Marzano tomatoes, it's nice to support many farmers and producers. Make notes of the ingredients you use and make your own decisions because taste is subjective. We keep a journal at home and a log at Claire's and we're always talking about ingredients and recipes (we're obsessed). This helps us to make the best decisions for ourselves and for our beloved customers.

Have fun experimenting with sauces, but remember, the rules for cooking are always the same: Use only the best, freshest, ingredients and cook for people you love, and you can never go wrong.

Penne Pasta with Mushroom-Vodka Sauce V GFO

Vodka sauces are very popular at Claire's. This recipe is delicious and a little less indulgent than our more traditional vodka sauces—the pink sauces made with tomatoes, butter, and cream. This recipe relies on the added flavors and health benefits from mushrooms and spinach, and it uses milk rather than cream for a healthier version that still tastes yummy.

Serves 6

½ stick butter or ¼ cup extra-virgin olive oil

2 shallots, coarsely chopped

3 cloves garlic, sliced

1 pound mushrooms, cremini and button, quartered

1 teaspoon red pepper flakes

½ cup chopped Italian flat-leaf parsley

6–8 fresh basil leaves

Salt and pepper

1 pound organic whole wheat or semolina penne pasta

1 pint sweet grape tomatoes, about 20 large, cut into halves

¼ cup vodka

1 7-ounce bag organic baby spinach

3 cups whole organic milk or organic plain soy milk

½ cup grated pecorino Romano cheese (optional)

1. Melt the butter or heat the oil in a large pot over medium-low heat. Add the shallots and garlic. Cover and cook, stirring occasionally for about 2 minutes, or until the shallots have softened. Add the mushrooms, pepper flakes, parsley, basil, and a little salt and pepper. Cover and cook, stirring occasionally, for about 10 minutes or until the mushrooms have released some of their moisture.

2. Meanwhile, bring a large covered pot of lightly salted water to a boil over high heat and cook the penne according to package directions. Before draining the pasta, reserve a cup of the cooking water. (I leave the measuring cup in a colander set in the sink so I'll remember to save the cooking water.)

3. Add the tomatoes and vodka to the mushrooms. Stir well to mix. Raise the heat to medium and bring to a medium boil. Cover and cook for about 10 minutes, stirring occasionally, until the tomatoes have softened. Slowly stir in the milk and the reserved cooking water and continue cooking, uncovered, stirring frequently, for about 10 minutes, until the sauce is heated through and has reduced slightly. Stir in the cooked pasta and mix well to coat. Stir in the grated cheese if using. Taste for seasonings.

Tip: Use gluten-free pasta to make this recipe gluten free.

Pasta alla Puttanesca V GFO

We used to joke with our mom whenever she made puttanesca sauce because in Italian, *puttana* means harlot, or a lady of the streets. The story goes that these women were very busy and eager to get back to their business so they made a quick sauce. Really, we always believed they'd be back to business faster with, say, a marinara. This always made my mother laugh and blush.

Serves 6

Sea salt

14.5 ounces whole wheat spaghetti or other pasta

¼ cup extra-virgin olive oil

6 cloves garlic, cut into thin slices

2 shallots, coarsely chopped

1 medium red onion, cut into thin ribs

1 14-ounce can quartered artichoke hearts, drained

½ teaspoon crushed red pepper flakes

10 fresh basil leaves

¼ cup chopped Italian flat-leaf parsley

½ teaspoon dried oregano

1 cup whole black olives, drained

1 cup whole Spanish pimento-stuffed green olives, drained

3 tablespoons capers, drained (if you're using salted capers, rinse and squeeze out excess moisture)

2 28-ounce cans whole peeled San Marzano tomatoes in juice

½ cup white wine

Pepper

Grated Parmesan or pecorino Romano cheese, if desired

1. Set a colander with a 1 cup measure in the sink for later in the recipe. Putting the cup in the colander will help you remember to reserve the cooking water you'll need.

2. Bring 4 quarts of lightly salted water to a boil in a covered pot over high heat. Cook the pasta according to package directions. Before draining the pasta, reserve 1 cup of the cooking water. Turn the drained pasta into a serving bowl.

3. Heat the olive oil in a deep pan over medium heat. Add the garlic, shallots, onion, artichoke hearts, red pepper flakes, basil, parsley, oregano, black and green olives, and capers. Stir to combine. Cook for about 7 minutes, stirring frequently until the onions are light brown but not burned.

4. Turn the tomatoes and juice into a bowl. Using your hands, crush the tomatoes, then add them to the pot. Add the wine, the reserved cooking liquid, and a little sea salt and pepper—go easy on the salt because the olives and capers tend to be salty. Stir well to combine. Cover and bring to a medium boil, stirring frequently.

5. Cook at a medium boil for about 15–20 minutes, stirring frequently, until the sauce reduces slightly. Taste for seasoning. Pour three-fourths of the sauce evenly over the spaghetti. Using two spoons, toss to coat and separate the spaghetti strands. Top with remaining sauce. Taste for seasoning. Serve topped with grated Parmesan or pecorino, if desired.

Tip: Use gluten-free pasta to make this recipe gluten free.

Pasta for Spring

Fresh English peas require shelling, and that's more work than buying frozen ones, but the flavor is astounding and worth the effort. Some of my best childhood memories are of my mother sitting around the kitchen table with a lady-friend or two, sipping lemonade, sharing stories, and shelling peas or snapping green beans.

Serves 4

Sea salt

12 ounces whole wheat pasta, penne or other

3 tablespoons extra-virgin olive oil

2 large cloves organic garlic, sliced

2 organic shallots, coarsely chopped

1 large bunch asparagus, tough bottom 2 inches trimmed and discarded, remainder cut into ½-inch pieces

1 large bulb fennel, base cut in half, then each half cut into thin half circles, and pale green stems cut into thin slices

2 sun-dried tomatoes, cut into thin slices

Pepper

1 pound English peas, shelled, about ¾ cup fresh peas

2 tablespoons chopped fresh organic tarragon or 1 teaspoon dried tarragon

1 35-ounce can whole peeled San Marzano tomatoes in juice, squeezed by hand

½ cup white wine

Pinch of saffron

1/8 teaspoon cayenne pepper

1. Bring a large covered pot of lightly salted water to a boil over high heat. Stir in the pasta and cook according to package directions. Before draining, reserve 1 cup of the cooking liquid.

2. Meanwhile, heat the olive oil in a heavy pot over medium heat. Add the garlic, shallots, asparagus, fennel, and sun-dried tomatoes. Sprinkle lightly with sea salt and pepper. Cover and cook, stirring occasionally, for about 10 minutes, until vegetables have softened slightly. Add the shelled peas, tarragon, tomatoes, white wine, saffron, and cayenne and stir well to mix. Cover and bring to a medium boil (about 5 minutes), stirring occasionally, for about 15 minutes, then add the reserved pasta cooking water, stir, and continue cooking for about 5 minutes until the sauce has reduced slightly. Taste for seasoning. Stir in the drained pasta. Serve immediately.

Tip: It's easy to remember to reserve the water if you set a measuring cup in a colander set in the sink.

Pasta with a Sauce of Eggplant, Sweet Cherry Tomatoes, Fresh Mozzarella, and Lemon GFO

Although we make this delicious sauce year round at Claire's, there's no denying it—summer produce tastes the best and we take full advantage of the work from our beloved farmers when we can.

Serves 6

3 small eggplants, cut into 1-inch cubes (about 8 cups)

Salt

1 pound pasta, homemade or other

¼ cup good extra-virgin olive oil

1 small sweet onion, diced

6 large cloves garlic, sliced

½ teaspoon crushed red pepper flakes

1 pint container cherry tomatoes

12 fresh basil leaves, whole

¼ cup fresh oregano, chopped

3 tablespoons freshly squeezed lemon juice (from about 1 lemon)

8 bocconcini (little balls of fresh mozzarella; found in the cheese section at the supermarket)

1. Place the cubes of eggplant in a large bowl. Sprinkle a tablespoon of salt evenly over the eggplant and toss to coat, using your hands or two wooden spoons. Set aside for about 25 minutes, tossing again every 5 minutes or so to allow some of the water from the eggplant to be released.

2. Meanwhile, bring 4 quarts of lightly salted water to a boil in a covered pot over high heat. When the water comes to a boil, add the pasta and cook according to package directions. Before draining, reserve 2 cups of the cooking liquid. (If you leave a measuring cup in a colander set in the sink, it's easier to remember to reserve the cooking liquid before draining.)

3. Heat the olive oil in a heavy pot over medium heat. Add the onion, garlic, crushed red pepper flakes, cherry tomatoes, and salt to taste. Cook for 3–5 minutes, stirring occasionally until the onions are softened but not browned.

4. Lift out a handful of the eggplant, and using two hands, squeeze out as much liquid as possible, leaving the dark liquid in the bowl. Add the squeezed eggplant to the pot with the onions. Continue with the remaining eggplant, again leaving the dark liquid in the bowl. Discard the liquid left behind from the eggplant.

5. Stir the eggplant to coat with the oil and to combine with the other ingredients in the pot. Stir in the basil and oregano. Cover and cook for 10–12 minutes, stirring occasionally until the eggplant is just tender. Add the lemon juice and the reserved cooking liquid from the pasta. Stir to combine.

6. Add the cooked and drained pasta to the pot and scatter the bocconcini over the top. Stir to combine and cook, uncovered, for about 5 minutes, stirring frequently until the bocconcini are nearly melted and the pasta sauce looks creamy. Taste for seasonings. Turn into a serving bowl.

Tip: Use gluten-free pasta to make this recipe gluten free.

Rigatoni Pasta with Butternut Squash, Chickpeas, and Spinach V GFO

Our customers love everything that includes butternut squash, and we love to please them. So in many months of the year, you'll see butternut squash in our produce cooler, waiting to be made into sauce, or soup, or risotto or roasted with our other organic vegetables for salads. It's loaded with vitamin A and fiber, too.

Serves 6

¼ cup extra-virgin olive oil

6 large cloves organic garlic, sliced

1 large sweet organic onion, cut into thick ribs, separated

1 large butternut squash, peeled, seeded, and cut into medium dice

1 bay leaf

$^{1}/_{8}$ teaspoon nutmeg

10 large fresh organic basil leaves

1 small bunch Italian flat-leaf parsley, coarsely chopped

Sea salt and pepper, to taste

1 pound organic rigatoni or other pasta

1 15-ounce can organic chickpeas, drained

1 7-ounce bag organic baby spinach

2 ounces grated pecorino Romano cheese (optional)

1. Heat the olive oil in a large heavy pot over medium-low heat. Add the garlic, onion, butternut squash, bay leaf, nutmeg, basil, and parsley, and a little sea salt and pepper. Stir to coat with the oil. Cover and cook, stirring occasionally, for about 25 minutes, or until the squash is just tender and has released some of its moisture.

2. Meanwhile, bring a large covered pot of lightly salted water to a boil over high heat.

3. When the pot of salted water reaches a rapid boil, cook it according to package directions, but before draining, reserve 3 cups of the cooking water. Set the drained pasta and the reserved water (separately) aside while you continue to cook the sauce. When the squash is tender, add the chickpeas, spinach, and reserved pasta cooking water. Using two wooden spoons, toss to combine. Cover and cook for about 5 minutes, stirring occasionally, until the chickpeas are heated through. Stir in the cooked pasta. Taste for seasonings. If desired, serve with grated cheese and additional pepper on top.

Tip: Use gluten-free pasta to make this recipe gluten free.

Pasta with Local Herbs and Eggs GFO

Enjoy this easy-to-prepare dish made with as many locally grown foods as you can find, straight from the farmers' market or your local farm stand. This pasta dish is rich in protein, fiber, vitamin A, and iron.

Serves 4–6

Sea salt

1 pound organic whole wheat or semolina penne

3 tablespoons local butter, cut into small pieces

1 pound local organic spinach, washed well and drained

5 local eggs, lightly beaten

¼ cup grated Parmesan and Romano cheese mixture

3 tablespoons snipped fresh local chives

Pepper

2 tablespoons lightly toasted pine nuts

1 tablespoon white truffle oil

1. Bring a large covered pot of lightly salted water to a boil over high heat. Cook the pasta according to package directions. Before draining, reserve 2 cups of cooking water. (Note: If you leave a measuring cup in a colander set in the sink, it's easier to remember to reserve the water.) Drain the pasta.

2. Return the drained pasta to the pot. Place the pot over low heat. Add the butter, spinach, and reserved cooking water. Stir well to combine and until the butter melts and the spinach wilts, about 2–3 minutes. Stir in the beaten eggs and the grated cheeses, and stir for about 2 minutes, until the eggs are just cooked. Stir in the chives, pepper, and toasted pine nuts. Taste for seasonings. Turn onto a serving platter. Drizzle with truffle oil.

Tip: Use gluten-free pasta to make this recipe gluten free.

"The heart of the city is sandwiched on a cozy corner in New Haven. Claire's is more than healthy eating—it's an experience! The moment you enter the door, your taste buds soar, the music uplifts your soul, and the atmosphere, cozy and charming, gives you pause to stay awhile."

—Ann Amrose, LMT, Reiki Master

Peas in Paradise   GFO

This dish is made with organic pasta and a combination of protein- and fiber-rich green peas and edamame, which are sweet young soybeans. You can find these delicious green soybeans already shelled in the freezer section in most supermarkets. Buy an extra bag and eat them as a snack—you'll love them.

Serves 4

Salt

1 10-ounce package frozen shelled organic edamame

1 10-ounce package frozen green peas

2 large cloves organic garlic, sliced

2 large organic shallots, sliced

Pepper

¼ cup chopped fresh dill

12-ounce box organic whole wheat spaghetti

3 tablespoons extra-virgin olive oil

½ teaspoon crushed red pepper flakes

1 bunch broccolini, coarsely chopped

1. Bring a large covered pot of lightly salted water to a boil over high heat to cook the spaghetti. Meanwhile, place the edamame and peas in a separate heavy pot. Add water to cover plus 2 inches. Cover and bring to a boil over high heat. Add the garlic, shallots, and a little salt and pepper. Cook at a boil for about 2 minutes, stirring occasionally until the peas are tender. Stir in the dill and remove from the heat. When the water for the spaghetti comes to a boil, add the spaghetti. Stir well and cook according to package directions. When it is cooked to your preference, drain and turn into a bowl.

2. Working in batches, spoon some of the cooked peas and edamame with some of the cooking water into a processor bowl fitted with a metal blade. Cover and process until smooth. Pour the pea/edamame sauce over the spaghetti. Process the remaining peas, edamame, and cooking water, adding the sauce to the spaghetti. In a medium skillet, heat the olive oil over medium heat. Add the crushed red pepper flakes, broccolini, and a little salt and pepper. Cook, stirring occasionally, for about 2 minutes, until the broccolini turns bright green. Add to the spaghetti. Using two large spoons, toss the spaghetti to coat with the pea/edamame sauce and the broccolini. Taste for seasonings.

Tip: Use gluten-free pasta to make this recipe gluten free.

Pasta with String Bean and Heirloom Tomato Sauce V GFO

Choose a variety of string beans—green, yellow, purple, and Italian flat beans—for this flavorful and healthful recipe. It's loaded with fiber and vitamins C and A, and it's a good source of protein.

Serves 6

Salt

1 pound Italian organic whole wheat pasta, such as penne or fusilli

3 tablespoons extra-virgin olive oil

4 cloves organic garlic, sliced

1 large sweet organic onion, cut into thin ribs

1 pound assorted organic string beans, stems trimmed

10 organic cherry or teardrop tomatoes

6 large organic heirloom tomatoes, diced, reserving juices

Black pepper, to taste

½ teaspoon crushed red pepper flakes

¼ cup white wine (optional)

10–12 large basil leaves

¾ cup hand-packed ricotta cheese (optional)

1. Bring 6 quarts of lightly salted water to a boil in a large covered pot over high heat. Cook the pasta according to package directions, then reserve 2 cups of the cooking liquid before draining. (A good way to remember to reserve the cooking liquid is to put a measuring cup in a colander set in the sink.) Meanwhile, heat the oil in a large, deep skillet over a medium heat. Add the garlic, onion, string beans, and tomatoes. Add the salt, pepper, and crushed red pepper flakes. Cover and cook, stirring occasionally, for about 20 minutes, until the tomatoes have softened and released some of their juices.

2. Add the white wine (if using), the basil leaves, and the reserved cooking liquid from the pasta. Stir to combine. Cook at a low-medium boil for about 10 minutes, stirring occasionally until the string beans are tender to your preference. Stir in the cooked pasta. Turn into a serving bowl. Serve in large, rimmed bowls. Top with additional black pepper and dollops of hand-packed ricotta cheese, if desired.

Tip: Use gluten-free pasta to make this recipe gluten free.

Italian Cauliflower in Tomato Sauce [V] [GFO]

I love this dish! There's a lot of sauce and cauliflower and a little bit of angel hair pasta, so it's beautiful, delicious, healthful, and satisfying while saving calories—better for you than eating a big bowl of pasta with a little sauce. If my calculations are correct, each serving is less than 475 calories.

Serves 4

¼ cup plus 1 tablespoon extra-virgin olive oil

1 small red onion, coarsely chopped

1 medium yellow onion, coarsely chopped

6 cloves garlic, sliced

1 small jalapeño pepper, seeded and chopped

1 large head cauliflower, cored and coarsely chopped

8 fresh basil leaves, torn into pieces

Sea salt

1 35-ounce can San Marzano whole peeled tomatoes in juice

2 cups water

Black pepper

8 ounces angel hair pasta

Grated pecorino Romano cheese (optional)

1. Heat the olive oil in a heavy pot over medium heat. Add the onions and garlic. Cover and cook for about 5–6 minutes, stirring occasionally until the onions are softened. Add the jalapeño, cauliflower, and basil leaves. Sprinkle with sea salt. Stir to combine. Cover and cook for about 15 minutes, stirring occasionally, until the cauliflower is softened.

2. Add the tomatoes and water. Using a potato masher, mash the mixture to crush the tomatoes and break up the cauliflower into smaller pieces. Cover and raise the heat to high. Bring to a simmer (this will take about 7 minutes), then reduce the heat to medium, cover, and cook at a simmer for about 30 minutes, stirring occasionally until the sauce is cooked to your preference. Stir in the black pepper to taste. Taste for seasonings.

3. Turn off the heat and leave the sauce on the stove to keep it warm while you cook the pasta according to package directions. Drain the pasta and turn into a serving bowl. Spoon one-fourth of the sauce over the top of the pasta. Using two wooden spoons, toss to coat. Spoon the remaining sauce over the pasta. Serve with grated pecorino Romano cheese on top, if desired.

Tip: Use gluten-free pasta to make this recipe gluten free.

Cauliflower

In the vegetable world, color is usually power. The deeper the color, the more powerful the vitamins, minerals, and antioxidants—that is, with one delicious exception: cauliflower. What this creamy white vegetable lacks in color, it makes up for in healthful nutrients. It contains a terrific amount of vitamin C and a good amount of iron, and because it's a cruciferous vegetable, researchers associate it with potential for cancer prevention.

There are hybrid varieties of cauliflower in vivid colors of orange, green, and purple, but they're far less available than the more familiar creamy white variety, and that's a

pity. The orange and green varieties contain much more vitamin A than the white. And the hybrid purple cauliflower gets its deep color from the same antioxidant that produces the red in red cabbage and the red in red wine, and thereby it offers similar health benefits.

I have to admit, I'm partial to the white cauliflower when I'm using it in a traditional Italian tomato sauce, like the one in the previous recipe. But for fritters, mashing, and roasting, if you can find a colorful head of cauliflower, that will be an added bonus to your health. Either way, cauliflower has a mild, cabbage-like flavor, is low in calories, and is easy to love.

Fettuccine with Braised Cabbage and Cremini Mushrooms V GFO

If you are like me and always on the lookout for delicious new ways to serve pasta, this is a healthful solution. You can use small heads of cabbage or a full-size head of Savoy cabbage, the curly-leaf, milder variety. Either way, it pairs nicely with the rich and earthy flavor of cremini mushrooms. Offer grated Parmesan or pecorino Romano cheese to sprinkle on top, if desired.

Serves 4

Sea salt

12 ounces fettuccine noodles

2 tablespoons extra-virgin olive oil

2 tablespoons trans fat–free buttery spread

1 local shallot, chopped

4 cloves local garlic, chopped

1 large local onion, sliced into thin rings, separated

5 little heads of local cabbage, or 1 large head local Savoy cabbage, cored and coarsely chopped

1 pound cremini mushrooms, rinsed and cut in half

Pepper

¼ cup chopped local dill weed

Freshly grated Parmesan or pecorino Romano cheese, if desired

1. Bring a large covered pot of lightly salted water to a boil over high heat. When it reaches a boil, cook the fettuccine according to the package directions. Reserve a cup of the cooking liquid, then drain the fettuccine.

2. Heat the olive oil and the buttery spread in a large, deep skillet over medium-low heat. Add the shallot, garlic, and onion. Cook, stirring frequently, for about 5 minutes, until golden but not burned. Add the cabbage and cremini mushrooms. Sprinkle with sea salt and pepper. Stir to coat with the oil. Cover and raise the heat to medium. Cook for about 20 minutes, stirring occasionally, until the cabbage is tender.

3. Stir in the dill and the reserved cooking liquid from the fettuccine, mixing well to combine. Add the drained fettuccine and stir to combine. Turn into a serving bowl, using a rubber spatula to scrape the skillet of any juices. Serve immediately.

Tip: Use gluten-free pasta to make this recipe gluten free.

Mafalda Pasta with Braised Arugula Sauce and Chickpeas V GFO

Mafalda pasta noodles look like thin, ribbonlike lasagna noodles. I love the name and the pasta. Of course, you can use any pasta you like for this delicious dish. This is a healthful one-dish meal you can prepare in less than 30 minutes. It supplies needed protein, fiber, vitamins, and minerals, and the colors are beautiful, too.

Serves 8

Sea salt

3 tablespoons extra-virgin olive oil

2 medium red onions, cut in half, then into ribs, separated

4 cloves garlic, sliced

7 ounces baby arugula, about 8 cups

¼ teaspoon crushed red pepper flakes

16 ounces mafalda pasta or other pasta of your choice

1 15-ounce can chickpeas, rinsed and drained

1 cup pasta cooking water

4 ounces goat cheese, crumbled (optional)

4 tablespoons grated pecorino Romano cheese (optional)

Grated lemon zest from 1 lemon

1. Bring a large covered pot of lightly salted water to a boil over high heat. Meanwhile, heat the olive oil in a large skillet over medium heat. Add the onions and garlic, and sprinkle with a little sea salt. Cook, stirring occasionally, for about 5 minutes, until the edges of the onions and garlic begin to brown but not burn. Add the arugula, red pepper flakes, and a little sea salt. Using tongs, turn the arugula to coat with the oil and onions. Cook for just several seconds, turning the arugula with the tongs until it just wilts. Turn off the heat and leave the skillet on the stove.

2. Once the pot of water reaches a rapid boil, stir in the pasta and cook according to package directions, but add the drained chickpeas during the last minute of cooking to heat them. Before draining the pasta, remove 1 cup of the pasta cooking water and stir it into the cooked arugula. Taste for seasoning, keeping in mind that if you plan to use pecorino Romano cheese later in the recipe, you should go easy on the salt as the cheese tends to be salty. Drain the pasta and chickpeas and turn them into a serving bowl.

3. Spoon the arugula and all the juices onto the cooked pasta. Using two wooden spoons, gently toss the pasta to coat it with the arugula sauce. If using goat cheese, scatter the pieces evenly over the pasta. Then, if using the pecorino Romano cheese, sprinkle this evenly over pasta. Scatter the grated lemon zest evenly over the pasta and serve immediately.

Tip: Use gluten-free pasta to make this recipe gluten free.

Whole Wheat Linguine with Zucchini, Kale, Tomatoes, and Parmesan V GFO

For many years, students at the Common Ground High School in New Haven grew organic Toscano kale for us. You can use organic Toscano kale in this recipe or substitute any other variety of kale. Either way, it's delicious and a wonderful source of vitamin A, beta-carotene, calcium, and iron.

Serves 6

3 tablespoons extra-virgin olive oil

4 cloves garlic, coarsely chopped

1 large sweet onion, cut into thin rings, separated

2 medium zucchini, about a pound, halved crosswise and then quartered lengthwise into spears

Salt and pepper, to taste

2 large heirloom or other tomatoes, cut into thin wedges

½ cup white wine

1 bunch Toscano kale or other variety, any tough stems removed and discarded, leaves cut into strips

10 fresh basil leaves

1 tablespoon fresh oregano

12 ounces whole wheat linguine

1½ cups reserved cooking liquid from the linguine

Freshly grated Parmesan cheese (optional)

1. Heat the olive oil in a deep pot over medium heat. Add the garlic, onion, zucchini, salt, and pepper. Cover and cook for about 20–25 minutes, stirring occasionally, until the onions and the zucchini are golden brown. Add the tomatoes, wine, kale, basil leaves, and oregano. Raise the heat to medium-high. Cover and continue cooking for about 10 minutes, stirring occasionally, until the tomatoes are broken down.

2. Meanwhile, cook the linguine according to package directions, reserving 1½ cups of the cooking liquid just before draining. When the tomatoes have broken down, stir in the cooked linguine and the reserved cooking liquid from the pasta. Cook, uncovered, for just 30 seconds or so, using two wooden spoons to toss the ingredients to blend the flavors. Taste for seasonings. Turn into a serving bowl. Serve with freshly grated Parmesan cheese and additional black pepper, if desired.

Tip: Use gluten-free pasta to make this recipe gluten free.

Whole Wheat Spaghetti with Olive Oil, Garlic Chips, and Romaine Strips V GFO

The romaine adds fiber, folate, and vitamins A and C to this delicious old Italian favorite.

Serves 6

Salt

1 pound whole wheat spaghetti

¼ cup extra-virgin olive oil

10 large cloves garlic, cut lengthwise into thick slices

½ teaspoon red pepper flakes

1 small head romaine, leaves cut into thin strips (about 10 cups)

Pepper

Grated pecorino Romano cheese (optional)

1. Bring a large covered pot of lightly salted water to a boil over high heat and cook the spaghetti according to package directions. Before draining the spaghetti, reserve 2 cups of the cooking water.

2. Heat the oil in a large, deep skillet over medium-low heat. Add the garlic and cook, stirring occasionally, for 2–3 minutes, until the garlic is golden brown but not burned. Add the red pepper flakes, the strips of romaine, a little pepper, and the reserved cooking water. Cook at a medium boil for about 2 minutes, stirring frequently until the romaine wilts. Add the cooked spaghetti. Using two wooden spoons, toss to mix well. Sprinkle with pecorino Romano cheese, if desired. Taste for seasonings.

Tip: Use gluten-free pasta to make this recipe gluten free.

Pasta with Fresh Tomato and Zucchini Sauce V GFO

This quintessential summer sauce is luscious atop any pasta. I also like it over cheese ravioli. Serve it alone or topped with grated pecorino Romano or ricotta salata cheese. Ricotta salata is a sheep's milk cheese (pecorino Romano is also made from sheep's milk) and is perfect for grating onto a sauce or cubed for a salad. You can buy it in the cheese section of most markets. For a complete dinner, I like to pair this pasta dish with a simple arugula salad tossed with chickpeas, lemon juice, and extra-virgin olive oil. I'd serve a lovely rosé wine with this dish, too.

Serves 6

Sea salt

1 pound pasta of choice

¼ cup extra-virgin olive oil, plus 1 teaspoon for coating the pasta

¼ large red onion, chopped

4 cloves garlic, coarsely chopped

1–2 pepperoncini peppers or other tiny hot peppers, chopped (optional)

6 large ripe local tomatoes, coarsely chopped, juices reserved

1 medium local zucchini, cut in half lengthwise, then into ¾-inch slices

½ cup chopped Italian flat-leaf parsley

12 fresh basil leaves

Pepper, to taste

Grated pecorino Romano or ricotta salata cheese, if desired

1. Bring a large covered pot of lightly salted water to a boil over high heat. Cook the pasta according to package directions until al dente. Drain, then drizzle with a teaspoon of olive oil. Turn into a serving bowl.

2. Meanwhile, heat the oil in a large skillet over medium heat. Add the onion, garlic, and pepperoncini peppers if using. Cook for about 2–3 minutes, stirring occasionally until the onions are just golden but not burned. Add the tomatoes and their juices, the zucchini, and the parsley. Tear the basil leaves and add them to the skillet. Sprinkle with salt and pepper. Stir to coat. Cover and cook for about 20 minutes, stirring occasionally until the tomatoes are broken down and the zucchini is tender. Taste for seasonings.

3. Turn the sauce over the pasta in the serving bowl. Using two wooden spoons, toss to coat with the sauce. Taste for seasonings. Serve topped with grated pecorino Romano or ricotta salata cheese, if desired.

Tip: Use gluten-free pasta to make this recipe gluten free.

Porcini Mushroom Tortelloni with Pistou

Tortelloni are big tortellini, so you get more yummy filling in them. Packages of dried tortelloni are available in the pasta section of most supermarkets. They're delicious and so convenient, and they're available with a variety of fillings, so you can have fun with the selection. If you're making the pistou, you'll want to prepare it and use it on the same day for the freshest flavor. Leftover Tortelloni with Pistou will keep in the refrigerator for up to a day and it's delicious served chilled, too.

Serves 4

Sea salt

1 8-ounce package porcini mushroom tortelloni

3 cloves garlic, peeled

2 cups fresh basil leaves, loosely packed

¼ cup plus 2 tablespoons extra-virgin olive oil

Pepper

1. Bring a covered pot of lightly salted water to a boil over high heat. When the water reaches a boil, add the tortelloni and cook according to package directions. When it is tender to your preference, drain the tortelloni, then return it to the empty pot.

2. Meanwhile, prepare the pistou. Place the garlic cloves and basil leaves in the bowl of a food processor fitted with a metal blade. Sprinkle with sea salt and pepper. Add the olive oil. Cover and process for a few seconds until blended but there's still some texture (not pureed). Taste for seasonings. Spoon the pistou over the cooked tortelloni and toss to coat.

Mother's Day

Anyone who knows me or who comes to my restaurant regularly knows my mother. And everyone loves her. That's really easy to do because she always has a smile for everyone, she has the prettiest blue eyes, and she has a kind word for everyone she meets. And she's the most patient person I've ever known. Also, she's the one who never, ever misses a chance to say that she's my mother. I have no doubt that this unstoppable sense of pride she has always had for me has given me a proper moral barometer and the encouragement to take risks and challenge myself, never wanting to let her down, or for her to lose faith in me. I adore her, on Mother's Day and every day.

If we're really lucky, we also have other women in our lives who are "like a mother to us." These are the women who aren't our birth mothers but who help nurture us. They are the aunts, the friends, the coworkers, and the neighbors who show us love, who celebrate our joys, and who help us through our sorrows. They are the special women who listen to and hold our secrets, who guide and teach us to be the best we can be while still liking us for being less than perfect. These are the women who help us to navigate this busy and often confusing world we live in.

On Mother's Day I salute all mothers and those many other women who "are like a mother to us."

For my dear friend, Sue Wilson, her aunt Jo (Josephine Signor) is "like a mother to her." Aunt Jo often refers to their warm and loving relationship as a *compagna*—friends, dear old friends. Over the years I've heard about their days together, their regular once-a-week schedule of shopping trips, visits to the salon, lunch out, and, of course, their times in the kitchen, with Aunt Jo sharing family recipes, passing on treasured family traditions. Aunt Jo's Ricotta Cavatelli (pronounced kah-vah-TEHL-lee) (page 172) is a recipe passed on from her mother (Sue's grandmother) and her mother's mother, so this is one of those recipes that really needs to continue being passed down for generations to come.

Cavatelli are incredibly tender, short pasta shells, usually ridged. You can make your own cavatelli in an hour. Sue has made Aunt Jo's Ricotta Cavatelli for Frank and me, and I've made it for us as well, but last week Aunt Jo herself came to Sue's house to let us observe the two of them making her cavatelli together. It was a day I will not forget, touching and sweet, watching the sharing of a longtime family recipe, made together by compagna.

Aunt Jo told us that she made cavatelli for her family by hand until several years ago, when she bought a manually operated cavatelli maker that really shortens the job of shaping the hundreds of little shells. If you don't have a cavatelli maker, you can shape old-fashioned, beautiful cavatelli completely by hand. Still, the cavatelli maker is

fun and it makes the job go much quicker. This works well for Aunt Jo because she makes several batches at a time and freezes them for her family to pick up for their own meals.

You can toss your cavatelli with your favorite sauce, maybe a marinara or a puttanesca sauce. Or you can toss the pasta with lots of fresh broccoli cooked in extra-virgin olive oil with plenty of garlic, a little bit of crushed red pepper flakes, and a little of the pasta cooking water. Serve with a tossed salad, maybe with a handful of chickpeas included for extra flavor, texture, fiber, and protein. Thank you, Aunt Jo, for sharing your beautiful recipe and your lovely stories.

Aunt Jo's Ricotta Cavatelli

These cavatelli are special. They're tender and delicate and worth the effort, because they're homemade, and homemade tastes . . . well . . . homemade, and that's always special.

Serves 8–12, makes about 3 pounds

4 cups unbleached all-purpose flour, plus additional for rolling the dough

½ teaspoon baking powder

½ teaspoon salt

1 pound whole milk ricotta cheese

1 extra-large egg

¼ cup whole milk

1. Measure the flour, baking powder, and salt onto a large wooden board or onto your counter. Make a well into the center, then measure the ricotta, egg, and milk into the well. Using your hands, start mixing the ingredients together, scooping and squeezing until the ingredients begin to come together into a dough. Knead the dough for about 10 minutes, until it is smooth and you can form it into a large ball. A good sign that the dough is ready is when your hands are clean rather than sticky with wet dough and flour. Cover the dough with a kitchen towel and let it rest for about 10 minutes.

2. Set a few sheet pans nearby for holding the cavatelli as you shape them later. Line the sheet pans with either kitchen towels or parchment paper, then lightly dust them with flour. Lightly flour your work surface for hand-shaping the cavatelli (or set up your cavatelli maker, if available).

3. To shape the cavatelli by hand, cut the dough in half and set half of your dough on your lightly floured work surface. Dust the top of the dough with a little flour. Using a rolling pin, roll the dough into a rectangle about 11 by 12 inches and about ¼ inch thick. Lightly dust the top with a little flour to prevent sticking when you shape the cavatelli.

4. Cut the rolled out dough into ½-inch-wide strips, then cut the strips into ½-inch pieces. Using your index and middle fingers, press your fingers into each piece, gently pushing into the dough while pulling your finger toward you to form a free-form shell. Place the shells on the flour-dusted lined cookie sheets and repeat until you run out of dough.

Note: If using a cavatelli maker, set a lined cookie sheet under it. Feed one strip of dough at a time into the machine with one hand, while turning the hand-crank with the other. The shaped cavatelli will come out onto the cookie sheet. Spread them out in a single layer as you form more cavatelli; this will prevent them from sticking to each other. Continue with the remaining dough, filling the sheet pans with cavatelli.

5. You can cook the cavatelli right away or freeze them for up to 3 months. To freeze them, place the cookie sheets on a flat shelf in the freezer and leave them for a couple of hours. Turn the frozen cavatelli into bags or other freezer containers (label and date them) and keep them in the freezer for future use.

6. To cook your cavatelli, bring a covered large pot (an 8-quart pot is perfect) of lightly salted water to a boil over high heat. When the water reaches a boil, carefully add the cavatelli (fresh or frozen) and don't stir them for about a minute or they'll stick together. After about a minute, stir the cavatelli. After about 5–8 minutes, you'll see the cavatelli float to the top. (The exact time will depend on whether they're fresh or frozen, and how long it takes the water to return to a boil.) Stir the cavatelli again. Taste for doneness. When they are cooked to your preference, drain them into a colander placed in your sink.

7. Turn the cavatelli into a serving bowl and top with your favorite sauce; toss gently. Serve with grated cheese, such as pecorino Romano or Parmigiano Reggiano, and freshly cracked black pepper, if desired.

Soy Turkey Cannelloni with Three-Tomato Marinara Sauce

For an added treat, just before serving the cannelloni, drizzle a teaspoon or two of white truffle oil evenly over the top. Magic!

Serves 8

Crespelle (Italian pasta crepes):

2 cups organic white whole wheat flour

4 eggs

2 cups water

Sea salt and pepper, to taste

Three-Tomato Sauce:

3 tablespoons organic extra-virgin olive oil

4 large cloves garlic, cut into thin slices

1 medium organic spring onion, finely chopped

1 pint sweet grape tomatoes, cut in half

4 sun-dried tomatoes, cut into thin slices

1 35-ounce can whole peeled Italian San Marzano tomatoes in juice, crushed by hand

½ cup chopped Italian flat-leaf parsley

8 large basil leaves, cut in half lengthwise

1 bay leaf

¼ cup white wine

Pinch of cayenne pepper

Sea salt and pepper, to taste

1. To make the crespelle, sift the flour into a bowl. In a separate bowl, whisk the eggs, water, salt, and pepper. Pour this mixture all at once over the flour. Mix well using a whisk or fork until the batter is smooth.

2. Let the batter rest for 10 minutes. Meanwhile, line a sheet pan with waxed paper and set by the stove. Heat a small skillet or a crepe pan for about 30 seconds over medium heat. Carefully remove the heated skillet from the stove and spray it with cooking spray. Stir the batter. Spoon about 3 tablespoons of the batter into the center of the heated skillet, tilting the pan to coat the bottom with a thin layer of the batter. Cook for about 25–30 seconds, or until the crespelle is set. Carefully turn the crespelle and cook the other side for 10–15 seconds or until it no longer looks wet. Transfer the cooked crespelle to the lined sheet pan. Repeat the process with the remaining batter. Transfer the cooked crespelle, overlapping slightly, onto the sheet pan as you cook them.

3. To make the sauce, heat the oil in a large skillet over medium heat. Add the garlic and onion. Stir to coat.

4. Cover and cook, stirring occasionally, for about 7 minutes, until the garlic and onion are light brown but not burned. Add the remaining ingredients and stir well to mix. Cover and cook at a medium boil, stirring occasionally, for about 20 minutes, until the sauce reduces slightly. Taste for seasonings. You can prepare the filling while the sauce is cooking.

5. Meanwhile, to make the filling, heat the oil in a large skillet over medium heat. Add the onion and the ground soy turkey. Using a spoon or a potato masher, break up the pieces of ground soy turkey. Cook for about 1 minute, stirring occasionally. Add the water, salt, and pepper and continue cooking for about 2 minutes, until the onions have softened. Taste for seasonings. Turn this into a bowl. Add the remaining ingredients and stir well to combine. Taste for seasonings.

6. To assemble and bake the cannelloni, preheat the oven to 400°F. Spoon 1 cup of the sauce into a 13 x 9-inch glass baking dish. Lay a crespelle on your hand and spoon about 3 tablespoons of the filling along the center. Roll one side over the filling, then roll into a tube shape. Place the filled cannelloni, seam side down, into the baking dish. Fill the remaining crespelle and arrange them in a single layer in the dish. Spoon the remaining sauce evenly over the top.

7. Bake for 30 minutes, or until the sauce is hot and bubbling and the cannelloni are warm inside when tested with a fork. (Insert a fork into the center of the cannelloni; if the tines are hot when you remove the fork, the cannelloni are ready.) Serve immediately; refrigerate any leftovers.

Filling:

1 tablespoon organic extra-virgin olive oil

1 small spring onion, coarsely chopped

1 12-ounce pack ground soy turkey

2 tablespoons water

Sea salt and pepper, to taste

1½ pounds ricotta cheese, hand-packed if possible

2 eggs

3 tablespoons finely chopped Italian flat-leaf parsley

¼ cup freshly grated Parmigiano-Reggiano cheese

4 ounces fresh mozzarella, shredded

Claire's Classic

Baked Rigatoni with Amalfitan Sauce GFO

Every family has its way of distinguishing between maternal and paternal grandparents. We used the cities ours resided in to differentiate between them. "Grandma and Grandpa in New Haven" were from Amalfi, Italy, and this grandma cooked with more vegetables, fish, beans, and cheese than "Grandma in Bridgeport," who used more meats and pastas. Luckily, both showed their great love for us by spoiling us with our favorite meals during every visit. This luscious sauce was the Sunday sauce at "Grandma in New Haven's." It's still one of my favorites, and I like seeing my customers enjoy it at Claire's in the restaurant and at their parties—it's a popular dish on our catering menu, too.

Serves 6

1 pound rigatoni, cooked according to package directions, drained

4 cups marinara sauce, brought to room temperature or chilled

4 eggs, lightly beaten

¼ cup grated Parmesan cheese

1 pound low-fat ricotta

4 ounces shredded low-fat mozzarella

Salt and black pepper, to taste

Preheat the oven to 375°F. Put all the ingredients in a large bowl and toss well. Turn into a rectangular glass baking dish sprayed with a nonstick cooking spray. Bake about 30 minutes, until heated through and lightly browned on top.

Tip: Use gluten-free pasta to make this recipe gluten free.

Springing to the Table

In my fantasy world, Mother Nature coordinates with our calendar and on March 20th, when the calendar reads "first day of spring," the asparagus and spring onions rise from the soil, and the vines filled with pods bursting with tender spring peas climb toward the sun, awaiting our hands to gently pick what will be the first spring vegetables. All right, it doesn't exactly work like that. But still, as soon as the calendar says that spring has arrived, particularly after "those winters that never end," I'm headed to the kitchen, ready to cook with asparagus, peas, and scallions because I desperately need to eat a meal that feels like spring has arrived, even if in early spring these vegetables come from other places where spring really has arrived.

To welcome spring, I created the Spring Vegetables with Four-Cheese Tortellini recipe (see page 178). For this recipe, I made a vegetable sauce with a little pasta rather than what is usually the opposite for us, lots of pasta with a little sauce. After reading the label on the package of tortellini I was reminded that a serving size is 1 cup, that's *1 cup,* which, by the way, is the serving size for most pastas. I wanted to try actually sticking with a serving size of pasta, so I figured that if I add a sauce that's loaded with vegetables, we can still eat our pasta without feeling the least bit slighted—and it turned out to be a completely satisfying dish. One serving of this pasta dish will provide you with more than four servings of vegetables, so it's very healthful in addition to being beautiful, delicious, and satisfying.

This time, I used a four-cheese tortellini from the frozen foods section at the grocery store, but sometimes I use a vegan, dairy-free "cheese" tortellini that you can buy in the freezer section at the supermarket where frozen veggie burgers and other meatless items are displayed.

Asparagus, peas, onions, broccoli, and tomatoes are packed with antioxidants, vitamins A and C, fiber, and many other nutrients that help boost our immune system. I hope you'll make this sauce when your local asparagus, peas, and spring onions are available.

Spring Vegetables with Four-Cheese Tortellini V

This dish really is sauce with pasta rather than the usual pasta with sauce. It's a delicious way to eat lots of healthful vegetables while enjoying enough pasta to satisfy you and resisting going overboard with the calories. I still can't believe that a serving size for pasta is 1 cup! Seems unfair, but it's true.

Serves 4

Sea salt

4 cups water

2 cups green peas, fresh or frozen

½ pound asparagus, tough stems trimmed and discarded, remaining stems cut into 1-inch lengths, with tips separated

4 cups (about ½ pound) broccoli florets

1 pound (about 4 cups) four-cheese tortellini or vegan "cheese" tortellini

3 tablespoons extra-virgin olive oil

1 large spring onion, cut in half, then into thin ribs

3 large cloves garlic, sliced

1 teaspoon fennel seeds

¼ teaspoon red pepper flakes

4 sun-dried tomatoes, sliced

Black pepper

2 14.5-ounce cans (or 1 28-ounce can) no-salt-added chopped tomatoes

4 medium basil leaves

Grated pecorino Romano cheese or vegan cheese alternative (optional)

1. Bring 4 cups of lightly salted water to a boil in a small pot over high heat. Set a rimmed sheet pan by the stove. When the water reaches a boil, add the peas and cook them for 2–3 minutes if using fresh peas, or for 1 minute if using frozen peas. Using a mesh hand strainer, scoop out the peas, shaking off excess water back into the pot, and transfer them to the sheet pan, spreading them on the pan to cool.

2. Add the asparagus stems to the boiling water and cook for 1½ minutes, then add the tips and continue cooking for another minute. Using the strainer, scoop out the asparagus, shaking off excess water, then scatter the asparagus onto the pan, again spreading it across the pan to help cool it more quickly.

3. Add the broccoli florets and cook for 3 minutes, then scoop out, shake off excess water, and transfer to the pan, spreading them across the pan, over the other vegetables. Set the pan aside. Remove the cooking water (you'll have about 3 cups) from the heat and set aside until later in the recipe.

4. Bring 6–8 quarts of lightly salted water to a boil over high heat. Cook the tortellini according to package directions. When they are tender to your preference, drain them and turn them into a serving bowl.

5. Meanwhile, prepare the sauce. Heat the olive oil in a large, deep skillet over medium-high heat. Add the onions, garlic, fennel seeds, red pepper flakes, and sun-dried tomatoes. Sprinkle lightly with sea salt and pepper. Cover and cook for about 5 minutes, stirring occasionally, until the onions are softened and lightly golden. Add the reserved cooking liquid from the vegetables. Cover and bring to a boil; this will take about a minute. Cook at a medium boil for about 10 minutes, stirring occasionally, until the liquid reduces a bit; then stir in the tomatoes and their liquid. Cover and cook at a medium boil for about 15 minutes, stirring occasionally until the tomatoes have broken down a bit and the sauce has thickened slightly.

6. Stir in the cooked vegetables and the basil. Cover and cook for about a minute, stirring occasionally until heated through. Stir in the cooked tortellini. Taste for seasonings. Turn into the serving bowl. Top with additional black pepper and grated cheese, if desired.

Summer Sauce with Pasta [V] [GFO]

This lovely sauce came about directly after my visit to our farmers' market, where I found freshly harvested vegetables and inspiration.

Serves 4–6

3 medium-size locally grown organic carrots, cut into 1-inch julienne

3 tablespoons extra-virgin olive oil

6 cloves fresh organic garlic, cut into thick slices

1 large leek, white part and 3 inches of green, coarsely chopped and washed well to remove any grit

2 medium locally grown organic red onions, cut into thick ribs, separated

8 medium-size locally grown organic tomatoes, cut into wedges

5 basil leaves

¼ cup chopped fresh parsley

¼ cup white wine

Sea salt and pepper, to taste

1 pound organic pasta, cooked according to package directions

1. Place the carrots in a small pot and cover with water. Cover the pot and bring to a boil over high heat. Cook for about 2 minutes until crisp-tender. Remove from the heat and set aside (do not drain).

2. Heat the oil in a large, deep skillet over medium-high heat. Add the garlic, leek, red onions, tomatoes, basil, parsley, and white wine. Sprinkle with sea salt and pepper. Stir to combine. Cover and bring to a boil, then lower the heat to medium and cook at a low-medium boil, stirring occasionally, for about 20 minutes or until the sauce reduces by about half.

3. Stir in the carrots and cooking liquid. Continue cooking, uncovered for about 3 minutes, stirring occasionally until the carrots are tender. Taste for seasonings. Add the cooked pasta to the sauce and stir to combine. Taste for seasonings.

Tip: Use gluten-free pasta to make this recipe gluten free.

Fazzoletto

Fazzoletto means "handkerchief" in Italian, and these little pasta crepes are folded into triangles in a way that always reminds me of the way my grandmother neatly folded her little handkerchief. *Fazzoletto* is the word she always said while I watched her iron those lovely little flowered handkerchiefs that she always had in her purse.

I was making crepes for manicotti one day when my sister-in-law Kathy came by. To let her taste one crepe right away, I just folded it into a triangle and dipped it into my marinara sauce. I told her about my grandmother's *fazzoletti*, and these little pasta triangles became a favorite. Now we serve them as a pasta dish, topped with a good San Marzano marinara sauce, a sprinkle of pecorino Romano cheese, and just a drizzle of white truffle oil. It's so delicious, and both the shape of the pasta crepe and the truffle oil elevate this humble dish to rather elegant standards, making it perfect for company. But it's easy enough to make for a weeknight supper, too.

Makes 24 pasta crepes

2 cups unbleached all-purpose flour

4 eggs

1 cup whole milk

1 cup water

Sea salt and freshly cracked black pepper

Olive oil spray

1 quart marinara sauce, warmed

2 teaspoons white truffle oil

¼ cup freshly grated pecorino Romano cheese

1. Measure the flour into a bowl. In a separate bowl, whisk the eggs, milk, water, and a little salt and pepper. Pour the mixture all at once over the flour. Mix well with a whisk until the mixture is smooth.

2. Line a cookie sheet with parchment paper or waxed paper and set it by the stove. Heat an 8-inch heavy skillet or crepe pan over medium heat. Spray it with olive oil spray. Stir the pasta crepe batter. Spoon about 3 tablespoons of the batter into the center of the heated skillet, tilting the pan to coat the bottom but being careful to avoid the sides to facilitate turning. Cook for about 25 seconds, or until the crepe is set. Carefully turn the crepe using a long spatula, and cook the other side for about 10 seconds or until the crepe no longer looks wet when you lift it to check. Transfer the cooked crepe to the lined cookie sheet. Repeat the process with the remaining batter, heating and spraying the pan in between batches. Transfer the cooked crepes, overlapping slightly on the cookie sheet as you cook them.

3. To serve, spoon about a cup of the warmed marinara sauce onto a platter to create a pool. Fold each crepe in half, then in half again, creating a triangle. Arrange the triangles on the platter, overlapping slightly. Spoon additional sauce evenly over the fazzoletti. Sprinkle with grated pecorino and drizzle with the truffle oil. Sprinkle with a little black pepper. Serve with additional marinara sauce.

Arugula Pesto Pasta V

Arugula, also known as rocket, is a bitter green with an assertive mustard flavor. It has a long history in the Italian community. Now many American cooks, looking for healthful greens with lively flavors, have discovered arugula. They appreciate its rich flavor and healthy dose of vitamins A and C, calcium, and iron.

This pasta dish is delicious served right away or chilled, making it a perfect choice for a picnic. And the meatless bacon adds 6 grams of good soy protein to every serving.

Serves 4

Sea salt

3 cups uncooked organic rigatoni, half wheat and half white semolina, or any other pasta

5–6 ounces organic arugula, well washed, drained, and torn into large pieces, about 5 packed cups

3 large cloves local garlic, sliced

8 strips meatless bacon, cut into thirds

1 teaspoon fennel seeds

½ teaspoon crushed red pepper flakes

7 tablespoons extra-virgin olive oil

Pepper, to taste

1. Bring 4 quarts of water to a boil in a covered pot over high heat. Cook the pasta according to package directions. When cooked al dente or to your preference, drain the pasta and turn into a bowl.

2. While the pasta is cooking, place the arugula, garlic, bacon, fennel seeds, red pepper flakes, olive oil, and a little salt and pepper into the bowl of a food processor fitted with a metal blade. Cover and process for about 25 seconds, until fairly smooth with small flecks of the meatless bacon visible.

3. Turn the arugula pesto into the bowl with the pasta. Use a rubber spatula to scrape the processor bowl. Using two wooden spoons, toss the pasta with the pesto to coat. Taste for seasonings.

Sicilian Pistachio Pesto V GF

The recipe is pure Sicilian, but the pistachios that we use at my restaurant are purely American, grown right in sunny California. Use it to toss pasta or as a dip for vegetables or a topping for crostini, carrot sticks, or pretzels. Any way you serve it, it's loaded with flavor and rich in essential fatty acids.

Makes about 1 cup sauce (for 1 pound of pasta)

1½ cups shelled pistachios

⅓ cup extra-virgin olive oil

4 tablespoons each organic flax oil and olive oil

Sea salt, to taste

Place the shelled pistachios in the bowl of a food processor fitted with a metal blade. Cover and process for about 45 seconds until finely minced. With the motor running, slowly add the extra-virgin olive oil, the flax oil, and the salt, and continue processing for about 15–20 seconds until the sauce is well blended. Taste for seasonings.

Claire's Classic

Marinara Sauce I V GF

There's nothing quite like a simple marinara. The delightful aroma will fill your kitchen, tempting all who enter. This wonderful sauce is quick and easy to make, requiring only staple ingredients and allowing you to offer last-minute dinner invitations to your friends. Invite them back to the house after a day at the beach or an evening of theater. Put your water for pasta on to boil while you prepare this delicious sauce and make a simple salad, and within the hour you and some very grateful friends will be enjoying a lovely meal.

Serves 6

½ cup olive oil

6 large cloves garlic, minced

2 28-ounce cans whole peeled San Marzano tomatoes

½ cup chopped fresh basil

1 teaspoon crushed red pepper flakes

Salt, to taste

Black pepper, to taste

Heat the oil in a large skillet over low heat. Add the garlic and cook for 3 minutes, stirring frequently, until golden brown. Do not let the garlic burn or your sauce will be bitter. Add the tomatoes and raise the heat to medium. Simmer for 10 minutes, stirring often. Using a spoon, break up the tomatoes into small pieces. Add the basil, red pepper flakes, salt, and pepper. Simmer, stirring frequently, for another 15–20 minutes, until the sauce is thick. Taste for seasonings.

Marinara Sauce II V GF

I think that every Italian family has its own marinara recipe. In our case, we have several variations that can include white or red wine and contains onions or garlic or both. My mother occasionally makes a sweet marinara using lots of sliced onions and no garlic. She learned this from a neighbor from Apuglia. This recipe is one of my favorites and I hope it becomes one of yours, too.

Makes about 5 cups

3 tablespoons extra-virgin olive oil

6 large cloves garlic, cut into slices

1 small yellow onion, coarsely chopped

1 35-ounce can whole peeled San Marzano tomatoes in juice, squeezed with your hands to crush

½ cup white wine

10 leaves fresh basil

¼ cup Italian flat-leaf parsley

1 bay leaf

Sea salt and pepper, to taste

Heat the oil in a large pot over medium heat. Add the garlic and onion. Cover and cook, stirring occasionally, for 7–10 minutes or until the garlic and onions are lightly browned but not burned. Add the remaining ingredients and stir well to mix. Cover and cook at a medium boil, stirring occasionally, for about 20–25 minutes or until the sauce reduces slightly. Taste for seasonings.

Claire's Classic

Basil-Scented Marinara Sauce V GF

I enjoy a good marinara sauce more than any other, and this one is perfect for fettucine.

Makes about 5 cups (plenty for 1 pound of pasta)

3 tablespoons extra-virgin olive oil

6 large cloves garlic, cut into thick slices

1 small yellow onion, finely chopped

1 35-ounce can Italian whole peeled tomatoes in juice, crushed by hand

½ cup dry red wine

10 large fresh basil leaves

¼ cup coarsely chopped Italian flat-leaf parsley

2 bay leaves

Salt and pepper

Heat the oil in a large pot over medium heat. Add the garlic and onion. Cover and cook, stirring occasionally, for 7–10 minutes, or until the garlic and onion are light brown but not burned. Add the remaining ingredients and stir well to mix. Cover and bring to a medium boil (this should take about 5 minutes), stirring occasionally. Cook for about 20 minutes, or until the sauce reduces slightly. Taste for seasonings.

Claire's Classic

Fresh Tomato Sauce I V GF

This quick sauce is perfect for the summer months. Use ripe plum tomatoes to make a delicious sauce for pasta, pizza, or rice.

Makes about 6 cups

3 tablespoons extra-virgin olive oil

4 large cloves garlic, cut into thin slices

1 medium red onion, finely chopped

24 ripe plum tomatoes, coarsely chopped, including juices

3 tablespoons finely chopped Italian flat-leaf parsley

5 large fresh basil leaves, coarsely chopped

5 medium fresh sage leaves, finely chopped, or 1 teaspoon dried sage

3 tablespoons dry white wine

Salt and pepper, to taste

Heat the oil in a large skillet over medium-high heat. Add the remaining ingredients and stir to mix. Cover and bring to a medium boil, then lower the heat to medium and cook, stirring occasionally, for about 20 minutes, or until the sauce reduces by about half. Taste for seasonings.

Fresh Tomato Sauce II   V GF

At the end of the season, I buy as many plum tomatoes as I can fit in my freezer because if you rinse your tomatoes, freeze them in a single-layer on cookie sheets, then transfer them to plastic bags, you can "save summer" for up to six months. When you plan to use "fresh" tomatoes out of season, just run one at a time under hot water (be careful not to burn your hands) until the skin bursts, then place them into a bowl to defrost. When they defrost, just use your fingers to remove the skin and to squeeze the tomatoes for your sauce.

You can also extend your season by making basil cubes for use during the winter. Place washed and drained basil leaves with just enough water necessary to puree them in a blender. Turn this puree into ice cube trays and freeze for future use.

Makes about 3 cups, enough for 12 ounces to a pound of pasta

3 tablespoons extra-virgin olive oil

1 medium yellow onion, coarsely chopped

4 large cloves garlic, cut into thin slices

15 plum tomatoes, fresh or frozen and defrosted, peeled and coarsely chopped or squeezed by hand or in a processor, juices reserved

5 leaves fresh basil or 2 basil "ice cubes"

Sea salt and pepper, to taste

Heat the oil in a large skillet over medium-high heat. Add the remaining ingredients and stir to mix. Cover and bring to a medium boil, then lower the heat to medium and cook, stirring occasionally, for about 15 minutes or until the sauce is reduced by about half. Taste for seasonings.

Hunter's Sauce ▣

This is every bit as good as the classic Italian sausage and pepper sauces I enjoyed in grinder sandwiches at carnivals during my teens. At Claire's we serve this richly flavored sauce over pasta to grateful customers, who are happy to have a cholesterol-free, absolutely delicious "sausage." We use Tofurky® or LightLife® Italian meatless sausage links. You can find them in the frozen food section of most health food stores.

Serves 6

½ cup olive oil

1 10-ounce package frozen tofu sausage, each link cut into 4 pieces while partly frozen

6 large cloves garlic, chopped

3 bell peppers (1 each yellow, red, and green), seeded and chopped

1 medium red onion, chopped

1 pound mushrooms, sliced

½ teaspoon fennel seeds

¼ teaspoon crushed red pepper flakes

½ teaspoon dried rosemary

Salt and black pepper, to taste

2 28-ounce cans Italian whole peeled tomatoes, crushed by hand

1 pound rigatoni or other pasta

1. Heat 2 tablespoons of the olive oil in a heavy skillet over medium heat. Add the sausage and brown all sides evenly. Set aside. In a heavy pot, heat the remaining ¼ cup plus 2 tablespoons olive oil over low heat. Add the garlic and cook 2 minutes, stirring frequently, until softened. Add the peppers, onion, mushrooms, fennel seeds, red pepper flakes, rosemary, salt, and pepper. Cover, raise the heat to medium-low, and cook for 15 minutes, stirring frequently, until the peppers are softened. Add the tomatoes, bring to a low boil, and simmer for 30 minutes, stirring frequently. Taste the seasoning. Keep the sauce warm.

2. Cook the pasta according to the package directions. Drain and turn into a serving bowl. Spoon one-fourth of the sauce over the top and toss to coat the pasta. Spoon the remaining sauce over the top. Grind additional black pepper over the top, if desired.

Claire's Classic

Amatriciana Sauce V

This is our meatless, cholesterol-free version of the pancetta-flavored tomato sauce so many of us enjoyed before the problem of cholesterol was posed. The flavor is rich, and Fakin Bakin has a familiar smokey taste. Prepare this delicious sauce for anyone who loves bacon or pancetta in a sauce but cannot have the cholesterol. You'll make that person very happy.

Serves 6

½ cup olive oil

1 medium yellow onion, chopped

4 large cloves garlic, chopped

1 8-ounce package meatless bacon, chopped

¼ cup chopped Italian flat-leaf parsley

½ teaspoon crushed red pepper flakes

2 28-ounce cans Italian whole peeled tomatoes, crushed by hand

¼ cup chopped fresh basil

Salt and black pepper, to taste

1 pound rigatoni

1. Heat the oil in a large skillet over low heat. Add the onion, garlic, and bacon. Cook, stirring occasionally, for 15 minutes, until the bacon browns. Add the parsley, red pepper flakes, tomatoes, basil, salt, and pepper. Bring to a boil and simmer for 40 minutes, stirring occasionally, until the sauce is thickened.

2. Cook the pasta according to the package directions. Drain and turn into a serving bowl. Spoon a little sauce over the top and toss well. Spoon the remaining sauce over the top.

entrees

Our everyday menu of entrees at Claire's consists mainly of Mexican food, but we make dozens of entrees throughout the day for our deli case and for our specials boards and they run the gamut, globe-trotting across the world for variety. We love exploring different cuisines, and we know that this is a wonderful way to learn about different cultures. I'm so grateful that we have access to amazing ingredients from good people whom we like to support. In turn, they help support our work, our community, our staff, and me.

During the summer when we have the most flavorful corn, zucchini, and tomatoes, you'll find specials that take advantage of these treasures from our farmers, like our Fresh Corn Fritters, Vegetarian Chicken Provençal, and Grilled Polenta Slices with Tomato Bruschetta Topping. Or we'll make our Tomato-Coconut Curry with Yellow Squash, Corn, and Kale.

During the fall we'll make Butternut Squash Pancakes or Moroccan Stuffed Sweet Lightning Squash with squash fresh from the farm. On my day off, Frank and I often take a road trip to our favorite farms to bring back fresh produce for Claire's and, of course, to enjoy the natural beauty of our beloved farms. Every season brings beautiful ingredients and we are so blessed to have them available to us, so grateful to our farm workers who work so hard to grow our food.

I hope you'll use this section to explore new foods and to revisit old favorites.

Black Bean Burgers V

Black beans are rich in protein and fiber, and they contain a fair amount of iron. These burgers are delicious and satisfying and are vegan, too, which means they are free of all animal products and also cholesterol-free. Serve them on a potato bun or other bun, with a slice of fresh mango, or with the more traditional organic romaine leaves, sliced tomato, red onion, and ketchup. Either way, they are really good.

These burgers freeze well and are easy to cook from frozen. When ready to serve, bake them in a preheated 400°F oven for about 5 minutes until heated through. Just remember, they are fragile, so handle them gently.

Makes 8 burgers

2 cups dry organic black beans, about 12 ounces, sorted for stones, rinsed

¼ cup organic brown rice

1 small organic red bell pepper, seeded and finely chopped

½ small sweet onion, finely chopped

¼ small organic jalapeño pepper, minced

1 tablespoon extra-virgin olive oil

2 tablespoons organic bread crumbs

Sea salt and pepper

1 teaspoon dried organic oregano

2 teaspoons organic chili powder

1. Measure 3 quarts of water into a heavy pot. Add the black beans and rice. Cover and bring to a boil over high heat. After the water reaches a boil, which takes about 5 minutes, reduce the heat to medium and cook at a medium boil for about 1 hour or until the beans are tender. (The time will vary depending to how old and dry the beans are.) When the beans are tender, drain them into a colander, then turn the drained beans into a bowl. Using a fork or a potato masher, mash the beans, not completely smooth, but leaving some beans partially whole. Add the remaining ingredients. Stir well to combine. Taste for seasonings.

2. Center the oven rack. Preheat the oven to 425°F. Line a baking sheet with parchment paper and spray it with olive oil spray, or just spray a baking sheet with the spray. Using a half-cup measure, pack some of the bean mixture into the cup, then tap it out onto one hand. Using your free hand, press lightly to form a burger about 4 inches in diameter. Carefully place the burger on the prepared baking sheet, then continue forming and placing the remaining burgers, leaving a little space between the burgers to make turning easier. Spray the tops of the burgers lightly with olive oil spray. Bake the burgers in the preheated oven for about 25–30 minutes until the tops are just firm to the touch. Using two metal spatulas, carefully turn the burgers and spray the tops lightly with olive oil spray. Bake for about 30 minutes, until just firm to the touch. Remove from the oven and set aside for about 10 minutes to allow the burgers to firm up enough for handling.

Sloppy Moes ⓥ

Serve this flavorful, soy-enriched version of Sloppy Joes on whole grain buns or with baked organic corn tortillas for a delicious and healthful supper. Pair it with a salad of organic mixed greens with sliced avocado and red onion drizzled with a little extra-virgin olive oil and freshly squeezed lemon juice.

Serves 4

2 teaspoons extra-virgin olive oil

1 large sweet onion, coarsely chopped

4 large cloves garlic, coarsely chopped

2 large organic bell peppers (1 red and 1 yellow), seeded and coarsely chopped

Salt and pepper, to taste

1 28-ounce can whole peeled Italian tomatoes, crushed by hand

1 13-ounce container ground soy beef (found in the produce section of the supermarket)

1 13-ounce can organic kidney beans, drained

2 tablespoons yellow mustard

2 teaspoons dried oregano

4 whole grain buns, split

1. Heat the olive oil in a heavy pot over low-medium heat. Add the onion, garlic, peppers, salt, and pepper. Cover and cook, stirring occasionally, for about 15 minutes, until the vegetables have released some of their liquids.

2. Add the tomatoes and the soy beef. Using a hand masher (the type you would use to mash potatoes), break up the ground soy beef into small pieces. Cover and cook for about 20 minutes, stirring occasionally.

3. Add the beans, mustard, and oregano. Stir well to combine. Continue cooking, uncovered, for about 10 minutes, stirring occasionally until heated through. Taste for seasonings. Spoon the filling into the buns and serve immediately.

Claire's Classic

Soy Bacon and Pepper Burgers VO

This recipe is vegetarian but can easily be made vegan by replacing the dairy egg with a vegan egg substitute. Serve on your favorite burger bun.

Serves 4

3 slices whole wheat bread

1 14-ounce package meatless ground soy beef (found in the refrigerated produce section at the supermarket)

¼ cup chopped organic Italian flat-leaf parsley

¼ small organic onion, finely chopped

2 cloves organic garlic, finely chopped

1 small organic red bell pepper, finely chopped

2 strips meatless bacon, finely chopped

2 tablespoons extra-virgin olive oil, divided

Salt and pepper, to taste

1 organic egg or equivalent egg substitute

4 hamburger rolls

1. Tear the bread into small pieces and place in a mixing bowl. Add the ground soy beef and the parsley, onion, garlic, bell pepper, meatless bacon, 1 tablespoon of the olive oil, and a little salt and pepper. Using your hands, mix the ingredients until well combined. Taste for seasoning. Add the egg and mix well to combine. Form into 4 burgers.

2. Heat a large skillet over medium-low heat. Add the remaining tablespoon of olive oil and swirl it around the skillet to cover the bottom. Arrange the burgers in a single layer in the heated oil. Cover and cook for about 8 minutes, or until the undersides are well browned but not burned. Turn the burgers, cover, and cook for about 5 minutes, or until the burgers are well browned but not burned.

Soy Sausage and Pepper Burgers VO

Enjoy these flavorful burgers for a delicious and healthful alternative to the higher fat pork sausages and you'll get the heart-healthful benefits of eating soy protein.

Note: If using ground soy beef in place of soy sausage, mix 1 teaspoon ground sage and ½ teaspoon crushed red pepper flakes into the ground soy beef.

Serves 4

1 1-inch slice Italian bread or other, fresh or day-old

½ small onion, finely diced, about ¼ cup

2 small bell peppers (1 red and 1 green), seeded, and finely diced (about 1 cup total)

1 12- or 14-ounce container ground soy sausage or soy beef (see note above)

1 teaspoon fennel seeds

2 cloves garlic, finely chopped

½ teaspoon crushed red pepper flakes

1 teaspoon extra-virgin olive oil, plus additional oil for coating the grill if using

Salt and pepper, to taste

1 egg or cholesterol-free egg substitute

4 hamburger rolls

1. Set the bread in a bowl. Cover with hot water. Set aside for a minute or two, or until the bread absorbs some of the water and softens. Drain the water and, using your hands, squeeze out as much liquid as possible. You should have about a quarter of a cup of soft and wet bread. Turn into a bowl large enough to mix the remaining ingredients.

2. Add the remaining ingredients except the egg. Using your hands, break up the soy sausage, and mix to combine the ingredients. Taste for seasonings. Add the egg, and, using your hands, mix well to combine.

3. Form the mixture into 4 patties. Spray a nonstick skillet with olive oil cooking spray and heat over low-medium heat. Arrange the burgers in the heated skillet, cover, and cook for about 10 minutes until medium brown. Turn, cover, and cook the other side for 7–10 minutes until medium brown.

Spicy Zucchini and Soymeat Burgers $\boxed{\text{V}}$

I love a good burger, and this one is a favorite of mine because it combines summer onions and zucchini with a nice shot of heat from chipotle chile powder and a little seeded jalapeño pepper.

Serves 6

2 slices organic whole grain flax bread

2 teaspoons extra-virgin olive oil, plus another tablespoon for pan-frying the burgers

½ medium local organic red onion, finely chopped

1 small local organic zucchini, cut into small dice (about 1 cup)

Sea salt

1 teaspoon chipotle chile pepper (found in the spice section at the supermarket)

Black pepper

1 14-ounce package ground soy beef (found in the refrigerated produce section at the supermarket)

3 cloves local organic garlic, minced

½ small local organic jalapeño pepper, seeded and finely chopped

1. Hold the 2 slices of bread (stacked) in your hands and run warm water over them just until the bread slices are wet, then squeeze the slices in your hands to soften and to remove as much water as possible. Turn the bread into a bowl, breaking up the slices into small pieces using your fingers. Heat the 2 teaspoons of olive oil in a small skillet. Add the chopped onion, zucchini, and a little sea salt. Stir to coat. Cook for about 5 minutes, stirring occasionally, until the zucchini is just tender and has turned golden. Stir in the chipotle chile pepper and a little black pepper.

2. Place the ground soy beef in the bowl with the bread, then add the sautéed zucchini and onion mixture, using a spoon to scrape the skillet of any brown bits. Add the minced garlic and jalapeño pepper. Using a potato masher, mash the ingredients to mix well. Taste for seasoning.

3. Form 6 burger patties using about ½ cup of the mixture per burger. Heat a large skillet over medium heat, then spray the skillet with olive oil spray. Add the remaining tablespoon of olive oil, and swirl the pan to coat it with the oil. Arrange the burger patties on the heated oil. Spray the tops with olive oil spray. Cover and cook for about 5–6 minutes until medium brown and firm on the underside, then using a spatula, turn each burger patty, and cook the other side for about 5 minutes until medium brown and firm on the underside. Serve hot.

Chinese Big Bowl V GFO

This is a popular dish at home and at Claire's and it's so much fun to prepare. It's a cross between a soup and a stew and it has a healthful array of vegetables. Really, any and all of your favorites can go into it.

Serves 4

1 8-ounce package soba noodles

2 tablespoons sesame oil

4 scallions, white part and 4 inches green, cut into thin slices

2 shallots, peeled and finely chopped

1 large clove garlic, finely chopped

2 small zucchini, diced

1 sweet potato, peeled and diced

1 2-inch piece fresh ginger, peeled and thinly sliced

2 large stalks broccoli, stems separated from florets; stems diagonally cut into ¼-inch slices and florets cut into small pieces

Sea salt and pepper

½ teaspoon crushed red pepper flakes, or more, to taste

3 tablespoons tamari sauce

1 pound soft tofu, drained and cut into small cubes

7 ounces baby organic spinach

¼ cup sweet miso, whisked into 2 cups warm water

3 tablespoons organic flax oil

1. Cook the soba noodles according to package directions. Before draining, set a colander into a large bowl in your sink. Drain the soba noodles, reserving the liquid. Set the reserved liquid aside. Rinse the soba noodles while in the colander, then drain them right into the sink—you don't need to reserve this water. Set aside the cooked noodles and the reserved cooking liquid separately.

2. Heat the sesame oil in a large pot over medium heat. Add the scallions, shallots, garlic, zucchini, sweet potato, ginger, and the stems from the broccoli. Sprinkle lightly with salt and pepper and the red pepper flakes. Stir well to combine. Cook for 5 minutes, stirring occasionally, until the scallions soften. Add the tamari sauce and 6 cups of the reserved cooking liquid. Stir well to combine. Cover and bring to a boil. Cook at a low-medium boil, stirring occasionally for about 8 minutes until the potatoes are tender-soft.

3. Stir in the broccoli florets, tofu, and baby spinach. Stir well to combine. Cook for 2–3 minutes, stirring occasionally, until the broccoli florets are crisp-tender. Turn off the heat. Stir in the miso-water mixture, the flax oil, and the cooked soba noodles, mixing well to combine. Taste for seasonings.

Tip: Use gluten-free noodles to make this recipe gluten free.

Vietnamese Spring Rolls V GFO

These light and tasty spring rolls are so colorful and pretty, and each roll is like a salad in tender rice paper. Buy spring roll skins in an Asian grocery store and keep them on hand at home. They keep for a long time in the cabinet, ready for you to make these spring rolls.

Makes 16 spring roll halves; serves 6–8 for lunch

Filling:

3 small organic carrots, cut into thin julienne sticks, 4 inches long

½ large organic red bell pepper, seeded and cut into thin strips

½ small head organic Savoy cabbage or soft leaf lettuce (such as romaine), cut into thin strips

½ cup organic cilantro, leaves and tender stems

½ cup organic frozen edamame or lima beans, defrosted

16 large leaves organic basil, cut in half

16 small leaves organic mint

1 2-inch piece organic ginger, peeled and finely minced

2 medium cloves organic garlic, finely chopped

½ organic jalapeño pepper, seeded and finely chopped

Dressing:

1½ tablespoons toasted sesame oil

Juice from 1 organic lime (about 2 tablespoons)

1 tablespoon organic brown rice vinegar

½ teaspoon organic brown sugar

Sea salt and pepper, to taste

8 spring roll skins

1. To prepare the spring roll filling, place the carrots and pepper strips into a bowl. Into a separate bowl, place the cabbage, cilantro, edamame, basil, mint, ginger, garlic, and jalapeño. Using two wooden spoons, toss to combine.

2. To prepare the dressing, in a separate small bowl combine the toasted sesame oil, lime juice, rice vinegar, brown sugar, salt, and pepper. Whisk, then taste for seasonings.

3. Pour the dressing evenly over the cabbage mixture, tossing to coat the vegetables well. Taste for seasoning.

4. Place a clean kitchen towel on the counter by the sink. Arrange the vegetables in their bowls by the towel. Place 1 spring roll skin on a 12-inch dinner plate. Turn on the water in the sink at a slow stream, adjusting the temperature until the water is warm. Hold the plate with the "skin" under the facet and add just enough warm water to cover the skin. Using your hand, push the skin into the water to allow it to soften for 12–15 seconds, until the skin has just softened. Don't let it get too soft or it will tear when you attempt to transfer it to the towel-lined counter. Lift the softened skin out of the water and hold it by the top and sides to allow a little water to drip off onto the plate.

5. Transfer the softened skin to the towel. Place 2–3 carrot and pepper strips into a row horizontally down the center of the softened skin, leaving about 1½ inches around the filling to roll up. Arrange about ¼ cup of the cabbage mixture over the carrots and peppers, horizontally down the center of the skin. Lift the side of the skin closest to you over the filling, bring the two sides in to meet the filling, then roll up the spring roll as tightly as you can without tearing the skin. Turn seam side down; then, using a sharp knife, cut the roll in half on the diagonal, being careful to cut only through the skin, not through the towel. Carefully transfer the filled spring roll to a serving platter. Repeat with the remaining skins and filling, placing them in a single layer on the platter. Serve with the Pineapple-Lime Dipping Sauce (page 136) or the Peanut-Tamari Dip (page 136).

Tip: Use gluten-free rice wrappers to make this recipe gluten free.

"Chicken" and Bean Burrito with Pipian Verde VO

My introduction to Mexican foods was in the early 1980s, when Javier Lopez came to work with us from his homeland in Tlaxcala, Mexico. It became a love affair that continues today. He taught me so much about his family recipes, but I think the most important lesson he taught me had to do with the use of chiles. Until then, I always thought of chiles as hot peppers, and I used them (mainly jalapeños) as a spice to add heat to a dish. Javier taught me to use chiles as a vegetable. He taught me how to use poblano chiles—big, deep-green-colored peppers that have a rich, spectacular pepper flavor and a mild to medium heat—in sautéed vegetable dishes, in fillings for quesadillas and enchiladas, and in burritos.

This delicious recipe is very healthful. It contains good protein, complete because the beans are paired with corn and tortillas, and it has loads of fiber and powerful antioxidants from the chiles, onions, and garlic. The pipian verde salsa is made with pumpkin seeds. These seeds are among the Native American foods that became New World treasures. They are rich in important nutrients, such as manganese, iron, copper, zinc, and protein. They also contain anti-inflammatory monounsaturated fats and phytosterols, plant sterols that contribute to a strong immune system.

Serves 8

Pipian Verde:

2 cups shelled pumpkin seeds, divided

5 large organic tomatillas, husk removed and discarded, fruit rinsed well and quartered

½ large sweet onion, coarsely chopped

2 cloves organic garlic, sliced

¼ cup coarsely chopped organic cilantro

1 medium organic jalapeño pepper, sliced

Sea salt and pepper

1½ cups organic vegetable broth, divided

1 tablespoon organic canola oil

1. To make the pipian verde, lightly toast the pumpkin seeds in a dry skillet over medium-high heat, stirring frequently, until they are just golden-green, fragrant, and begin to make a "popping" noise, about 1–2 minutes. Reserve 3 tablespoons of toasted seeds to garnish the burritos before serving.

2. Spoon the toasted pumpkin seeds into the bowl of a food processor fitted with a metal blade. Cover and process for about a minute or until the seeds are finely ground. Add the tomatillas, onion, garlic, cilantro, and jalapeño. Sprinkle lightly with sea salt and pepper. Add vegetable broth to cover the vegetables, about a cup of broth. Cover and process for about a minute until well blended. Taste for seasonings. Heat the tablespoon of canola oil in a large skillet over medium-high heat. Add the processed pumpkin seed mixture and the remaining broth. Bring to a boil and cook, stirring frequently, for about 30 seconds, until the mixture is heated through. Taste for seasonings. Remove from the heat and reserve ¾ cup for your burritos. (Store the remainder and use to top sides like baked or roasted potatoes.)

3. To make the burritos, measure the beans into a 4-quart pot. Fill the pot with cold water and bring to a boil over high heat. Boil the beans for about 1¼ hours or until just tender but not soft, stirring occasionally, adding water if needed to keep the beans covered plus 1½ to 2 inches. When the beans are tender, drain them and set aside.

4. Meanwhile, put the garlic, cilantro, and jalapeño into the bowl of a food processor fitted with a metal blade and process for about 10 seconds or until finely minced. Set aside.

5. Heat the olive oil in a large, deep skillet over medium heat. Add the onion, poblano, and corn kernels. Sprinkle lightly with sea salt and pepper, the chile powder, and oregano. Stir well to combine. Cover and cook for about 5–6 minutes, stirring frequently until the crisp-tender. Add the meatless chicken strips, the cooked pinto beans, and the ¼ cup water. Stir to combine. Cover and cook for about 2 minutes, until the chicken strips have defrosted and are limp. Add the processed cilantro mixture and stir to combine. Taste for seasonings.

6. Preheat the oven to 400°F

7. Line a cookie sheet with parchment paper or spray it with nonstick cooking spray. Lay one tortilla on a plate and spread about a heaping cup of the filling in a row along the center of the tortilla, leaving about an inch bare on each end. Tuck in the sides to meet the filling, then roll the tortilla and place this burrito, seam side down, on the prepared cookie sheet. Continue filling and rolling the remaining tortillas. Spoon about ¾ cup of the pipian verde over the burritos, then divide the crumbled cheese evenly over top of the pipan verde. Bake in the preheated oven for about 10 minutes until the sauce is heated through. Sprinkle with a few toasted pumpkin seeds if desired before serving.

Burrito:

1 cup dry organic pinto beans, picked over for stones

4 cloves organic garlic, sliced

¼ cup coarsely chopped organic cilantro

1 medium organic jalapeño pepper, sliced

3 tablespoons extra-virgin olive oil

1 large sweet onion, cut into thick ribs, separated

2 medium poblano chile peppers, seeded and cut into strips

2 ears of fresh corn, kernels cut to make about 2 cups of kernels

Sea salt and pepper

1 tablespoon chile powder

1 teaspoon oregano

1 8-ounce package meatless chicken strips, added frozen

¼ cup water

6 8-inch whole wheat flour tortillas

4 ounces queso fresco or Cotija cheese (can substitute feta cheese or ricotta salata), crumbled

Farmers' Market Burrito GFO

Use the freshest vegetables you can get for this tribute to summer.

Serves 6

2 small carrots, chopped

1 tablespoon extra-virgin olive oil or organic corn oil

3 cloves garlic, sliced

2 sweet onions, cut into thick wedges

18 string beans (green, yellow, or purple), trimmed and cut into 1-inch pieces

Salt and pepper

1 teaspoon ground cumin

1 teaspoon ground chipotle chile powder, found in the spice section of the supermarket

3 bell peppers, seeded and cut into thin ribs

1 small yellow summer squash, cut into ¼-inch slices

1 small zucchini, cut into ¼-inch slices

2 cups fresh corn, cut from 2 to 4 large ears

¼ cup chopped cilantro

1 large organic heirloom tomato, cut into thin wedges

1 12-ounce can organic pinto beans, drained, rinsed, and drained again

4 ounces shredded low-fat mozzarella

4 ounces goat cheese, crumbled, or shredded low-fat cheddar cheese

6 10-inch whole wheat tortillas

1 ripe avocado, sliced (optional)

1. Preheat the oven to 350°F. Line two cookie sheets with parchment paper or spray them with olive oil spray. Place the chopped carrots into the bowl of a food processor fitted with a metal blade. Cover and process until finely minced and nearly pureed. Set aside.

2. Heat the oil in a large, deep sauté pan over low-medium heat. Add the garlic, onions, and string beans. Sprinkle with salt and pepper, the cumin, and the chipotle powder. Stir to coat. Cover and cook for 6 minutes, stirring frequently. Add the peppers, the yellow squash and zucchini, the corn, cilantro, and the minced carrots. Stir to combine. Cover and continue cooking for about 4 minutes, until the vegetables are crisp-tender, or cook a few minutes longer until they are cooked to your preference. Add the tomato and the drained beans. Stir to combine. Cover and cook for 2 minutes until heated through. Taste for seasonings.

3. Arrange 3 tortillas on each of the prepared cookie sheets. Divide the filling on the center of each tortilla, leaving 1 inch on each end without filling. Sprinkle a little of each cheese over the filling. Pull the sides of the tortillas in just to meet the filling. Take one side of the tortilla and cover the filling, then roll the tortilla until the seam side is down. Bake in the preheated oven for about 12–15 minutes until the tortillas are soft-crispy. Remove from the oven and arrange avocado slices, if desired, over each burrito.

Tip: Use gluten-free tortillas to make this recipe gluten free.

Claire's Classic

Enchiladas GF

These enchiladas first appeared at Claire's as a special for the day. We sold out every time we offered them, so we added them to our permanent "big board" menu. They remain popular today at lunch and dinner. Try with Claire's Classic Salsa (page 138).

Serves 6

4 tablespoons (½ stick) butter, cut into 4 pieces

1 small onion, chopped

2 cloves garlic, minced

1 pound mushrooms, sliced into ¼-inch pieces

Corn kernels cut from 3 ears, or 1 10-ounce box frozen kernels

2 10-ounce bags fresh spinach, washed and chopped

1 teaspoon chili powder

12 ounces shredded Monterey Jack cheese, divided

2 cups of low-fat sour cream

Black pepper, to taste

12 6-inch corn tortillas

Soybean or vegetable oil for brushing the tortillas

2 cups salsa

Avocado slices (optional)

1. Preheat the oven to 400°F. Melt the butter in a large skillet over medium-low heat. Add the onion, garlic, mushrooms, and corn. Cook about 15 minutes, stirring occasionally, until the onions are softened. Add the spinach and chili powder. Cover and cook for 20 minutes, stirring occasionally, until the spinach is wilted. Stir in half the cheese. Mix well until melted. Add the sour cream and pepper; mix well. Remove from the heat and cool slightly.

2. Brush both sides of each tortilla with a little oil. Spoon just less than 1/3 cup of the filling into the center of each tortilla. Roll one side of the tortilla over the filling, the roll the other side over. Place the filled tortilla, seam side down, in a rectangular glass baking dish. Repeat with remaining tortillas, placing them in the baking dish in a single layer. Spoon the salsa over the enchiladas and sprinkle with the remaining cheese.

3. Bake for 15 minutes, or until the salsa is hot and bubbly and the cheese has melted. Serve with slices of ripe avocado, if desired.

Nachos di Alma   GFO

Customers had been requesting nachos with tomatoes, olives, mushrooms, and jalapeño peppers for a long time before this recipe became a permanent fixture at Claire's. Why have just organic corn chips with cheese when you can step it up with the addition of healthful vegetables?

Serves 4

3 8-inch sprouted whole wheat or other whole wheat tortillas

8 ounces (a heaping $2/3$ cup) shredded manchego cheese, divided

¼ cup sliced black olives

8 organic cremini mushrooms, thinly sliced

12 organic sweet grape tomatoes, quartered

1 small organic red onion, finely chopped

1 medium jalapeño pepper, finely minced

Smokey store-bought salsa and low-fat sour cream for dipping (optional)

1. Preheat the oven to 400°F.

2. Cut each tortillas into 16 pieces. (First cut each tortilla in half, then cut each half into quarters, then cut each quarter in half.) Spray two cookie sheets with nonstick canola oil spray. Arrange the whole wheat tortilla pieces evenly on the two sheets, in a single layer if possible or overlapping slightly. Scatter about ⅓ cup of the shredded cheese evenly on the tortilla pieces. Then, in the order listed, scatter the remaining ingredients evenly over the tortilla pieces. Scatter the remaining shredded cheese evenly over the tortillas. Bake in the preheated oven for about 10 minutes, until the cheese is melted. Using a long metal spatula, transfer the nachos to two large platters. Serve alone or with salsa and/or sour cream for dipping.

Tip: Use gluten-free tortillas to make this recipe gluten free.

Claire's Classic

Spinach Empanadas Gallega

I first learned of this entree from one of our favorite former staffers, Lori Sav, who studied in Spain for a semester. She came back and told me about *empanadas gallega,* something popular in the Galicia area of Spain. I fell instantly in love and hope to one day visit Galicia to see and taste these empanadas myself. Empanadas gallega are savory turnovers big enough for a family, and spinach is one of the many fillings you can use to create a lovely dinner pie. Serve this with Black Bean and Wheat Berry Salad (page 107) for a lovely supper.

Serves 6

1 double unbaked crust for 9-inch pie (homemade or store-bought)

3 tablespoons olive oil

2 medium sweet onions, finely chopped

2 10-ounce bags spinach, washed and finely chopped

Salt and pepper

½ cup shredded Monterey Jack cheese, divided

1. Preheat the oven to 400°F. Place 1 piecrust in a 9-inch glass pie plate. Set aside while you prepare the filling.

2. Heat the olive oil in a large, deep skillet over medium-high heat. Add the onions. Cook for 5 minutes, stirring occasionally. Add the spinach (with the water clinging to the leaves). Sprinkle with salt and pepper to taste. Cover and cook for about 15 minutes, stirring occasionally, until the spinach is tender. Remove from the heat. Taste for seasonings. Drain the spinach in a colander set into a bowl.

3. Sprinkle half of the Monterey Jack cheese evenly over the piecrust. Using a slotted spoon, transfer the cooked spinach and onions to the piecrust. Arrange the spinach evenly. Scatter the remaining Monterey Jack cheese evenly over the spinach. Place the top piecrust over the pie. Seal the edges all around by gently pressing the top and bottom crusts together using the tines of a fork. Cut four small slits into the top crust, using a sharp knife. Place the pie on a cookie sheet to catch any drippings. Bake for about 40 minutes or until the piecrust is light brown. Serve immediately or chilled.

Spinach Quesadillas with Avocado–Sour Cream Sauce GFO

Out of all the fillings, spinach remains my favorite and that's a good thing because it's loaded with iron, vitamins A and C, and fiber.

Serves 4

Quesadillas:

2 tablespoons extra-virgin olive oil, divided

1 medium red onion, cut in half, then into thin rings, separated

Sea salt and pepper

7 ounces (about 3 heaping cups) organic baby spinach, rinsed and drained

6 8-inch whole wheat flour tortillas

1 cup shredded cheese

Sauce:

1 ripe avocado

½ cup low-fat sour cream or yogurt

2 tablespoons chopped cilantro

1 tablespoon freshly squeezed lime juice (from about ½ lime)

Sea salt and pepper

1. Preheat the oven to 200°F.

2. To prepare the quesadillas, heat 1 tablespoon of olive oil in a large skillet over medium-low heat. Add the onion, sprinkle lightly with sea salt and pepper, then stir to coat. Cover and cook for about 5 minutes, stirring occasionally until the onions have softened. Add the spinach and sprinkle with sea salt and pepper. Using tongs, turn the spinach to coat with the oil. Cover and continue cooking for about 5 minutes, using the tongs to turn the spinach until it's tender to your preference. Arrange 3 of the tortillas on a cookie sheet. Sprinkle each tortilla evenly with about 2 heaping tablespoons of the shredded cheese. Using tongs, arrange about one-third of the spinach mixture evenly over the cheese, first allowing as much of the juices as possible to drip back into the skillet as you lift out the spinach. Sprinkle about 2 heaping tablespoons of the shredded cheese evenly over the spinach mixture. Repeat with the remaining 2 tortillas on the tray. Top each with a tortilla. Using your hands, gently press the tortillas together.

3. Transfer the tray of assembled quesadillas to the counter by the stove. Have a second cookie sheet handy so you can keep the finished quesadillas warm in the preheated oven while you cook the rest. Wash and dry the skillet to reuse it—you'll appreciate having one less pan to wash after supper. Measure 1 of the remaining teaspoons of olive oil in a skillet over medium heat, then tilt the skillet to spread the oil around. Carefully transfer a quesadilla to the heated skillet. Carefully press the quesadillas together again to keep them together. Cover and cook for about 4–5 minutes, until the underside is golden brown. Using two large spatulas, carefully turn the quesadilla and cook the other side for about 2 minutes until it is golden brown.

4. Transfer the cooked quesadilla to the spare cookie sheet and set it in the preheated oven to keep it warm as you cook the remaining quesadillas. Add another teaspoon of the remaining olive oil, tilt the skillet to coat the bottom, and repeat the process until you've cooked all 3 quesadillas. Keep the quesadillas warm while you prepare the sauce.

5. To prepare the sauce, cut the avocado in half and remove the seed. Using a spoon, scoop the pulp into a bowl. Using a fork, mash it somewhat smooth. Add the sour cream, cilantro, lime juice, and a sprinkle of sea salt and pepper. Using the fork, mash the ingredients together. Taste for seasonings.

6. To serve, cut each quesadilla into quarters. Serve with the sauce on the side and encourage everyone to dip in.

   Tip: Use gluten-free tortillas to make this recipe gluten free.

Sweet Corn and Goat Cheese Tamales, with a Roasted Tomato and Chipotle Salsa `GF`

Tamales are basically corn cakes covered with a filling then wrapped in corn husks and steamed. I use a three-tier bamboo steamer over a metal pan that I bought at a Chinese grocer, and it works great. You can use a setup like this, or any steamer you have. This recipe makes about 15 tamales and you can freeze any leftovers for up to 3 months. Defrost frozen tamales in the refrigerator, then reheat them by steaming for about 15 minutes, or until heated through.

Serves 8

20 or more dry corn husks (look for them in the Mexican-foods section of the supermarket)

Masa:

1¼ cups corn kernels, from about 2 ears of corn

1¼ cups plus 2 tablespoons soy milk

2 tablespoons orange juice

Sea salt and pepper

¹⁄₃ cup organic trans fat–free spread or buttery spread

2 cups masa harina

1 teaspoon baking powder

2 tablespoons canola oil

Filling:

2 teaspoons olive oil

½ large red onion, finely chopped

1 large red bell pepper, finely chopped

Juice from ½ lime, about 4 teaspoons

2 tablespoons finely chopped cilantro

Sea salt and pepper

2 ounces goat cheese

1. Place the dry corn husks in a loaf pan and cover with hot water. The husks need to soak until pliable, about 30 minutes.

2. Meanwhile, to prepare the masa, heat a heavy, 10-inch skillet over high heat. Spray with canola oil spray. Add the corn kernels and cook, stirring frequently, for about 4 minutes until the corn turns bright yellow and smells sweet and smokey. Remove from the heat.

3. Measure the soy milk and the orange juice into a blender cup. Add the corn kernels and a little salt and pepper. Cover and blend on high speed for about 30 seconds, until the mixture is well mixed and the kernels are broken up. In a large bowl, beat the buttery spread, using a wooden spoon, until smooth. In a separate bowl, combine the masa harina, 1 teaspoon salt, and the baking powder. Whisk to combine. Add the masa harina mix to the buttery spread ½ cup at a time, alternating with ¼ cup of the liquid mixture. Use a wooden spoon to beat well after each addition until the ingredients are combined. Beat in the canola oil. Set aside.

4. To prepare the filling, heat the olive oil in a medium skillet over medium heat. Add the red onion, bell pepper, lime juice, and cilantro. Sprinkle with a little salt and pepper. Cook for about 15 minutes, stirring occasionally until the vegetables are tender. Taste for seasonings. Stir in the goat cheese, stirring until melted and blended, about 2 minutes. Remove from the heat.

5. To assemble the tamales, lift the softened, pliable corn husks out of the water and drain them into a colander. Separate the corn husks if they are stuck together. Tear 2 or 3 of the corn husks into lengthwise

strips about the width of thick string. You'll need about 40 "strings" of torn corn husks to tie the tamales later in the recipe. Open a corn husk and hold it flat and open in one hand. Spread about 2 tablespoons of the masa along the center of the corn husk, about 5 by 1½ inches. Spread about 1 heaping tablespoon of the filling evenly over the masa. Pull one side of the corn husk lengthwise over the filling, then roll the corn husk into a cylindrical shape. Using two pieces of the corn husk "string" that you made, tie each end just at the end of the filling. Place the tamale into a steamer basket tray. Continue filling and tying the tamales, arranging them in a single layer on the steamer basket trays, trying to gauge the mix so as to use up both the masa and the filling by the last tamale. (The last few may have a little extra or a little less masa and filling.)

6. To cook the tamales, fill the bottom pan of the steamer with warm water about three-fourths full. Stack the trays onto the bottom pan. Place over high heat. Steam the tamales for about 40 minutes, carefully rotating the steamer trays after 20 minutes to steam evenly. Open one tamale to check for doneness. The masa should be fairly firm; if it isn't firm, continue to steam for another 5 minutes and then check again for doneness.

7. Meanwhile, to prepare the salsa, preheat the oven to 350°F. Spray a cookie sheet with canola oil spray. Arrange the sliced tomatoes and the tomatillos in a single layer on the prepared cookie sheet. Bake in a preheated oven for about 25 minutes, turning once with tongs until softened. Turn the cooked tomatoes and tomatillos and their liquids into a blender cup. Add the chopped garlic, the lime and orange juices, the banana slices, and a little salt and pepper. Lift the softened chipotle pepper out of the soaking liquid. Remove and discard the stem. Coarsely chop the pepper. Add the chopped pepper to the blender cup. Cover the blender and blend on high speed for about 30 seconds until smooth. Taste for seasonings.

8. To serve the tamales, heat the salsa over low-medium heat for about 5 minutes, stirring occasionally until heated through. Pour the salsa into a gravy boat. Using tongs, remove the tamales from the steamer and arrange on a platter. To eat, untie and unroll a tamale, leaving the corn masa and the filling exposed on the corn husk. Spoon a little salsa over the filling or serve alongside for dipping.

Salsa:

1 large red tomato, cut into ½-inch-thick slices

1 large yellow tomato, cut into ½-inch-thick slices

2 large tomatillos, husked, rinsed, and cut into ½-inch-thick slices

1 clove garlic, finely chopped

Juice from ½ lime, about 4 teaspoons

2 tablespoons freshly squeezed orange juice (from about ½ orange)

½ large, ripe banana, cut into ½-inch slices

1 dried chipotle pepper, soaked in hot water to cover until softened, about 15 minutes

Sea salt and pepper, to taste

Quesadilla with Caramelized Onions, Quince Preserves, and Cheddar with Horseradish `GFO`

Recipe ideas come from so many places. This one began after I tasted a cheddar cheese that was infused with horseradish. Cabot* makes it, and it's amazing! The combination of sweet, caramelized onions, with a little kick of heat from chipotle powder and with the sweet-tartness from the quince preserves, is terrific paired with the cheese. Everyone at my house loves it. If you don't have a horseradish cheddar cheese, you can spread the tortilla with a layer of horseradish mustard and use a plain sharp cheddar cheese. It's delicious either way.

Serves 4

1 tablespoon extra-virgin olive oil

2 medium organic onions, cut into thin rings, separated

2 cloves organic garlic, sliced

Sea salt

¼ teaspoon chipotle powder

½ teaspoon ancho chile powder

¼ cup quince preserves

2 12-inch wheat tortillas

4 ounces cheddar with horseradish, shredded, about 1 cup

Low-fat organic sour cream

1. Heat the oil in a large skillet over medium heat. Add the onions and garlic. Sprinkle with a little sea salt and the chipotle and ancho chile powders. Stir to coat with the oil. Cook for about 15 minutes, stirring occasionally, until softened and golden. Taste for seasoning. Remove from heat. Using the back of a spoon, spread the quince preserves evenly on one side of each tortilla. Using tongs, arrange half the onions evenly over half the preserves on each tortilla. Sprinkle half the cheese over the onions on each tortilla. Fold the tortilla over onto the filling, pressing the edges together gently to encase the filling.

2. Heat a large, heavy skillet over medium heat. Wearing oven mitts, lift the hot skillet away from the heat and carefully spray it with olive oil spray. Return the skillet to the heat. Arrange the filled tortillas in a single layer on the heated, sprayed skillet. Cook over medium heat for about 8 minutes, or until the underside is golden brown when you lift one end with a metal spatula. Carefully turn the tortillas and cook the other side for about 3–4 minutes until the underside until golden brown. Transfer to a platter and cut each quesadilla into four triangles. Serve with low-fat sour cream.

Tip: Use gluten-free tortillas to make this recipe gluten free.

"Beefy" Chili [V]

When I make chili, I use Lightlife® Gimme Lean® Beef, or for a "chicken" chili, I crumble up four Gardenburger® Chik'N Grill veggie patties. Both are delicious in the chili. Serve this chili with warm cornbread or warm corn tortillas.

Serves 8

3 quarts water

1 pound organic pinto beans, sorted for any stones

2 large organic onions, coarsely chopped

3 organic bell peppers (1 each of red, yellow, and orange), seeded and coarsely chopped

4 cloves garlic, finely chopped

1 small local butternut squash, peeled, seeded, and diced

1 teaspoon chili powder

2 teaspoons cumin

2 teaspoons oregano

1 small jalapeño pepper, finely chopped

1 28-ounce can San Marzano whole peeled tomatoes in juice, squeezed using your hands

Sea salt and pepper, to taste

1 12-ounce tube ground soy "beef" or 4 meatless chicken patties, defrosted and crumbled

1 10-ounce box frozen organic sweet corn kernels, defrosted

1. Put the water and the beans in a large pot over high heat. Cover and bring to a boil. Lower the heat to medium and simmer the beans, covered, for about 30 minutes, stirring occasionally. Add the onions, peppers, garlic, butternut squash, chili powder, cumin, oregano, jalapeño, tomatoes, sea salt, and pepper. Stir well to mix. Cover, raise the heat to high, and bring to a boil, stirring occasionally. This should take about 10 minutes.

2. Once the mixture reaches a boil, lower the heat to medium-low and cook at a slow boil, covered, for about 45 minutes, stirring occasionally, until the beans are tender. Stir in the soy beef or crumbled veggie patties; stir in the corn. Cover and cook for about 5 minutes, stirring frequently, until the meat substitute and corn are heated through. Taste for seasonings.

Dark Chocolate: Good for Your Health!

When you think of Valentine's Day, of course you think of chocolate. In my household on Valentine's Day, I always say to my honey, "Make sure you eat your fruits and vegetables—and your dark chocolate, too."

No, you're not dreaming; eating a little piece of dark chocolate each day fits into a diet for good health. Researchers have determined that cocoa beans contain the same antioxidants—plant phenols called flavonoids—that are found in red wine, the other "can you believe I'm drinking this for my health?" discovery. These compounds found in plants help to lower blood pressure, and scientists say the darker the chocolate, the better. Now, this information does not give us the license to eat a bar at a time, and certainly not instead of a diet that consists mainly of fruits, vegetables, beans, and whole grains, along with low-fat dairy, fish, and lean meats. Rather, you might want to include a 1.5-ounce piece of dark chocolate along with your healthful diet.

Of course you can nibble on a piece of dark chocolate, especially on Valentine's Day, but I think it's more fun to include it in cooking and baking, as I do in my Cincinnati Chili (page 216). It's a chili made using black beans, carrots, and onions, combined with an interesting and flavorful mole. The mole is a blend of charred onions, plantain, tomatoes, garlic, sesame seeds, corn tortillas, and dark chocolate, first blended to a rough paste, then stirred into the beans.

I also use this healthful treat in my Dark Chocolate–Dipped Walnut-Coated Apricots (page 318), which pairs vitamin A, fiber, and iron-rich dried apricots with walnuts for another antioxidant boost, dipped in more antioxidant-rich dark chocolate. This is pure pleasure with health benefits to boot. What a delicious way to show your love for that special someone.

You can bake a Dark Chocolate Almond Cake with Rich Dark Chocolate Espresso Glaze (page 355) for friends, family, and coworkers and remind them that, while it looks like a pure indulgence, there is redeeming health value in the dish from the dark chocolate and from the almonds and soy, two more heart-healthy foods. Again, don't down a huge slice of cake, because it's still a decadent dessert that contains plenty of calorie-rich sugar. But for Valentine's Day—and, really, any other special day—chocolate is a must.

Cincinnati Chili V GF

Many years ago, a favorite customer of ours, Joe, told us about a chocolate-infused black bean chili that he enjoyed at a couple of restaurants when he lived in Cincinnati. To please him, I developed this recipe to remind him of his old hometown. This chili is made up of two components, the mole and the bean chili. Serve it alone or with brown rice or corn tortillas. Add a simple salad of organic mixed greens with sliced avocado, red onion, and tomatoes, dressed with a dressing of extra-virgin olive oil and lime juice, and you'll have a delicious and healthful supper in less than an hour. The mole was inspired by my dear friends in Mexico and it can be used separately as a dip with corn tortillas or as a sauce over enchiladas, grilled fish, or soy chicken patties. If you plan to use the mole as a sauce, just thin it a bit with a little more grapefruit juice or a vegetable broth until it is thinned to your preference.

Serves 4

Mole:

1 pasilla chile pepper, stem removed

¼ cup water

3 large pitted prunes

1 medium yellow organic onion, cut into thick ribs, separated

2 large cloves garlic, unpeeled

1 medium tomato, cut into thick slices

¼ cup sesame seeds, about 1 ounce

2 trans fat–free corn tortillas, torn into pieces

1 large ripe (yellow/black) plantain, peeled and cut into thick slices

2 ounces dark chocolate, finely chopped

Juice of ½ grapefruit (about 1/3 cup)

Salt and pepper, to taste

1. To prepare the mole, heat a large griddle pan or skillet over medium-high heat. Add the chile pepper and toast lightly for about a minute, using tongs to turn frequently until just evenly toasted and not burned. Pour the ¼ cup of water (careful, it will sizzle) over the chile pepper. Using the tongs, move the chile pepper around until it softens and most of the water evaporates, about a minute. Remove the softened chile pepper from the pan and transfer to the bowl of a food processor fitted with a metal blade. Add the 3 prunes. Set aside.

2. Arrange the onion, garlic, tomato, sesame seeds, torn tortillas, and sliced plantain on the hot grill pan. Grill for about 4 minutes, until you've charred some parts of each ingredient, using the tongs to turn individual pieces every minute or so. Remove the 2 cloves of garlic and peel them, then return them to the grill pan. Set aside. Cover the processor and process on high for about 30 seconds to chop the chile pepper and the prunes.

3. Using the tongs, add the charred ingredients to the processor. Add the chopped dark chocolate. Add the grapefruit juice and a little salt and pepper. Cover and process for about 1 minute, until finely mixed. It won't be smooth, but it will be blended like a rough paste. Set aside.

4. To prepare the chili, heat the olive oil in a medium-size heavy pot over medium heat. Add the onion and the carrots. Sprinkle lightly with salt and pepper. Cook for about 3 minutes, stirring occasionally until the onions have softened slightly. Add the beans and their liquid and the 2 cups of water. Cover the pot, and bring to a medium boil. Once it reaches a boil (in a few minutes), cook for about 7–8 minutes, stirring occasionally until the carrots are tender. Stir in the mole, using a rubber spatula to scrape the processor bowl. Stir well to combine. Continue cooking, uncovered, for about 2 minutes, stirring frequently until mixed into the bean mixture, then occasionally until heated through. Taste for seasonings. Serve hot.

Chili:

1 tablespoon extra-virgin olive oil

½ medium organic yellow onion, coarsely chopped

2 medium organic carrots, diced

Salt and pepper, to taste

1 15-ounce can organic black beans

2 cups water

"As a graduate student I spent hours at Claire's. Her corn walnut muffin was a version of my childhood favorite—with less sugar and more protein. It was healthy and deliciously familiar. And it eased my transition to more conscious and healthy eating. At Claire's you find healthy favorites conceived and prepared with love. Nothing could taste better."

—Frank Mitchell, Yale graduate and Claire's customer and friend

Cuban-Style Black Beans and Rice V GF

I have watched the popularity of black beans soar over the past ten years and I couldn't be happier to see the people I care for eating and enjoying these protein-, fiber-, and iron-packed beans.

Serves 6–8

1 pound organic black beans, about 2 cups, picked over for stones

3 tablespoons extra-virgin olive oil, Spanish or other

3 medium green bell peppers, seeded and coarsely chopped

8 cloves garlic, finely chopped

1 bay leaf

Salt and pepper, to taste

1¹/₃ cups organic long grain brown rice

2 tablespoons organic flax oil

Rinse the beans. Place them into a large heavy pot. Add 4 quarts of water, the olive oil, peppers, garlic, and bay leaf. Cover and bring to a boil over high heat. Once it reaches a boil in about 25 minutes, lower the heat to medium and cook at a medium boil, stirring occasionally, for about 1 hour, until crisp-tender. Carefully scoop out about half of the beans from the pot and place them into the bowl of a food processor fitted with a metal blade. Cover and process for about 20 seconds until fairly smooth. Return the beans to the pot. Add salt and pepper, and the brown rice. Cover and cook at a medium boil, stirring occasionally for about 20 minutes, then remove the cover and continue cooking uncovered for about 35 minutes, until the rice and the beans are tender soft and the liquid has reduced to about 1 inch above the beans and rice. Remove from the heat. Stir in the flax oil. Taste for seasonings.

Rice and Cabbage V GF

This flavorful combination remains a favorite in our house. It's so healthful—it's rich in important nutrients, and cabbage is a cruciferous vegetable highly recommended by researchers who believe it may help prevent many cancers. Serve a bowl topped with a little Parmesan cheese for a most delicious meal. A nice salad of sliced avocado and tomato wedges tossed with a little olive oil, fresh lime juice, cilantro, salt, and pepper will be wonderful and will cost less than ten dollars.

Serves 4

2 cups brown rice

1 bay leaf

Salt

5 tablespoons extra-virgin olive oil

6 large cloves garlic, sliced

1 large onion or 2 smaller ones, coarsely
   chopped

1 large (a little more than 3 pounds) head
   green cabbage, coarsely chopped

½ cup coarsely chopped Italian
   flat-leaf parsley

Salt

Pepper, if desired

Grated Parmesan cheese, if desired

1. Measure the rice into a heavy pot. Add 7 cups cold water, the bay leaf, and a little salt. Cover and bring to a boil over high heat. When it reaches a boil, reduce the heat to low and simmer the rice, covered, for about 25 minutes, until it is just tender and remains covered with water (my mom uses a wet rice for this dish). Drain most of the remaining water, but leave a little, about ¼ cup, in the rice. Set aside.

2. In a heavy 4-quart pot, heat the olive oil over low-medium heat. Add the garlic, onion, cabbage, and parsley. Sprinkle with salt. Cover and cook the cabbage for about 30 minutes, stirring occasionally until the cabbage is softened and has released some of its liquid. Add 2 cups of water, cover, and continue cooking for about 30 minutes, stirring occasionally, until the cabbage is soft. Stir in the cooked rice and any remaining water and continue cooking, covered, for another minute just to heat it through. Taste for seasonings. Serve with pepper and Parmesan cheese to sprinkle on top, if desired.

Mushroom and Spinach Risotto GF

Risotto dishes are always popular at Claire's, and we take advantage of all the lovely organic vegetables we get to create new recipes throughout the year. This is one of our oldest recipes, and it has remained a favorite.

Serves 6

5½ cups water

1 tablespoon butter

8 cups (about ¾ pound) organic baby spinach

Sea salt and pepper

3 tablespoons butter, cut into 3 slices

3 shallots, peeled and finely chopped

½ red onion, finely chopped

1 pound assorted mushrooms (I like to use button, cremini, and shiitake), cut into quarters (remove tough stems from shiitake mushrooms, if using)

2½ cups Arborio rice

¼ cup white wine

¼ cup grated pecorino Romano cheese, or other

1. Prepare the broth. Measure the water into a large pot. Add 1 tablespoon of the butter, spinach, and a little sea salt and pepper. Cover and bring to a boil over high heat, stirring once or twice to combine. Cook at a boil for just a minute, stirring once to combine. Taste for seasonings. Turn off the heat and keep this spinach broth covered on the stove.

2. Melt the 3 tablespoons of butter in a large skillet over medium-low heat. Add the shallots, onion, and mushrooms. Sprinkle lightly with sea salt and pepper. Cook, stirring occasionally, for 5 minutes, or until the onions and mushrooms are softened. Add the rice. Cook for 2–3 minutes, stirring frequently. Add the wine. Cook, stirring constantly, for about 1 minute, until the wine is absorbed into the rice. Add 1 cup of the spinach broth. Cook, stirring constantly, for about 2 minutes, or until the rice absorbs the broth. Add ½ cup of the broth and stir continuously for 2 minutes, or until the broth is absorbed into the rice. Continue adding ½ cup of the broth at a time, using the remaining broth except for ½ cup that you will add at the end; stir continuously for 2 minutes, or until the rice absorbs the broth.

3. Taste the rice for doneness. The risotto should be barely tender, fairly thick, and creamy when it is done. Remove the skillet from the heat. Stir in the final ½ cup of broth. Stir in the cheese. Taste for seasoning. Serve immediately.

Spring Asparagus Risotto GF

Although asparagus is available year round, and we do enjoy that convenience, we treasure our Connecticut crop every late spring because as with everything else, freshly harvested always tastes better.

Serves 6

7 cups water

3 ribs organic celery, cut into ½-inch slices, including leaves

2 tablespoons organic butter or organic vegan buttery spread

1 spring onion, finely chopped

Sea salt and pepper

2 tablespoons organic extra-virgin olive oil

2 organic shallots, finely chopped

1 large bunch (about 1¼ pounds) local asparagus, tough stems trimmed and discarded, remaining stem and tips cut into ½-inch pieces

2½ cups Arborio rice

3–4 tablespoons freshly grated Parmigiano-Reggiano cheese

1. Measure the water into a medium pot. Add the celery, butter, onion, and a little salt and pepper to taste. Cover and bring to a boil over high heat. When it reaches a boil, reduce the heat to medium. Cook, covered, at a medium boil for about 30 minutes, stirring occasionally, until the celery is barely tender. Turn off the heat but leave the pot, covered, on the hot stove. Taste the broth for seasonings.

2. Heat the olive oil in a large, deep skillet over medium-low heat. Add the shallots and half of the asparagus. Sprinkle with a little salt and pepper. Cook, stirring occasionally, for about 5 minutes, or until the shallots and asparagus are softened. Add the Arborio rice. Stir well to coat with the oil. Cook for 3 minutes, stirring frequently. Add 1 cup of the broth. Stir well to combine.

3. Cook, stirring constantly, for about 2 minutes, until the rice absorbs the broth. Stir in the remaining asparagus. Add another ½ cup of the broth. Cook, stirring constantly, for about 2 minutes, or until the rice absorbs the broth. Continue adding the remaining broth, ½ cup at a time, stirring continuously for 2 minutes after each addition, or until the broth is absorbed into the rice. Taste for doneness. The risotto should be barely tender, thick, and creamy when done. Stir in the cheese. Taste for seasonings.

Artichoke, Basket Cheese, and Parmesan Risotto GF

My grandmother loved basket cheese and we continue to enjoy it just as she did, every Easter, when cheesemakers make this mild, somewhat firm ricotta cheese. It's delicious cut into cubes for a salad or tossed with a simple penne marinara and it's lovely in this risotto. It's highly perishable, so plan to use it within 3 days of purchase. You can always serve it with crostini for breakfast, too, with apricot preserves.

Serves 6

2 tablespoons organic butter or organic buttery spread, divided

1 9-ounce package frozen artichoke hearts

Sea salt and pepper

7 cups water

2 ribs organic celery, including leaves, finely chopped

1 medium carrot, finely chopped

1 10-ounce bag organic baby spinach

3 tablespoons extra-virgin olive oil

2 small organic shallots, finely chopped

2½ cups Arborio rice, found in the rice section at the supermarket

¼ cup white wine

½ cup crumbled basket cheese or feta

¼ cup grated Parmesan cheese

3 tablespoons chopped pistachios

1. Melt 1 tablespoon of the butter in a skillet over medium heat. Add the artichoke hearts and some sea salt and pepper and stir to coat. Cover and cook for about 4 minutes, stirring occasionally until the artichoke hearts are softened. Turn the softened artichoke hearts and any juices into the bowl of a food processor fitted with a metal blade. Cover and process for about 15 seconds, until smooth. Set aside.

2. Bring the 7 cups of water to a boil in a large covered pot over high heat. Add the remaining tablespoon of the butter and the celery, carrot, and some sea salt and pepper. Cover and cook at a boil for about 2 minutes, stirring occasionally, until the vegetables are crisp-tender. Stir in the baby spinach. Cover and turn off the heat. This will be your broth for the risotto. Leave it covered on the stove to keep warm.

3. Heat the olive oil in a large skillet over medium-low heat. Add the shallots and sprinkle with sea salt and pepper. Cook, stirring occasionally, for about 2 minutes, or until the shallots are softened. Add the rice and stir to coat. Cook for 2 minutes, stirring frequently. The rice will turn from white to a creamy beige. Add the wine and stir to combine. Cook, stirring constantly, for about 2 minutes, until the wine is absorbed. Stir in the blended artichoke hearts, using a rubber spatula to scrape the processor bowl. Add 1 cup of the broth, stirring well to combine. Continue stirring for about 2 minutes, until the rice absorbs much of the broth but is not dry. Add ½ cup of the broth and stir constantly for about 2 minutes, until the rice absorbs much of the broth.

4. Continue adding the broth and the vegetables in the broth, ½ cup at a time, stirring constantly for 2 minutes after each addition or until the rice mostly absorbs into the rice, but is not dry. Taste for doneness; the rice should be barely tender, thick, and creamy when done. Remove from the heat. Stir in the basket cheese and the Parmesan cheese. Taste for seasonings. Turn into a serving dish. Sprinkle the chopped pistachios evenly over the top.

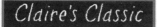

Claire's Classic

Sicilian Rice Balls

I like to serve these with warm marinara sauce for dipping. Bite-size rice balls make a lovely appetizer for a cocktail party.

Serves 8

5 cups water

1 pound Arborio rice (found in the rice or Italian section of supermarkets)

1 cup shredded mozzarella cheese

¼ cup grated Parmesan cheese

½ cup minced fresh Italian flat-leaf parsley

Salt and pepper

4 eggs or equivalent egg substitute, lightly beaten

3 cups plain dry bread crumbs

½ cup olive oil

1. Bring the water to a boil in a covered pot over high heat. Stir in the rice. Lower the heat to low. Cover and cook the rice for about 25 minutes, stirring frequently, until the water is absorbed and the rice is tender. Remove from the heat. Turn the rice into a bowl. Stir in the mozzarella, Parmesan, and parsley, mixing well to melt the mozzarella. Add the salt and pepper to taste. Cover and refrigerate for at least an hour, until cool enough to handle.

2. Scoop ¼ cupful of the rice mixture into your hand and roll into a ball. Set the rice ball on a cookie sheet. Continue forming all of the rice mixture into balls; you'll have about 24 balls.

3. In a shallow bowl, beat the eggs lightly. Measure the bread crumbs into a separate bowl. Roll each rice ball into the beaten eggs to coat, then lift out and shake off excess. Roll the rice ball in the bread crumbs to coat. Shake off the excess. Place the breaded rice balls back on the cookie sheet and repeat with the remaining rice balls until they are all breaded.

4. Preheat the oven to 350°F. Spray a separate cookie sheet with nonstick cooking spray. Set aside. Heat ¼ cup of the olive oil in a large skillet over medium-high heat. Place as many rice balls in the heated oil as you can fit without crowding. Brown the rice balls evenly on all sides, cooking 1 to 2 minutes per side, until evenly browned. Transfer the browned rice balls to the prepared cookie sheet. Heat the remaining ¼ cup olive oil. Continue browning the remaining rice balls. Bake the rice balls for 20 minutes to heat through. Serve alone or with lemon wedges or warm marinara sauce.

Lentils and Chard V GF

Enjoy this winning combination of flavor and nutrients from a healthy dose of protein, fiber, iron, phosphorus, and vitamins A and C. You can have it on the table in under an hour from start to finish!

Serves 6

1 pound dried lentils

2 quarts water

1 bay leaf

1 whole clove garlic

2 shallots, coarsely chopped and divided

Sea salt and pepper

¼ cup extra-virgin olive oil

1 red onion, cut in half and then cut into thick ribs, separated

5 cloves garlic, sliced

3 stalks celery, leaves included, cut into ¼-inch slices

2 bunches Swiss chard, about 2 pounds, green, red, or rainbow, well washed and drained, stalks cut in half lengthwise, then cut into ½-inch pieces, and leaves cut into 1-inch slices

7–8 large leaves basil

1. Sort the lentils for any stones, then rinse the lentils and drain. Put the sorted lentils and the water in a heavy pot. Cover and place the pot over high heat. Add the bay leaf, garlic, and about a teaspoon of the chopped shallots to the lentils. Sprinkle with a little sea salt and pepper. Bring to a boil, then reduce the heat to medium and cook the lentils at a low-medium boil for about 20–25 minutes, stirring occasionally, until the lentils are tender to your preference. The time will vary depending on how old the lentils are; the older they are, the drier they are and the longer they need to cook to become tender.

2. Meanwhile, heat the oil in a large skillet over medium heat. Add the remaining shallots, the red onion, and the sliced garlic. Sprinkle with a little sea salt and pepper. Stir to coat. Cook, stirring occasionally, for about 7 minutes or until the onions are golden brown. Add the celery and the chard. Sprinkle with a little sea salt and pepper. Using two wooden spoons, toss the celery and chard with the onions to coat with the oil. Cover the skillet and cook for about 5 minutes, using two wooden spoons to occasionally toss until the chard stalks are tender to your preference. Tear the basil leaves, then stir them into chard, stirring well to combine. Taste for seasonings.

3. Remove from the heat and cover the chard to keep it warm until the lentils are tender to your preference. When the lentils are tender, add the cooked chard and all the juices to the lentils and stir to combine. Taste for seasonings.

Claire's Classic

Lentils, Brown Rice, and Spinach V GF

Lentils and rice were always a welcome combination at our house. My mom still uses a lot of lentils in her cooking. We love their delicious flavor, and we like knowing that lentils are rich in protein and iron and are also fat-free. At Claire's, we often use twenty or more pounds per week.

Serves 6

1 pound lentils, picked over

3 quarts water

1 cup brown rice, uncooked

2 bay leaves

1 cup chopped Italian flat-leaf parsley

¼ cup olive oil

4 large cloves garlic, chopped

1 10-ounce bag fresh spinach, rinsed well
   and chopped

½ cup chopped fresh basil

Salt and black pepper, to taste

Grated Romano cheese (optional)

1. Put the lentils and water in a large pot. Cover and bring to a boil over high heat. Stir in the brown rice, bay leaves, and parsley. Lower the heat to medium and cook, uncovered, stirring frequently, until the beans and rice are very soft, about 1¼ hours. Keep the mixture warm. In a large skillet, heat the olive oil over medium-low heat. Add the garlic. Cook, stirring frequently, for 3 minutes, until softened but not brown.

2. Add the spinach, basil, salt, and pepper. Cover and cook for 5 to 10 minutes, stirring occasionally, until the spinach is wilted. Add the spinach mixture to the lentils and stir to combine. Taste for seasonings. Serve with plenty of good bread for dunking, and sprinkle with grated Romano, if desired.

Sweet Peas with Eggs GF

Freshly shelled peas are rich in protein and iron, and are so tender and sweet. And, it takes only a few minutes to shell enough peas for a meal. Make it a family project; sit around the kitchen table, and chat as you shell the peas. You'll create memories as you create your lunch or dinner. This simple yet delicious dish can be enjoyed hot or chilled, which makes it perfect to take to an outdoor concert. Pack along some good wheat bread and maybe some local goat's milk cheese, a simple, calcium-rich arugula salad, and fresh local raspberries for dessert.

Serves 6

Sea salt

2 pounds English peas, shelled, about 2 cups

1 tablespoon extra-virgin olive oil

1 small organic scallion, cut into thin rings, separated

½ small jalapeño pepper, finely chopped

Pepper, to taste

1 dozen organic eggs

4 fresh mint leaves, chopped

1. Bring a small covered pot of lightly salted water to a boil over high heat. Place a colander into a large bowl and set this in the sink for draining the peas. When the water reaches a boil, stir in the shelled peas and cook for 2–3 minutes, until just tender. Drain the peas in the colander. If desired, reserve the cooking water for a future soup or risotto dish. If saving, cool it to room temperature, then refrigerate for up to 3 days or freeze it for up to a month.

2. Heat the olive oil in a large skillet over medium heat. Add the scallion and the jalapeño pepper. Sprinkle lightly with sea salt and pepper. Stir to coat. Cook for about 4 minutes, stirring occasionally until soft and golden in color. Meanwhile, break the eggs into a bowl. Add ¼ cup water, a little sea salt and pepper, and the mint. Using a fork or a small whisk, beat the eggs to blend. After the onions are golden, reduce the heat to low-medium. Add the beaten eggs. Cook, stirring occasionally until the eggs are just set, about 5–7 minutes. Stir in the cooked peas, mixing to combine. Taste for seasonings.

Salad in a Pizza Dough Boat

My neighbor Claudio Romano is from Bari, Italy, and he's one of the best chefs I know. Before he retired, he owned two highly successful restaurants, and Frank and I loved eating at them. And we always loved his salads, especially the one he made for me one evening during the middle of summer when his gardens were bursting with gorgeous tomatoes, lettuces, and radishes. He's also an amazing gardener! This is my interpretation of his glorious salad. It's served over what I affectionately refer to a "pizza boat" because you first bake plain pizza dough and after you bake it, you cut it in half lengthwise and bake it again to crisp it, and the resulting shape looks like a boat.

Serves 6

Pizza Dough Boat:

2 tablespoons coarse cornmeal

2 tablespoons unbleached all-purpose flour, or more for rolling the pizza dough

½ pound chilled pizza dough (homemade or store-bought)

1. To prepare the pizza dough boat, position one oven rack in the lowest position and one rack in the highest position. If you are using a pizza stone, place on the bottom rack. If you are not using a pizza stone, line a large cookie sheet with parchment paper. Preheat the oven to 500°F. Scatter the cornmeal evenly over a pizza peel or a large wooden cutting board, about 12 by 20 inches. Scatter the flour evenly on a counter top. Holding one end of the dough, slap the dough on the floured counter top a few times to stretch it a bit. Coat both sides of the dough with the flour on the counter.

2. Using a rolling pin, roll the dough into a large, thin oval, about 12 by 20 inches. Carefully transfer the oval to the cornmeal-coated pizza peel, then slide the dough onto the hot pizza stone. If you are not using a pizza stone, transfer the oval to a parchment-lined cookie sheet. Bake for about 8–10 minutes, until the dough puffs up and is golden brown on the underside. Carefully remove the baked pizza dough boat from the oven and set it on a cutting board. Using a long, sharp knife, carefully slice open the pizza dough, horizontally, to create two equal ovals. Carefully transfer one oval cut side down on the pizza stone and the other one directly on the upper oven rack. Bake for about 1–2 minutes, until both sides are golden brown and crisp. Set each oval on a large plate, cut side up.

3. To prepare the salad, place the mixed greens, radishes, tomatoes and juices, scallions, celery, peppers, basil leaves, garlic, olives, artichoke hearts, and cheese in a bowl. Using two wooden spoons, toss to combine.

4. To prepare the dressing, combine the oil and vinegar in a bowl. Sprinkle with salt and pepper. Whisk to combine, then taste for seasoning. Pour over the salad, using two wooden spoons to toss until coated.

5. To assemble the dish, divide the tossed salad evenly on each pizza dough boat. Using a sharp knife, cut each oval into thirds. Serve immediately.

Salad:

12 cups organic mixed greens

3 radishes, thinly sliced

2 large ripe tomatoes, cut into cubes, including juices

2 scallions, white part and 3 inches green, cut into ¼-inch slices

1 rib celery, thinly sliced

½ large bell pepper (orange, red, green, or yellow), seeded and finely chopped

4 pepperoncini peppers (pickled peppers; sold in jars in the supermarket), drained and cut in half lengthwise

8–10 fresh basil leaves

2 cloves garlic, sliced as thin as possible

18 pitted oil-cured black olives, cut in half lengthwise

4 canned artichoke hearts, drained and quartered

4 ounces provolone or ricotta salata cheese, cut into small cubes

Dressing:

3 tablespoons extra-virgin olive oil

2 tablespoons red wine vinegar

Sea salt and pepper

Summer Tomato and Basil Quiche

Served warm or chilled, quiche makes a lovely luncheon or dinner entree and it's perfect for a picnic or garden party.

Makes 1 10-inch quiche, enough for 6 luncheon or 4 supper servings

1 10-inch piecrust, prebaked in a 350°F oven for about 15 minutes until just golden brown

Quiche Liquid:

3 organic eggs

1 cup organic 2 percent milk

½ cup organic heavy cream

1/8 teaspoon ground nutmeg

Sea salt and pepper, to taste

Tomato-Basil Filling:

2 medium organic local heirloom tomatoes, thinly sliced

6 medium leaves local organic basil

¼ teaspoon extra-virgin olive oil

Salt and pepper, to taste

½ cup shredded organic mozzarella cheese

½ cup drained, crumbled feta cheese

1. Preheat the oven to 350°F.

2. To prepare the quiche liquid, crack the eggs into a bowl. Using a whisk, beat until light and blended. Add the milk, heavy cream, nutmeg, salt, and pepper. Whisk to blend. Cover and refrigerate while you prepare the filling. (You can prepare this a day or two in advance; just whisk the liquid again to blend the spices just before you use it.)

3. To prepare the filling, place the sliced tomatoes in a shallow bowl. Add the basil leaves. Drizzle the olive oil evenly over the tomatoes, then sprinkle lightly with sea salt and pepper. Toss gently to coat. Taste a little piece of a tomato for seasonings.

4. To prepare the quiche, spray a cookie sheet with nonstick oil spray or line it with parchment paper to catch any drips. Set the prebaked piecrust on the prepared cookie sheet. Scatter the mozzarella cheese evenly in the crust, then scatter the feta cheese over the mozzarella cheese. Pick out the basil leaves and arrange them over the cheese about an inch and a half apart so that every slice will have a basil leaf, then arrange the tomatoes evenly in the piecrust over the cheeses, in a circular patter, overlapping slightly if needed. Whisk the quiche liquid, then slowly pour the liquid over the filling.

5. Using your fingers, rearrange the tomatoes that may have shifted, but don't worry too much about them "floating" in the quiche liquid—the quiche will still be delicious if a bit uneven.

6. Bake the quiche in the preheated oven for 1 hour, until the top is golden brown and the center is just set. The quiche will be puffy when you first remove it from the oven, then it will flatten within 10 minutes or so—so don't get alarmed when it does. Let set for 15 minutes before cutting.

7. Serve hot or chilled. Refrigerate any leftovers for up to 2 days.

Fresh Corn Fritters

Pan-fry these wonderful fritters in an electric skillet outdoors and you won't even have to heat up your kitchen. Just be careful not to trip on the electrical cord. Serve the fritters with a dollop of Greek yogurt mixed with a chopped chipotle in adobo sauce.

Serves 4

2 cups fresh corn kernels, cut from about 2 to 4 ears of local corn

1 cup unbleached all-purpose flour

1 teaspoon baking powder

1 teaspoon ground cumin

Sea salt and black pepper

2 local organic eggs

½ cup organic milk, 2 percent or whole

1 teaspoon avocado oil or extra-virgin olive oil

½ small local organic red bell pepper, finely chopped

2 tablespoons finely chopped cilantro

½ cup organic canola oil or soybean oil for frying

1. Bring a covered pot of water to a boil over high heat. Cook the corn kernels for about 3 minutes, until crisp-tender. Drain and set aside. In a bowl, whisk together the flour, baking powder, and cumin, and a little sea salt and pepper. In a separate bowl, whisk together the eggs, milk, and avocado oil until blended. Pour the liquid ingredients over the dry ingredients, all at once. Using a spoon, mix until well combined. Stir in the corn, chopped pepper, and cilantro.

2. Set a cookie sheet by the stove or the electric skillet and line it with a double layer of paper towels. Heat ¼ cup of the oil in a large skillet over medium-low heat, or in an electric skillet set at 375°F. The oil is ready for frying when a pinch of batter dropped in quickly rises to the top.

3. Drop heaping tablespoons of the batter into the oil. Do not crowd the skillet or the fritters will be oily. Cook each side until golden brown, 2–3 minutes, using two slotted spatulas to turn the fritters. Drain the fritters on the paper towel–lined cookie sheet. Fry the remaining batter, heating the additional oil as necessary. Serve hot or at room temperature.

Polenta Campagnolo V GF

Polenta is a cornmeal "mush" that is a perfect base for a tomato or other sauce and a nice alternative to pasta. The possibilities for enjoyment are limited only by your imagination. Have some fun and try it with your favorite cooked vegetables stirred in before serving, then topped with a dollop of ricotta cheese on top or a little grated Asiago or other cheese. And do try it chilled and then pan-fried the next day for breakfast, topped with a little apricot fruit spread.

When making polenta, use caution because it "erupts" like a volcano as it boils and can burn you if you are not careful. I always use a deep pot set on the back burner of the stove, and I wear long oven mitts and use a long whisk to stay protected. Be careful.

Serves 4

Sauce:

3 tablespoons extra-virgin olive oil

1 large organic yellow onion

5 large cloves organic garlic, sliced

1 small carrot, finely chopped

¼ small organic jalapeño pepper, chopped

6 large leaves organic basil

¼ cup chopped organic Italian flat-leaf parsley

Sea salt and pepper

1 6-ounce can organic tomato paste

⅓ cup red wine

2 cups water

½ pound assorted mushrooms, sliced (about 4 heaping cups; I like to use cremini, oyster, portobello, or button)

4 meatless Italian sausage links, cut into 1-inch slices

1 14-ounce can chopped organic tomatoes

6 pitted and halved oil-cured black olives

Polenta:

8 cups water

Sea salt and pepper

2 cups cornmeal

½–1 cup ricotta cheese (optional)

1. To make the sauce, heat the oil in a large, deep skillet over medium heat. Add the onions, garlic, carrot, jalapeño, basil, and parsley. Sprinkle lightly (the sausage and olives that you add later tend to be salty) with sea salt and pepper. Cover and cook for about 7 minutes, stirring occasionally, until the onions have softened but are not burned. Stir in the tomato paste and cook, stirring constantly, for about 30 seconds, until the mixture is well blended and begins to darken a bit. Add the wine and the water, the mushrooms, sausages, tomatoes, and olives. Stir well to combine. Cover and cook at a medium boil, stirring frequently, for about 12 minutes, until the sauce has reduced slightly. Taste for seasonings. Cover and set aside while you make the polenta.

2. To make the polenta, measure the water into a heavy 8-quart pot set on the back burner over high heat. When it reaches a boil, add a little sea salt and pepper. Slowly and carefully pour the cornmeal in a stream into the boiling water with one hand while whisking continuously with the other hand. After the cornmeal is added, reduce the heat to medium and continue whisking the boiling polenta for about 3–5 minutes. Turn onto a serving dish. Using the bottom of a large spoon, create a well in the center of the polenta, then spoon the sauce into the well. Spoon ricotta cheese on top if desired. Serve hot.

Tip: If you're in the mood for something different, try topping your polenta with my Marinara Sauce (page 183) instead of the campagnolo sauce.

Grilled Polenta Slices with Tomato Bruschetta Topping, Avocado, and Lemon V GF

Enjoy this beautiful dish either hot or chilled, it's delicious either way. Organic flax oil with lemon adds both a tasty lemony flavor and the needed omega-3 fatty acids.

You can buy precooked organic polenta, sold in tubes in the refrigerated section of the supermarket, generally alongside the pizza dough and prepacked hummus.

Serves 4–6

1 18-ounce tube of precooked organic polenta

1 tablespoon extra-virgin olive oil

Sea salt and pepper

2 cloves organic garlic

½ organic jalapeño pepper, cut in half

1 large, ripe locally grown organic tomato, quartered

5–6 basil leaves

1 tablespoon organic flax oil with lemon

Sea salt and pepper

1 small ripe organic avocado

½ organic lemon, cut into wedges

1. Heat the grill to high. Cut the polenta into 8 slices, each ½ inch to ¾ inch thick. Set slices in a single layer on a plate. Brush both sides of each slice of polenta with the olive oil, then sprinkle each side lightly with sea salt and pepper. When the grill is hot, place the polenta slices in a single layer on the rack. Cover the grill and cook for about 6–8 minutes per side until deep brown marks appear. Using a metal spatula, turn to grill the other side.

2. Meanwhile, place the garlic cloves and the jalapeño pepper in the bowl of a food processor fitted with a metal blade. Cover and process for about 5 seconds until the garlic and pepper are finely minced. Add the tomato, basil leaves, flax oil, sea salt, and pepper. Cover and process for about 10 seconds until blended. Taste for seasonings.

3. After the polenta is grilled, arrange the slices on a platter. Spoon about a tablespoon of the tomato bruschetta topping on each slice of polenta, then turn the remaining topping into a bowl for your guests to use for dipping their tofu or for dipping baked tortilla chips. Peel, pit, and slice the avocado into thin slices and arrange these slices on the polenta. Squeeze the lemon wedges over the polenta.

Parmesan Grits with Braised Mushrooms GFO

Grits are real comfort food and we're all looking for comfort, so we turn to this homey dish.

Serves 6

Grits:

3 cups water

2 cups organic 2 percent milk

1 cup grits (do not use instant)

Sea salt and pepper

¼ cup freshly grated Parmesan cheese

1 tablespoon organic butter

2 teaspoons white truffle oil

Mushrooms:

2 small carrots, coarsely chopped

2 ribs organic celery, coarsely chopped

½ medium organic sweet onion, cut into large ribs

1 tablespoon organic butter

1 tablespoon extra-virgin olive oil

2 organic shallots, sliced

Sea salt and pepper

1 pound assorted organic mushrooms, sliced (I like to use shiitake, cremini, oyster, portobello, and button)

1 teaspoon dried organic thyme

1 teaspoon dried organic sage

$^1/_3$ cup red wine, anything you drink is fine

¼ cup finely chopped organic Italian flat-leaf parsley

1. To prepare the grits, bring the water and milk to a boil in a 4-quart heavy pot over high heat. When the liquid reaches a boil, slowly add the grits, whisking as you add them. Lower the heat to medium and whisk in a little sea salt and pepper. Cook, uncovered, at a low boil, whisking frequently, until the grits thicken, about 12 minutes. Remove from the heat and whisk in the Parmesan cheese until blended. Whisk in the butter until blended. Drizzle the truffle oil evenly on top, then whisk to blend. Cover the grits to keep them warm while you prepare the braised mushrooms.

2. To prepare the braised mushrooms, place the carrots, celery, and onion in the bowl of a food processor fitted with a metal blade. Cover and process for about 10 seconds until finely minced, but not pureed.

3. Heat the butter and the oil in a large, deep skillet over medium heat. Add the shallots and the processed carrot mixture. Sprinkle with salt and pepper. Cover and cook for about 2 minutes, stirring occasionally, until the vegetables have released some of their liquids. Add the mushrooms, thyme, sage, and red wine. Stir well to combine. Cover and continue cooking for about 5 minutes, stirring frequently, until the mushrooms are tender. Uncover and stir in the chopped parsley. Continue cooking, uncovered, for a minute until heated through; this will allow some of the alcohol to evaporate from the wine, leaving behind a gentler flavor. Taste for seasonings.

4. Turn the Parmesan grits onto a platter. Spoon the mushroom mixture with juices evenly in the center of the grits. Serve immediately.

Tip: Use corn grits to make this recipe gluten free.

Peruvian Corn Cakes with Garlic-Cilantro Dipping Sauce

These delicious corn cakes are light because they are not fried in lots of oil—they are "fried" in a hot skillet sprayed with canola oil, just enough to keep them from sticking and allow them get golden brown and crisp. Serve them with a zippy cilantro dipping sauce and a nice tossed salad or a black bean salad.

Serves 6, makes 13 corn cakes

Garlic-Cilantro Dipping Sauce:

1 cup coarsely chopped cilantro

½ cup coarsely chopped Italian flat-leaf parsley

3 cloves garlic, sliced

¼ cup canola oil

½ teaspoon salt

½ teaspoon red pepper flakes

2 teaspoons fresh lime juice

1 tablespoon white wine vinegar

Corn Cakes:

4 ears organic corn, kernels removed (or 2 cups frozen organic corn kernels, defrosted)

2 tablespoons canola oil

1/8 teaspoon sea salt

1 cup all-purpose flour

¾ cup milk

½ cup sour cream

2 eggs

½ teaspoon baking powder

¼ teaspoon baking soda

½ teaspoon ground aji amarillo pepper (or substitute ground pasilla chile powder)

½ cup mozzarella cheese, shredded

Canola spray oil

1. To prepare the sauce, place all the sauce ingredients in a blender and blend for about 20 seconds or until smooth. Taste to adjust seasoning and set aside.

2. To prepare the corn cakes, place the corn, oil, salt, flour, milk, sour cream, eggs, baking powder, and baking soda, and the pepper in the bowl of a food processor fitted with a metal blade. Cover and process for 15–20 seconds until well blended. Scrape into a bowl and stir in cheese.

3. Line a large plate or cookie sheet with paper towels and set by the stove. Spray a large skillet with canola oil spray and heat until medium. Spoon ⅓ cup of batter at a time into the skillet, repeating without crowding the pan. Cook for about 4 minutes, until golden, then flip and cook the other side for 2–4 minutes until golden. Remove to a plate lined with paper towels. Re-spray the skillet and continue cooking the remaining corn cakes.

4. Serve corn cakes with the dipping sauce.

Note: **Aji amarillo** can be bought in powder form, or you can buy the dried peppers and grind your own powder in a spice grinder. These lovely Peruvian peppers have a nice floral tone with a medium heat. I was introduced to this dish and many other wonderful Peruvian specialties through a really great guy, Walker, who came to join our team at Claire's on a J-1 visa back in the early 2000s. He was a joy to work with!

Organic Red Jewel Sweet Potato and Apple Latkes

Organic Red Jewel sweet potatoes are so healthy, loaded with vitamin A and fiber, filled with antioxidants and rich in flavor. Serve your latkes with a dollop of Lemon-Ginger Crème Fraîche (page 147) and drizzled with a little local honey for a nice juxtaposition between sweet and tart flavors.

Makes about 18 small latkes

3 large organic Red Jewel sweet potatoes, peeled and grated

1 medium organic Gala or other apple, cored and grated

1 medium organic red onion, coarsely chopped

¼ cup chopped organic Italian flat-leaf parsley

½ cup plain organic bread crumbs

¼ cup unbleached organic flour

5 organic eggs

Sea salt and pepper

5–7 tablespoons canola, sunflower, or other good oil

1. Place a cookie sheet on the counter by the stove. Line the sheet with either a brown paper bag or a double layer of paper towels.

2. Place the grated sweet potatoes, apple, onion, and chopped parsley into a bowl. Using two spoons, toss to combine. Add the bread crumbs, flour, eggs, about a ¼ teaspoon of sea salt, and a little pepper. Using a spoon, stir to mix the ingredients. Heat 4 tablespoons of the oil in a large skillet, about a 12-inch skillet, over medium-high heat. Using a ¼-cup measure, lightly pack some of the latke mixture into the cup and turn out into heated oil. Using the back of the cup, lightly flatten the pancake. Cook the latke for about 2–3 minutes until the underside is just golden brown, then, using two slotted spatulas, turn the latke and cook the other side for about 2 minutes until the underside is golden brown.

3. Transfer the cooked latke to the lined cookie sheet. Turn off the heat. As soon as the latke has cooled enough, taste it for seasonings. Add additional salt to the batter if needed. Set the heat back to medium-high, reheat the oil, and continue to add ¼-cupful portions of the mixture to the heated oil until you have 4–5 latkes. (Do not crowd or the oil temperature will drop and the latkes will be greasy.) Cook the pancakes for 2–3 minutes until the undersides are just medium brown, then, using two slotted spatulas, turn the latkes over to cook the other side for about 2 minutes until medium brown. Transfer the cooked latkes to the paper-lined cookie sheet. Continue frying the remaining mixture, adding and heating the remaining oil as needed. Serve hot or at room temperature.

Zucchini and Ricotta Latkes

The ricotta in this recipe produces a most tender and light latke. I like to serve these with warmed marinara sauce, but sour cream and applesauce are delicious choices, too.

Makes about 18 small latkes

3 medium organic zucchini

1 small organic sweet onion, finely chopped

6–8 leaves organic spinach, finely chopped

¼ cup ricotta cheese

6 organic eggs

¼ cup organic plain bread crumbs

¼ cup unbleached organic flour

Sea salt and pepper

5–7 tablespoons good oil, such as refined grapeseed, canola, sunflower, or almond

1. Place a cookie sheet on the counter by the stove. Line the sheet with either a brown paper bag or a double layer of paper towels. Place a box-style grater in a colander set in a bowl. Grate the zucchini against the large holes of the box grater. Using your hands, grab a handful of the grated zucchini and squeeze out as much liquid as you can. Place the squeezed zucchini into a clean bowl. Add the onion, spinach, ricotta, eggs, bread crumbs, flour, and a little salt and pepper. Using a spoon, stir the mixture well to combine.

2. Heat 4 tablespoons of the oil in a large skillet over medium-high heat. Using a ¼-cup measure, lightly pack some of the latke mixture into the cup. Turn out into heated oil. Using the back of the cup, lightly flatten the pancake. Cook the latke for about 2–3 minutes, until the underside is just golden brown; then, using two slotted spatulas, turn the latke and cook the other side for about 2 minutes, until the underside is golden brown. Transfer the cooked latke to the lined cookie sheet. Turn off the heat. As soon as the latke has cooled enough, taste it for seasonings. Add more salt to the batter, if needed.

3. Set the heat back to medium-high, reheat the oil, and continue to add ¼-cup portions of the mixture to the heated oil until you have 4–5 latkes. (Do not crowd or the oil temperature will drop and the latkes will be greasy.) Cook the pancakes for 2–3 minutes until the undersides are just medium brown; then, using two slotted spatulas, turn the latkes over to cook the other side for about 2 minutes, until medium brown. Transfer the cooked latkes to the paper-lined cookie sheet. Continue frying the remaining mixture, adding and heating the remaining oil as needed. Serve hot or at room temperature.

Butternut Squash Pancakes

This is a perfect dish to serve as a holiday appetizer or for a light supper, while celebrating our fall and winter bounty. These pancakes are pan-fried and need only 5 tablespoons of oil to obtain crisp and flavorful exterior, but it is important whenever you are frying to use a good-quality oil that has a high smoke point. (Avocado, almond, grapeseed, and sunflower oil are your best choices.) Serve these pancakes with sour cream and applesauce or with Prosecco and Cinnamon Poached Apples with Mascarpone (page 321) for a real celebration of our magnificent bounty.

Makes 18 pancakes, enough for 6 entree servings or for appetizers for 9–12

1 savory biscotto

½ medium locally grown butternut squash, peeled and seeded

¼ cup finely chopped locally grown onion, about ⅛ medium onion

1 cup coarsely chopped locally grown organic baby spinach or other local greens

¼ cup organic all-purpose flour

¼ teaspoon sea salt

¼ teaspoon ground black pepper

Pinch of freshly grated nutmeg

4 locally raised eggs

5 tablespoons grapeseed, avocado, almond, or sunflower oil, divided

1. Place a cookie sheet on the counter by the stove. Line the sheet with either a brown paper bag or a double layer of paper towels.

2. Using your hands, break up the biscotto into large pieces and place in the bowl of a food processor fitted with a metal blade. Cover and process for about 5 seconds, until you have coarse crumbs. Turn into a bowl. Cut the butternut squash in half, then cut each half into thirds. Fit the bowl of the food processor with a shredding disc attachment and process the butternut squash into large shredded strips, or do this by hand on a box grater. You should have about 6 cups of shredded butternut squash. Turn this into the bowl with the biscotto crumbs. Add the chopped onion, spinach, flour, sea salt, pepper, and nutmeg.

3. Using your hands or two spoons, toss well to combine. Add the eggs and mix with a spoon until well blended. Heat a large skillet, about a 12-inch skillet, over medium-high heat. Add 4 tablespoons of the oil and swirl to coat the bottom of the skillet. Using a ¼-cup measure, lightly pack some of the pancake mixture into the cup and turn out into heated oil. Using the bottom of the cup, lightly flatten the pancake. Continue adding ¼-cup portions of the mixture to the heated oil until you have 4–5 pancakes, but do not crowd or the oil temperature will drop and the pancakes will be greasy. Cook the pancakes for 2–3 minutes until just medium brown. Using a slotted spatula, turn the pancakes over to cook the other side for about 2 minutes until medium brown. Transfer the browned pancakes to the paper-lined cookie sheet.

4. Continue frying the remaining mixture, adding the remaining tablespoon of oil just before adding the last batch of pancakes to fry. Serve hot or at room temperature.

Moroccan Stuffed Sweet Lightning Squash V

For this recipe you may use any small winter squash—acorn, butternut, pumpkin, or other—as you please, so have fun and try a variety of squash straight from the farmer.

Serves 4

2 tablespoons extra-virgin olive oil

1 small red onion, coarsely chopped

2 cloves garlic, finely chopped

8 baby organic carrots, cut into thin slices

1½ teaspoons cinnamon

Sea salt and pepper

1 cup water

¼ cup organic raisins

¼ cup sliced almonds

2 teaspoons grated orange zest

Juice from 2 oranges (about 1 cup)

Pinch of saffron

1 cup organic whole wheat couscous

4 medium Sweet Lightning squash, or other winter squash

1. Preheat the oven to 450°F.

2. Heat the olive oil in a medium pot over medium heat. Add the onion, garlic, carrots, and cinnamon, and a little sea salt and pepper. Cook, stirring frequently for about 5–6 minutes, until the onions are softened. Add the water, raisins, almonds, orange zest, juice, and saffron, and a little more sea salt. Raise the heat to high and bring to a boil. Stir in the couscous, mixing to combine. Cover and remove from the heat and set aside for about 5 minutes, until the couscous absorbs the liquid. When the liquid is absorbed, use two forks to fluff up the couscous. Taste for seasonings.

3. Meanwhile, using a big, heavy knife and holding the squash on its side, carefully cut the tops off the squash, say about ½ inch. Using a teaspoon, scoop out the fleshy strings and fibers and the seeds, creating a cavity for the stuffing. Discard the fleshy strings and fibers, but reserve the seeds if you want to roast them for a snack. Set aside the top of the squash for a "lid" to cover the stuffing later in the recipe. Spoon about a cup of the stuffing into the cavity of each squash, mounding over the opening. Cover each squash with the reserved top. Transfer to a glass baking dish, about 9 x 14 inches or so. Pour about 3 cups of water around the squash (not over it), until the water is about an inch deep. Cover the baking dish with foil, tenting as needed. Bake in the preheated oven for about 70 minutes, or until the squash is tender when tested with a fork.

Stuffed Chayote Squash V

Chayote is a pale green member of the gourd family. It has a delicate flavor, somewhat like a combination of zucchini and cucumber. It's lovely. Note: To prepare annatto oil, heat ½ cup of canola oil in a small pot over medium heat. Add ¼ cup of ground annatto and stir to blend. Remove from the heat and strain into a jar, using a fine mesh strainer. Cool to room temperature and cover for future use to add a nice yellow color to rice or other dishes. It keeps for up to 3 months. You can buy ground annatto in the spice section of most supermarkets.

Serves 4

1 2-inch slice Italian or French bread

1 14-ounce package soy ground beef

1½ teaspoons annatto oil (see note above)

1 small yellow onion, finely chopped

2 cloves garlic, coarsely chopped

1 medium cubanelle or poblano pepper, seeded and finely chopped

1 strip meatless bacon, finely chopped

1 medium tomato, finely chopped, including juices

3 tablespoons finely chopped cilantro

8 pimento-stuffed Spanish olives, halved

½ teaspoon dried oregano

Sea salt and pepper, to taste

1 egg or the equivalent substitute for a vegan dish

4 medium chayote squash, halved and pitted

1 cup hot water

1. Place the bread in a bowl. Cover the bread with hot water. Let stand for a minute or two to soften. Turn into a colander. Squeeze out as much water as you can, pressing down with your hand. Turn the bread into a bowl (you should have about ¼ cup). Add the soy ground beef. Heat a large skillet over medium-high heat. Add the annatto oil, rotating the skillet to coat it. Add the onion, garlic, chopped pepper, meatless bacon, tomato, cilantro, olives, oregano, and a little sea salt and pepper. Cook, stirring occasionally, for about 3 minutes, until the vegetables have softened a little.

2. Preheat the oven to 425°F.

3. Turn the cooked vegetables into the bowl with the soy ground beef, using a rubber spatula to scrape the skillet of any juices. Add the egg. Mix well, using a spoon to break up the beef and to combine the ingredients. Once the mixture cools sufficiently, use your hand to mix the stuffing, squeezing the mixture together to combine evenly. Taste for seasonings. Spray a rectangular baking dish with canola oil cooking spray or brush the inside with canola oil. Sprinkle the chayote squash lightly with sea salt. Divide the stuffing evenly among the 8 halves, slightly less than a half cup of stuffing per half, mounding it as you fill the cavity and the top of each half. Arrange the stuffed halves in the prepared baking dish. Pour 1 cup of hot water around (not over) the chayote halves. Spray a sheet of aluminum foil with canola spray, then, with the sprayed side down, cover the dish with foil, tenting to avoid flattening the stuffing. Bake in the preheated oven for 1 hour until the squash is tender when tested with a fork.

Quinoa-and-Pecan-Stuffed Acorn Squash GF

Quinoa is a protein-rich grain that dates back to South America over 5,000 years ago. It has a nutty flavor and is most easy to digest, gluten-free, and easy to cook. Try it as a change from brown rice; you'll be glad you did. You can find quinoa in supermarkets and in natural foods stores.

Serves 4

1 cup quinoa

3 tablespoons extra-virgin olive oil

3 cloves garlic, finely chopped

2 small carrots, diced

1 medium red onion, cut into thick ribs

4 ribs organic celery, leaves included, finely chopped

5–6 cremini mushrooms, chopped

¼ cup chopped pecans

1 tablespoon chopped fresh sage leaves or ½ teaspoon dried sage

2 teaspoons fresh rosemary leaves or ½ teaspoon dried rosemary

Sea salt and pepper

1 cup crumbled goat's milk cheese

2 medium acorn squash, cut in half and seeded

1. Preheat the oven to 450°F.

2. Bring 2 cups of water to a boil in a covered pot over high heat. When the water comes to a boil, stir in the quinoa. Cover and cook at a medium-high boil for about 10 minutes, until the water is absorbed. Turn the cooked quinoa into a bowl.

3. Heat the olive oil in a large skillet over medium heat. Add the garlic, carrots, onion, celery, mushrooms, pecans, sage, and rosemary. Sprinkle with salt and pepper. Stir to coat. Cover and cook for about 5 minutes, stirring occasionally, until the vegetables have released a little of their liquid. Turn this mixture into the bowl with the cooked quinoa. Stir in the cheese. Taste for seasoning. Divide the stuffing evenly among the squash halves. Arrange the halves in a glass baking dish. Pour hot water into the baking dish to a depth of 1 inch, pouring around, not over, the stuffed squash.

4. Cover the baking dish tightly with foil. Bake for about an hour, or until the squash is tender when pierced with a fork.

Thanksgiving Stuffed Acorn Squash ▣

I look forward to a stuffed acorn squash at home every Thanksgiving, and at Claire's we serve this recipe throughout the fall and winter months. Our customers love it.

Serves 6

1 cup water

1½ cups organic apple juice or cider

½ stick butter or ¼ cup trans fat–free margarine

1 medium yellow onion, coarsely chopped

6 stalks celery, including leaves, sliced

1 tablespoon fresh thyme or 1 teaspoon dried thyme

6–8 fresh sage leaves, chopped, or ½ teaspoon dried sage

1 teaspoon fennel seeds

1 12-ounce package Italian or other meatless sausage links, cut into thin slices

Salt and pepper

1 loaf whole wheat Italian bread, cut into 1-inch slices, then each slice cut into quarters

¾ cup organic unsweetened applesauce

1 medium organic apple, McIntosh or other, cored and chopped

3 large acorn or butternut squash, cut in half and seeded

1. Preheat the oven to 450°F. Measure the water, apple juice, butter, onion, celery, thyme, sage, fennel seeds, and the meatless sausage into a large pot. Sprinkle with salt and pepper, then stir to combine. Cover and set over a high heat. Bring to a boil, then reduce the heat to medium and cook at a medium boil, stirring occasionally for about 5 minutes, until the celery just softens. Remove from the heat. Stir in the cut bread, applesauce, and apple, mixing well to combine. Taste for seasonings.

2. Divide the stuffing evenly among the squash halves, mounding as needed. Arrange the stuffed squash in a roasting pan (or two if needed). Pour water into the pan, around (not over) the squash, to a depth of 1 inch. Spray the non-shiny side of a large sheet of foil (if the shiny side is down, the stuffing will get too brown) with cooking oil spray, then cover the pan tightly, tenting as needed to avoid pressing on the stuffing. Bake for about 1½ hours, until the squash is tender when pierced with a fork.

Claire's Classic

Moroccan Sweet Potatoes V GF

Everyone knows how rich in beta-carotene sweet potatoes and carrots are, and this delicious, sweet combination also contains chickpeas for protein and additional fiber. This recipe is based on a traditional Moroccan dish of meat roasted with sweet potatoes, chickpeas, and raisins. Our customers love our cholesterol-free version.

Serves 6

6 medium sweet potatoes, cut into 1-inch cubes

3 medium carrots, cut on the diagonal into ½-inch slices

1 large yellow onion, sliced into ¼-inch rings

¼ cup olive oil

1 teaspoon cinnamon

¼ cup brown sugar

1 tablespoon vanilla extract

¼ cup golden raisins

Salt and black pepper, to taste

$1/3$ cup water

1 16-ounce can chickpeas, drained

¼ cup chopped walnuts

Preheat the oven to 400°F. In a large bowl, combine the sweet potatoes, carrots, onion, olive oil, cinnamon, brown sugar, vanilla extract, and raisins. Sprinkle lightly with salt and pepper. Toss well. Pour the water into a rectangular glass baking dish. Turn the potato mixture into the dish. Cover tightly with foil. Bake for 1 hour. Remove the foil and stir in the chickpeas and walnuts. Continue cooking, uncovered, for 10 minutes, until the potatoes are tender.

Sweet and Sour Stuffed Little Cabbages V

This version of stuffed cabbage is prepared in a casserole form, making it so much easier and quicker to prepare than stuffing individual leaves, and it's every bit as tasty.

Serves 4

3 little heads local cabbage, or 1 large one

2 tablespoons extra-virgin olive oil

½ small local organic onion, finely chopped

1 14-ounce container soy ground beef or other vegetable meat

Sea salt and pepper

1 cup cooked brown rice

1 35-ounce can San Marzano whole peeled tomatoes in juice

¼ cup pure granulated maple sugar

1 tablespoon pure maple syrup

2 tablespoons apple cider vinegar

1. Preheat the oven to 400°F. Spray a 9-inch square glass baking dish with olive oil spray. Cut the cabbages in half lengthwise. If you are using a large cabbage rather than 3 little ones, cut it in half, then cut each half into thirds so you'll have 6 wedges. Using a paring knife, carefully create a small cavity in the cut side of each half, about the size of a grape, reserving the cabbage (you'll have about ½ cup) from creating the cavity.

2. Heat the olive oil in a large skillet over medium heat. Add the reserved ½ cup of cabbage, the onion, and the soy beef. Using a fork, break up the soy beef to create little pieces. Sprinkle with sea salt and pepper. Cook for about 5 minutes, stirring occasionally until the onion and cabbage have softened and the ground beef is lightly browned. Stir in the cooked brown rice, mixing to combine. Taste for seasoning. Set aside.

3. Turn the tomatoes and their juice into a bowl. Using your hand, squeeze the tomatoes to crush them. Add the maple sugar, maple syrup, and vinegar. Sprinkle with sea salt and pepper. Stir to combine. Taste, and add a little more maple syrup if you prefer a sweeter sauce.

4. Arrange the cut cabbage halves in a single layer, cut side up, in the prepared baking dish. Spoon the soy ground beef mixture evenly over the top. Spoon the tomato mixture evenly over and around the cabbage halves and over the beef mixture to cover. Place in the preheated oven and bake for 1 hour, or until the cabbage is tender when pierced with a fork and the sauce is hot and bubbling.

Claire's Classic

Stuffed Pepper Halves ▣

My mother-in-law is one of my favorite cooks. This is her recipe for the best stuffed peppers in the world.

Serves 6

1 12-ounce loaf day-old Italian or French bread

4 cups warm water

6 bell peppers (red, green, and yellow)

5 large cloves garlic, finely chopped

¼ cup finely chopped fresh Italian flat-leaf parsley

1 medium zucchini, cut up into ¼-inch dice

6 large mushrooms (button and shiitake), thinly sliced

1 small onion, minced

3 tablespoons extra-virgin olive oil

1 teaspoon dried oregano

Salt and pepper

1 egg or egg substitute, lightly beaten

1 cup hot water

1. Preheat the oven to 400°F. Cut the bread into 10 pieces. Place the bread in a large bowl. Pour 4 cups of warm water over the bread. Using your hand, push the bread to the bottom of the bowl so that it will soften as it absorbs the warm water. Set aside for 5 minutes. Drain the bread in a colander. Squeeze out as much water as you can, pushing down on the bread. Turn the drained bread into a large bowl.

2. Cut ¼ inch off the top of each pepper. Mince the top pieces (discard the stems) and add them to the bread. Cut each pepper in half. Remove and discard the seeds and soft ribs from each pepper half. Set aside. Add the garlic, parsley, zucchini, mushrooms and onion to the bread. Toss well to mix. Drizzle the olive oil over the bread mixture. Add the oregano, salt, and pepper to taste. Add the eggs. Toss well to combine.

3. Divide the filling among the pepper halves, mounding as necessary. Place the pepper halves in a large roasting pan. Pour the hot water around (not over) the peppers. Cover tightly with foil. Bake for 45–60 minutes until the peppers are fork-tender.

Pierogi V

Pierogi are to the Polish people what ravioli are to the Italians and dumplings are the Chinese, and I love them all—the people and the filled creations.

Makes 13, enough for 6 entrees

1 cup warm water

7 tablespoons extra-virgin olive oil, divided

Sea salt

2½ cups organic all-purpose flour, plus extra for kneading and rolling

2 medium organic Yukon Gold potatoes, partially peeled, quartered

2 medium organic yellow onions, cut in half, then cut into thin slices

Sour cream (optional)

1. To prepare the dough, measure the warm water and 3 tablespoons olive oil into a large bowl. Sprinkle with sea salt, then whisk to combine. Add the flour, all at once, then stir to mix until the flour is blended in and you have a soft dough. Dust a countertop or a large cutting board with a little flour, then dump the dough onto the flour. Knead for about 2–3 minutes, adding more flour a little at a time (up to 3–4 tablespoons, depending on the moisture in the air and the dough) until the dough is soft and elastic but not sticky. Return to the bowl and cover with a kitchen towel for about 30 minutes while you make the filling and the topping.

2. To prepare the filling, place the partially peeled and quartered potatoes into a pot of lightly salted water, cover and bring to a boil over high heat. When it reaches a boil, remove the cover and boil for about 15 minutes or until tender when tested with a fork. Drain and return to the pot. Heat 2 tablespoons of olive oil in a skillet over medium heat. Add 1 sliced onion and sprinkle with a little sea salt. Cook for about 10 minutes, stirring occasionally until the onion is golden and soft. Add the onion and any juices to the drained potatoes. Using a potato masher or the back of a slotted spoon, mash the potatoes with the cooked onion slices until blended and roughly mashed but still a little chunky. Taste for seasonings.

3. To prepare the topping, heat 2 tablespoons of olive oil in a large skillet over medium heat. Add 1 sliced onion, and sprinkle with a little sea salt. Stir to coat with the oil. Cook for about 10 minutes, stirring occasionally until the onion is a little golden and soft. Remove from heat and cover the skillet to keep warm.

4. Bring a large pot of lightly salted water to a boil over high heat.

5. On a lightly floured countertop or cutting board, turn out the dough. Dust the top with a little flour, and lightly flour your rolling pin. Roll out the dough to about ⅛-inch thickness. Cut into 4-inch rounds, transferring the rounds to a flour-dusted cookie sheet. Continue cutting and re-rolling the scraps to cut more rounds until you've cut about 13 rounds.

6. One at a time, place a rounded tablespoonful of filling into the center of each round of dough, then lift the dough over to form a half circle. Lightly press the filling into the center of the half circle, and press the ends to seal. Continue until you've filled and formed all the pierogi. When the water reaches a boil, carefully drop the pierogi into the boiling water one at a time. Don't stir them until they begin floating to the top, in about 3 minutes, then give them a gentle stir with a large slotted spoon. Continue cooking for a total of 5 minutes from the time you dropped the pierogi into the boiling water. Using a large slotted spoon, not a colander, lift out the pierogi one or two at a time, holding the slotted spoon over the pot for a few seconds to allow the water to drain back into the pot. Transfer the pierogi to a platter.

7. To serve, reheat the cooked onions. Spoon them with their liquids evenly over the pierogi. Serve with sour cream, if desired.

Claire's Classic

Potato Croquettes

When I was a child, my mom served massive quantities of delicious mashed potatoes with dinner at least once a week. She often had leftovers to make into wonderful croquettes that we enjoyed with the next night's dinner. Today at Claire's we serve them with either homemade organic applesauce and sour cream or marinara sauce.

Serves 4

6 large red potatoes, quartered

2 tablespoons butter

2 tablespoons milk

2 tablespoons chopped Italian flat-leaf parsley

Salt and black pepper, to taste

2 eggs

1 cup bread crumbs

¼ cup or more olive oil for frying

1. Cook the potatoes in lightly salted boiling water until soft, about 20 minutes. Drain and turn into a bowl. Add the butter, milk, parsley, salt, and pepper. Thoroughly mash with a potato masher, mixing well. Taste for seasoning. Set aside until cool enough to handle.

2. Form ¼-cup measures of the mashed potatoes into cylinders about 2 by 4 inches. Arrange in a single layer on a cookie sheet and refrigerate until firm to the touch. Beat the eggs lightly in a bowl large enough to dip a croquette. Set aside. Measure the bread crumbs into a separate bowl. Set aside. Dip each croquette into the beaten eggs, turning to coat evenly, then shake off the excess and roll the croquette in the bread crumbs to coat evenly. Return to the cookie sheet while you repeat the process with the remaining croquettes.

3. Heat the oil in a large nonstick skillet over medium heat. Add as many croquettes as you can fit in the skillet without crowding. Brown all sides of the croquettes, about 1 minute per side, turning when golden brown. Heat additional oil, if needed. Drain on a plate lined with a double thickness of paper towels.

Soy Chicken and Potato Croquettes

Potato croquettes are perennial favorites at Claire's, and adding soy chicken to these made them into an entree that we all love.

Makes 13 large croquettes, enough for 6 entrees or for 12–13 appetizers

Sea salt

10 medium organic potatoes, Yukon Gold or other, cut into quarters

½ cup organic butter or organic buttery spread

½ cup organic milk

Pepper

2 tablespoons extra-virgin olive oil

4 organic shallots, chopped

1 tablespoon fresh organic thyme leaves or 2 teaspoons dried thyme

3 8-ounce packages meatless chicken strips

2 tablespoons chopped organic Italian flat-leaf parsley

6 organic eggs

3 cups organic bread crumbs

2 cups organic canola oil or other oil for frying

1. Bring a pot of lightly salted water to a boil in a covered pot over high heat. Add the potatoes and cook for about 12–15 minutes, until soft when tested with a fork. Drain, then turn into a bowl. Add the butter, milk, and a little sea salt and pepper. Mash well with a potato masher. Heat the olive oil in a medium-size skillet over medium heat. Add the shallots, a little sea salt and pepper, and the thyme, and cook for about a minute, stirring frequently until softened and golden. Add the meatless chicken strips and the parsley and stir to coat with the oil. Cook for about 2 minutes until heated through. Turn the shallot-and-chicken mixture into a food processor fitted with a metal blade. Cover and process for about 20 seconds until finely minced. Turn this into the mashed potatoes. Stir well to combine. Taste for seasonings.

2. Scoop a 1-cup measure into your hand, then, using two hands, form into a rounded log-shaped croquette. Place this on a cookie sheet and continue forming the remaining mixture.

3. Crack the eggs into a shallow bowl. Add a little sea salt and pepper; then, with a whisk or a fork, beat them until blended. Measure the bread crumbs into another shallow bowl. Using your hands, carefully dip one croquette into the beaten eggs, turning it to coat all sides. Then place the croquette into the bread crumbs and turn to coat. Place the breaded croquette back onto the cookie sheet and continue breading the remaining croquettes.

4. Heat the oil in a large skillet over medium-high heat. Add as many croquettes as you can fit in a single layer without crowding, leaving some space in between each croquette so that you can turn them. Cook for about a minute per side, using two slotted spatulas to turn until evenly browned but not burned. Transfer the browned croquettes to a platter and continue frying the remaining croquettes.

Grilled Lemon Herb Tofu Kebabs on Rosemary Skewers V GF

Remove the leaves from the rosemary branches by holding the branch with one hand at the top (the leaves grow up toward the top) and using the other hand to push the leaves down.

Serves 4

4 rosemary branches, rosemary leaves removed and reserved for other use

1 14-ounce package organic extra-firm tofu

2 large cloves organic garlic

1 tablespoon fresh organic oregano leaves or 1 teaspoon dried

4 tablespoons freshly squeezed lemon juice, from about 1 lemon

1 tablespoon extra-virgin olive oil

Sea salt and pepper, to taste

1. Soak the rosemary branches in cold water to cover.

2. Line a cookie sheet with a double layer of paper towels or a kitchen towel. Drain the tofu. Cut the block of tofu in half lengthwise, to create two thinner blocks of tofu, then cut the blocks each into thirds lengthwise and crosswise, giving you 18 cubes. Arrange the cubes in a single layer on the paper towels and place a double layer of paper towels on top. Press the cubes lightly to remove excess liquid. Set aside while you prepare the marinade.

3. Place the garlic cloves in the bowl of a food processor fitted with a metal blade. Cover and process for a few seconds to mince. Add the oregano leaves, lemon juice, olive oil, salt, and pepper. Cover and process for about 10 seconds to blend. Taste for seasonings. Transfer the drained tofu cubes to a clean plate. Spoon the marinade evenly over the tofu, using a rubber spatula to scrape the processor bowl. Set aside to marinate for a few minutes while you heat the grill, or cover and refrigerate overnight.

4. Heat the grill to medium. Remove the rosemary branches from the water. Carefully thread 4 tofu cubes onto each of two branches and 5 tofu cubes onto each of the remaining two branches. When the grill is heated, brush the grill rack with organic canola oil or organic sunflower oil. Arrange the kebabs in a single layer on the heated oiled rack and cook for about 3 minutes per side, until grill marks appear. Using tongs, carefully turn the kebabs to brown the other side. Transfer to a plate. Serve warm or chilled.

Macaroni and Cheese with Broccoli

When I was growing up, my mother made macaroni and cheese. She always added broccoli to it because broccoli was one of what we referred to as the Big Three: broccoli, carrots, and spinach, the three vegetables she served every single day. Her insistence paid off because we've grown to be "good vegetable eaters" and she was always proud of that. Today, mac and cheese is quite the comfort food. We make it as a special a few times a week.

Serves 8

Sea salt

1 pound organic whole wheat pasta, penne or other

2 medium organic broccoli crowns, cut into small bunches of florets (about 6 cups)

3 tablespoons organic butter, cut into slices, divided

1 quart organic whole milk

1 medium sweet organic onion, coarsely chopped

3 cloves organic garlic, sliced

8 ounces (2 cups) shredded organic cheddar cheese

4 ounces (1 cup) shredded low-fat organic mozzarella cheese

Pepper

Pinch of nutmeg

¼ cup dry organic bread crumbs

2 tablespoons grated Parmesan and Romano cheese mixture (optional)

1/4 cup organic flax meal

1. Bring a large covered pot of lightly salted water to a boil over high heat. Cook the pasta according to package directions, and about 2 minutes before the pasta is cooked to your preference, add the broccoli florets. Before draining, reserve ½ cup of the cooking water. (A good way to remember is to place a measuring cup in a colander set in the sink.) Drain the pasta and broccoli and turn back into the pot. Add 1 tablespoon (one-third) of the sliced butter and the reserved cooking water to the pasta. Using a wooden spoon, toss to coat. Set aside.

2. Preheat the oven to 350°F.

3. Cook the milk with the onion and garlic in a pot over medium-high heat, bringing it only to a simmer, stirring occasionally, until the milk is hot but not boiling or scorched and the onions are just tender, about 12 minutes.

4. Stir in the cheddar and mozzarella cheeses, a little sea salt and pepper, and the nutmeg, stirring constantly until the cheeses melt, about a minute. Pour the mixture over the pasta and broccoli, using a rubber spatula to scrape the pot. Using a wooden spoon, stir to combine. Taste for seasonings. Spray a 3-quart, 13 x 9 x 2-inch glass baking dish with organic olive oil spray. Turn the pasta and cheese mixture into the prepared baking dish, using a rubber spatula to scrape the bowl and to spread the mixture evenly in the dish. Measure the bread crumbs, grated Parmesan and Romano cheeses, and flax meal into a small bowl, then stir to mix. Melt the remaining 2 tablespoons of butter in a small pot over medium heat, stirring for about a minute until it melts, then add the bread crumb mixture and stir to coat with the melted butter. Spoon the buttered crumbs evenly over the top of the macaroni and cheese. Bake in the preheated oven for about 20 minutes until the topping is crunchy.

Mediterranean Flat Bread Pizza `GFO`

Even though we've served this pizza for many years, I am still struck by the beauty of the colors of green, red, purple, and white; the flavor, which is delicious; and the fact that it's so healthy to eat.

Serves 4

4 8-inch sprouted wheat or other whole wheat flour tortillas

1 tablespoon extra-virgin olive oil, divided

3 garlic cloves, thinly sliced

1 7-ounce bag organic baby spinach (about 2 cups)

16 organic sweet grape tomatoes, halved

1 medium organic red onion, cut into thin rings, separated

½ teaspoon dried organic oregano

Sea salt and pepper

2 ounces feta cheese, crumbled

4 ounces fresh fiore di latte (cow's milk) mozzarella, cut into tiny cubes

1. Preheat the oven to 400°F.

2. Spray two cookie sheets with nonstick canola spray. Arrange the tortillas in a single layer on the prepared cookie sheets, 2 tortillas on each. Brush each tortilla with 1 teaspoon of the olive oil, then scatter the garlic slices evenly over the tortillas. Arrange the spinach leaves evenly over the top, then scatter the halved tomatoes and onion rings evenly over the spinach. Scatter the oregano evenly over the top, then sprinkle lightly with sea salt and pepper. Drizzle the remaining 2 teaspoons of olive oil evenly over the top, then scatter the crumbled feta cheese and the cubes of mozzarella evenly over the top. Bake in the preheated oven for about 10 minutes, until the cheese is melted and the spinach is wilted. Serve hot.

Tip: Use gluten-free tortillas to make this recipe gluten free.

Panecotto V

Panecotto translates to "cooked bread," and from the time I was a child, it was the dish always made the night after my grandmother, my mother, or, later, my mother-in-law made her *Escarole e Fagioli*. It's made using leftover bread, some vegetables you might have on hand, and your leftover soup. We never wasted good food, and this was a delicious way to make another healthy meal with what you had on hand. Serve it as your entree or as a side dish to a frittata; either way, it's wonderful and remains a favorite in my house.

If you want to make this dish and don't have any leftover Escarole e Fagioli (page 27), substitute a 12-ounce can of drained white beans, a head of well-washed, chopped fresh escarole, a teaspoon of fennel seeds, and ¼ teaspoon crushed red pepper flakes.

Serves 4

3 tablespoons extra-virgin olive oil

½ medium Vidalia onion, cut into thick ribs and separated

3 cloves garlic, sliced

½–1 cup leftover cooked vegetables, such as broccoli, chard, cauliflower, or other (optional)

4 cups Escarole e Fagioli

4 1-inch slices leftover Italian bread, torn into pieces

Salt and pepper

Heat the olive oil in a large, deep skillet over medium heat. Add the onion ribs and garlic. Cook for about 4–5 minutes, stirring occasionally until the onions are golden brown. Add leftover cooked vegetables if using, the Escarole e Fagioli (page 27), and the torn bread. Sprinkle lightly with salt and pepper. Stir to combine. Cook, stirring frequently, for about 4–5 minutes, until the bread is soft and the ingredients are heated through. Taste for seasoning.

Italian-Style Kidney Beans and Sausages ■

You can serve this easy-to-prepare, fiber- and protein-rich entree with a simple salad of organic arugula tossed with good olive oil and fresh lemon juice for a wonderful supper.

Serves 4

3 tablespoons extra-virgin olive oil

1 small sweet onion, cut into thin rings, separated

3 cloves garlic, sliced

½ cup chopped Italian flat-leaf parsley

Salt and pepper

½ teaspoon crushed red pepper flakes

6 fresh basil leaves, cut in half

1 13-ounce can organic red kidney beans, drained, rinsed, and drained again

5 soy Italian sausages, cut into thick slices

Heat the oil in a large, deep skillet over medium heat. Add the onion, garlic, parsley, salt and pepper, the red pepper flakes, and basil leaves. Cover and cook for about 10 minutes, stirring occasionally, until the onions are softened and golden. Add the kidney beans and the sausages. Stir well to combine. Cover and cook for about 5 minutes, stirring occasionally, until the beans are heated through. Taste for seasonings.

Meatless Cutlets and Romesco Sauce

For this recipe I like to use Quorn™ Chick'n Cutlets, the praises of which some friends of mine in England had been singing for years before I tried them here. I always keep my freezer stocked with a couple of packages for delicious and quick entree ideas. They are a healthful source of vegetarian (not vegan) protein. You can buy them at the supermarket; they're in the frozen foods section.

Serves 4

2 large red organic bell peppers, cut in half and seeded

1 medium organic carrot, cut into 1-inch pieces

3 cloves organic garlic, peeled

3 large organic tomatoes, cut in half

¼ cup sliced almonds

1 slice whole wheat bread, torn into 4 pieces

2 tablespoons sherry wine vinegar

1 tablespoon extra-virgin olive oil

Sea salt and pepper, to taste

4 meatless chicken cutlets

1. Heat a large grill pan or a cast iron skillet (use two smaller ones if you don't have one large one) over high heat. Arrange the pepper halves (cut side up), carrot, garlic cloves, and the halved tomatoes (cut side down) on the hot pan. Cook for about 4–5 minutes until the tomatoes, garlic, and carrot get char marks on the underside. Using tongs, turn the tomatoes, the garlic, and the carrot to make char marks on the other side. The peppers will need about 7 minutes to get char marks before you turn them.

2. Continue cooking the vegetables for about another 2–3 minutes until the underside of the tomatoes have char marks and the skins burst, then add the sliced almonds to the pan and toast for about a minute. Turn the charred vegetables and the almonds into the bowl of a food processor fitted with a metal blade. Set aside the pan to use again later in the recipe. Add the torn wheat bread to the processor bowl. Cover and process for about 7–10 seconds until blended smooth. Stir in the vinegar, olive oil, sea salt, and pepper. Taste for seasonings.

3. Using a paper towel, wipe out the pan to remove any charred bits. Set the pan over a medium-high heat. Add the blended sauce to the pan and cook at a medium boil for about 18–20 minutes, stirring occasionally, until the sauce has thickened and reduced by about half. Taste for seasonings. Cook the cutlets according to package directions. Arrange them on a serving platter, then spoon the sauce over the cutlets and serve.

New England Boiled Dinner █ V

This hearty stew-type entree is aromatic and delicious. It's the perfect answer to a cold day.

Serves 6–8

⅓ cup extra-virgin olive oil

1 medium sweet onion, cut into thick wedges, separated

3 medium carrots, cut into thick slices

4 ribs celery, leaves included, cut into 1½-inch slices

3 medium red skin potatoes, quartered

1 small butternut squash, peeled, seeded, and cut into 1½-inch pieces

1 teaspoon dried sage

½ teaspoon dried thyme

1 teaspoon dried fennel seeds

Salt and pepper, to taste

½ 6-ounce package soy pepperoni, slices separated

½ 6-ounce package smoked tempeh strips, cut in half

2 quarts water

1 small head savoy cabbage, cored and cut into thick slices

6 tofu hot dogs, cut in half

1 2-pound bag sauerkraut, with liquid

Heat the oil in an 8-quart pot over low-medium heat. Add the onion, carrots, celery, potatoes, squash, sage, thyme, fennel seeds, salt, and pepper. Stir to coat. Cover and cook for 15 minutes, stirring occasionally. Add the pepperoni, tempeh, and water. Raise the heat to medium-high and bring to a boil, stirring occasionally. Cook at a medium boil for 30 minutes, stirring occasionally until the carrots are tender. Add the cabbage, hot dogs, and sauerkraut. Cover and cook for 5 minutes, then stir and continue cooking, covered for about 10 minutes, until the cabbage is tender. Taste for seasonings.

Claire's Classic

Green Bean, Tomato, Potato, and Meatball Stew V

This is the perfect stew for a cold winter night. All you need to add is some crusty Italian bread for a wonderful supper.

Serves 6

2 1-inch-thick slices hard Italian bread

1 14-ounce package meatless ground beef (I like to use Lightlife® Gimme Lean®)

½ cup finely chopped Italian flat-leaf parsley

4 large cloves garlic, finely chopped

1 egg

5 tablespoons extra-virgin olive oil

Salt and pepper, to taste

1 medium yellow onion, cut into thick ribs

¾ pound green beans, trimmed and cut into 1-inch pieces

3 large potatoes, peeled and cut into 2-inch pieces

2 28-ounce cans Italian whole peeled tomatoes, squeezed with your hands to crush

½ cup water

10 large fresh basil leaves

2 bay leaves

1 teaspoon dried oregano

1. Place the bread in a bowl and cover with hot water. Set aside for 5–10 minutes, or until cool enough to handle. Drain the bread in a colander and press out as much water as possible. Turn into a large bowl. Add the ground "beef," ¼ cup of the chopped parsley, one-fourth of the chopped garlic, the egg, 1 teaspoon of the olive oil, and salt and pepper. Mix well with your hands or a spoon. Taste for seasonings. Roll heaping tablespoons of the mixture into about 16 balls. Set aside on a platter or cookie sheet.

2. Heat the remaining olive oil in a large pot over medium heat. Add the remaining chopped garlic, the onion, green beans, potatoes, remaining chopped parsley, and salt and pepper. Cover and cook, stirring occasionally, for 15 minutes, or until the vegetables have released some of their juices. Add the tomatoes and their juices, the water, basil, bay leaves, and oregano. Stir well to mix. Cover and cook at a medium boil (it will reach a boil after about 5 minutes) for about 40 minutes, stirring occasionally.

3. Meanwhile, spray a large skillet with olive oil spray. Heat the skillet over the medium-high heat. Arrange the "meatballs" in the heated skillet without crowding them too much. Brown each side for about 2 minutes, then transfer them to the cookie sheet. Carefully lower the "meatballs" into the sauce, using a wooden spoon to gently push them into the sauce to cover. Cover and cook for 20 minutes without stirring, then stir gently to mix, trying not to break up the "meatballs." Taste for seasonings.

Soy Beef and Vegetables Paprikás

Enriched with cabbage and mushrooms and strips of soy beef, this traditional and inviting noodle-and-sour-cream dish is a lovely example of how Hungarian paprika can add warmth to a meal.

Serves 6–8

3 tablespoons extra-virgin olive oil

3 large cloves garlic, sliced

3 medium sweet onions, cut in half, then into thick ribs

2 6-ounce packages soy beef strips

4 medium carrots, cut on the diagonal into ¼-inch-thick slices

1 large head green cabbage, cored and cut into quarters, then cut into thick slices

10 medium cremini mushrooms, quartered

3 tablespoons Hungarian paprika

Salt and pepper

⅓ cup red wine

1 cup low-fat sour cream

1 pound wide whole wheat noodles, cooked according to package directions (optional)

Heat the oil in a large pot over medium heat. Add the garlic, onions, soy beef strips, carrots, cabbage, mushrooms, paprika, salt, and pepper. Stir to coat with the oil, using tongs. Cover and cook for about 15 minutes, turning occasionally. Stir in the wine. Cover and cook for about 20 minutes, stirring occasionally, until the vegetables are tender. Stir in the sour cream, mixing well to combine. Cook for about 2 minutes until heated through. Serve over the noodles, if desired.

Tempeh

We all have a food that we enjoy and that we know is really good for us, yet we rarely eat it. For me, this food is tempeh. Tempeh is a fermented soybean "cake" that is made by cooking and dehulling soybeans and then inoculating them (either alone or with other grains) with a culturing agent that causes the mixture to ferment and become firm. Later, the tempeh is cut into blocks and packaged for sale. You can buy tempeh in packages, ready to cook into a variety of dishes. It has a nice nutty flavor and it pairs well with strong flavors. I love it baked with a smokey barbecue sauce or crumbled and added to a tomato sauce for a healthful and delicious version of Bolognese sauce. It's loaded with protein—19 grams per serving—and one serving contains more than half the amount of fiber you need for a day. And it's rich in isoflavones and the minerals magnesium and riboflavin, which makes tempeh both heart-healthy and a great antioxidant—good food for your entire body.

You can buy tempeh in the produce section of most supermarkets. It keeps fresh in your refrigerator for weeks (there will be an expiration date on the package to guide you). Buy a few extra packs and store them in your freezer for convenience. Just take out a package to defrost in the refrigerator the night before you plan to cook with it. When you open the package, don't be alarmed by any black or grayish spots; these are normal and caused by the fermentation. Any pink, yellow, or blue spots mean the tempeh is too old and you should not eat it.

Cut the tempeh in cubes or into thick slices, then cook it in your favorite barbecue sauce and serve it with corn on the cob and a colorful tossed salad for an easy and very delicious supper. Or, for a lovely appetizer or a light entree, enjoy your tempeh in my Tempeh Cakes with Dipping Sauce (page 260). To make them, I first give chunks of tempeh a quick boil to soften them a bit. Then I blend the tempeh with cilantro, shallots, and jalapeño, form them into cakes, then pan-fry it for a Thai-inspired dish.

To turn these little cakes into a light supper, serve them with a vegetable slaw made with shredded cabbage, carrots, broccoli stems, a little grated ginger, a few fresh mint leaves, sea salt, and white pepper, tossed with a little sesame or soy oil and rice wine vinegar.

Tempeh was first made in Indonesia over 2,000 years ago. It was brought to Europe by the Dutch and then brought to the United States in the early 1900s. Now is the perfect time to enjoy this centuries-old protein source.

Tempeh Cakes with Dipping Sauce V GFO

Serve these little protein-rich cakes with Braised Kale, Carrots, and Shiitake Mushrooms (page 292) for a lovely dinner. The leftover dipping sauce from this dish goes wonderfully with a vegetable stir-fry or as a salad dressing.

Makes 18 little cakes, enough for a light entree for 4

Cakes:

1 8-ounce package organic tempeh, cut into 10 cubes

4 cloves organic garlic, sliced

4 organic scallions, coarsely chopped

1 medium organic jalapeño pepper, sliced

Grated zest of 1 organic lemon

Grated zest of 1 organic lime

¼ cup coarsely chopped organic cilantro

2 tablespoons freshly squeezed lime juice

1 tablespoon organic granulated sugar

1 tablespoon organic canola oil, plus additional ¼–½ cup for pan-frying the cakes

Sea salt and white pepper

1 cup plus 1 tablespoon organic all-purpose flour, divided

1. To prepare the cakes, bring a small pot of water to a boil over high heat. Add the tempeh cubes and boil for 5 minutes, then drain. When the tempeh is cool enough to handle, chop the cubes into small pieces. Place the chopped tempeh in a bowl. Add the garlic, scallions, jalapeño, lemon and lime zest, cilantro, lime juice, sugar, 1 tablespoon of canola oil, and a little sea salt and white pepper. Stir to combine. Turn this into the bowl of a food processor fitted with a metal blade. Process for about 25 seconds, or until the mixture is completely blended and nearly smooth. Turn this into a bowl.

2. Stir in ½ cup plus 1 tablespoon flour and mix well to combine. Taste for seasoning. Let rest for 15 minutes to absorb some of the flour and make it easier to handle. Place the remaining ½ cup of flour on a plate. Set a large plate next to the other plate. Measure a heaping tablespoon of the tempeh mixture into your hand. Using your other hand, gently pat the mixture into a small cake, about 2 inches. The mixture will be soft, so handle it gently. Carefully dredge both sides of the cake into the flour, gently shaking off any excess flour, then set the floured cake on the empty plate. Continue until you have formed all the cakes.

3. Place another large plate by the stove. Heat ¼ cup of canola oil in a large skillet over medium heat. Drop a pinch of flour into the oil; if it sizzles, you can begin frying the cakes. Arrange as many cakes as you can in the skillet without crowding so it will be easy to turn them. Fry for about 1½ minutes or until the underside is golden brown, then turn and cook the other side for about a minute. Transfer to the plate. Continue frying the remaining cakes, heating additional oil if needed.

4. To make the dipping sauce, measure the sauce ingredients into a bowl. Stir to combine. Use immediately and store leftover dipping sauce in the refrigerator for up to a week.

5. Serve the tempeh cakes immediately or at room temperature, with dipping sauce. Leftovers can be refrigerated for up to 3 days, then served chilled or at room temperature.

Tip: Use a gluten-free tamari to make this recipe gluten free.

Sauce:

$1/3$ cup plus 1 tablespoon organic rice vinegar

$1/3$ cup organic low-sodium tamari

3 tablespoons freshly squeezed organic lemon juice (from about ½ lemon)

¼ teaspoon crushed red pepper flakes

"The first time I arrived on campus, I stumbled upon a cool-looking place to get a cup of coffee: Claire's. Little did I know what a positive impact this special place would have on my time at Yale and beyond. Claire's quickly became my respite to celebrate personal and academic achievements as well as to "drown my sorrows" . . . in a cup of hazelnut coffee and, of course, a slice of that legendary Lithuanian Coffee Cake (always with frosting)! I completed my college thesis largely at Claire's at the middle table looking out on the Green. And here I am today, twenty-three years later and still at the same table. I live in Boston now but travel back to Yale periodically. And no trip is complete or possible without going to Claire's. Today the Lithuanian Coffee Cake/hazelnut coffee combination brings me back to that twenty-something-year-old guy, and I am instantly reminded that life is great!"

—Dennis Pardo, Yale Class of 1988

Vegetarian Chicken Provençal V

This dish could stand alone as a lovely luncheon dish. For dinner, serve it over fluffy mashed or roasted organic Yukon Gold potatoes.

Serves 4

2 tablespoons extra virgin olive oil

3 tablespoons organic trans fat–free butter substitute, or butter, divided

2 shallots, finely chopped

2 medium organic zucchini, cut into small-medium dice

1 pint grape tomatoes or 1 14-ounce can Italian cherry tomatoes in juice

2 packages soy chicken strips, or 1 9.7-ounce package meatless cutlets, cut into strips or chunks

6–8 fresh sage leaves, torn into thirds

2 tablespoons fresh oregano leaves

1 tablespoon fresh thyme leaves

7–8 large fresh basil leaves

½ cup white wine, Chardonnay or other

Sea salt and pepper

1. Heat the extra-virgin olive oil and 1 tablespoon of the trans fat–free butter substitute or the butter in a large, deep skillet over medium heat. Add the shallots, zucchini, tomatoes, vegetarian chicken, sage, oregano, thyme, basil, white wine, and a little sea salt and pepper. Stir to coat with the oil. Cover and bring to a simmer for about a minute. Cook, covered, at a simmer, for about 5 minutes, stirring occasionally, until the zucchini are crisp-tender to your preference. (When you stir the mixture, use the back of the spoon to press the tomatoes to crush them.)

2. Uncover and continue cooking for a minute to reduce the liquid slightly. Taste for seasonings.

Claire's Classic

Vegetarian Meat Loaf with Roasted White and Sweet Potatoes, Onions, and Carrots Ⓥ

The most enticing aroma will fill your kitchen as this one-pan meal bakes in the oven. Any leftover meat loaf makes a terrific sandwich on Italian bread with sliced tomato and onion and a little mayonnaise. You don't even need to reheat it. Note: You can find meatless beef in the produce section at your supermarket.

Serves 6–8

Meat Loaf:

8 1-inch-thick slices Italian bread

1 14-ounce package meatless ground beef

½ cup coarsely chopped Italian flat-leaf parsley

2 large cloves garlic, finely chopped

1 small sweet onion, finely chopped

1 egg or ¼ cup egg substitute

1 tablespoon extra-virgin olive oil

Salt and pepper, to taste

Roasted Vegetables:

6 medium baking potatoes, cut lengthwise into 6 wedges

2 large sweet potatoes, cut lengthwise into 6 wedges

2 large carrots, peeled and cut into ½-inch slices

2 medium sweet onions, cut in half, then into thick ribs

3 large cloves garlic, coarsely chopped

1 tablespoon extra-virgin olive oil

Salt and pepper, to taste

1 cup Basil-Scented Marinara Sauce (page 185)

1. Center the oven rack. Preheat the oven to 375°F. Spray a large roasting pan with olive oil spray.

2. To prepare the meat loaf, place the bread in a bowl. Cover with hot water. Set aside to soften for about 5 minutes. Turn into a colander and press out as much water as you can. Turn the drained bread into a large bowl. Add the ground "beef," parsley, garlic, onion, egg, and oil. Sprinkle with salt and pepper. Mix well with your hands to combine. Taste for seasonings.

3. Place the meat mixture in the center of the prepared baking pan. Using your hands, form it into a loaf about 8 by 5 inches. Pat the loaf smooth.

4. To prepare the vegetables, place the potatoes, carrots, onions, and garlic in a large bowl. Toss well to mix. Drizzle with the olive oil, sprinkle with salt and pepper, and toss well to combine. Taste for seasonings.

5. To assemble and cook the dish, arrange the vegetable mixture in the pan around the meat loaf. Pour the marinara sauce over the meat loaf. Cover the pan tightly with foil. Bake for 40 minutes, then remove the foil and continue baking for 35 minutes, or until the potatoes are fork-tender to your preference.

Vegetable Fried Rice GFO

This one-bowl supper is delicious. I scramble the eggs separately so that my customers can enjoy big pieces of tender egg.

Serves 4–6

3 cups water

1¾ cups brown rice

2 tablespoons butter

5 large eggs, lightly beaten

Sea salt

White pepper

2 tablespoons extra-virgin olive oil

1 medium red onion, finely chopped

3 cloves garlic, finely chopped

2 shallots, finely chopped

1 1-inch piece ginger, peeled and minced

3 medium carrots, cut into quarters lengthwise, then cut into ¼-inch pieces

2 broccoli crowns, stems coarsely chopped and florets separated

8 cremini or button mushrooms, cut in half

1 cup frozen green peas

¼ cup low-sodium tamari or soy sauce

1. Measure the water and the brown rice into a pot. Cover and bring to a boil over high heat. Reduce the heat, cover, and cook at a simmer for about 20 minutes, until the rice is tender but the water is not completely absorbed. Move the covered pot of rice to a cool burner on the stove for later in the recipe.

2. Melt the butter in a small skillet over medium heat. Add the beaten eggs. Sprinkle lightly with sea salt and a little white pepper. Cook for about 2 minutes, until the edges are just set. Mix the eggs with a fork to break them up into big pieces, and continue cooking and mixing for about a minute until the eggs are cooked but not dry. Set aside.

3. Heat the olive oil in a large skillet over medium heat. Add the onion, garlic, shallots, and ginger. Sprinkle lightly with sea salt and white pepper. Stir to combine. Cook for about 5 minutes, stirring occasionally until the shallots are golden and the onions have softened. Add the carrots, broccoli, and mushrooms. Use two wooden spoons to toss and mix. Continue cooking for about 4 minutes, occasionally tossing the vegetables until the carrots are crisp-tender. Stir in the frozen peas and the tamari. Cook for 1–2 minutes, tossing occasionally until the peas are heated through. Add the cooked rice, using a rubber spatula to scrape the pot of the rice and any liquid. Stir well to combine. Add the scrambled eggs and stir to combine. Taste for seasonings.

Tip: Use a gluten-free tamari to make this recipe gluten free.

Claire's Classic

Stir-Fried Veggies over Brown Rice V GFO

We prepare a combination of stir-fried vegetables every day at Claire's, depending on the selection from the farm. Choose your favorite vegetables of the season. When we want a change, we serve our stir-fries on a bed of couscous instead of rice—either way it's a healthful, appealing meal.

Serves 4

¼ cup sesame oil

3 cloves garlic, chopped

1 teaspoon crushed red pepper flakes

1 1-inch piece fresh ginger, peeled and minced, or 2 teaspoons ground ginger

1 small red onion, chopped

2 medium carrots, cut into large matchsticks

¼ small green cabbage, chopped

1 small bunch broccoli, stems separated from florets, then chopped

1 small yellow bell pepper, cut in half, seeded, then sliced into ¼-inch ribs

¼ cup chopped walnuts (optional)

¼ cup low-sodium soy sauce or tamari

2 tablespoons bottled mango chutney (found in the condiment section of most supermarkets) or honey

Salt and black pepper, to taste

3 cups cooked brown rice

Heat the oil in a large skillet over medium-high heat. Add the garlic, red pepper flakes, ginger, and onion. Cook, stirring frequently, until the onion softens, about 5 minutes. Add the carrots, cabbage, broccoli stems, and bell pepper. Cook, stirring frequently, until the vegetables are crisp-tender, about 10 minutes. Add the walnuts (if using), broccoli florets, soy sauce or tamari, and chutney or honey. Continue cooking, stirring frequently, for 3 minutes. Taste for seasoning. Add salt and pepper to taste. Spread the cooked brown rice in a large serving dish. Spoon the stir-fried veggies and their juices evenly over the rice.

Tip: Use gluten-free tamari to make this recipe gluten free.

Stir-Fried Vegetables with Organic Tofu over Organic Brown Rice V GF

This colorful stir-fry is rich in beta-carotene, vitamins A and C, fiber, good fats, whole grains, and flavor. Vary the vegetables as the season allows, first cooking the hardest vegetables like winter squash and carrots and later adding the quicker-cooking vegetables like tender organic baby spinach, broccoli florets, baby bok choy, and shiitake mushrooms.

Serves 6

2 tablespoons extra-virgin olive oil

4 cloves garlic, sliced

½ teaspoon crushed red pepper flakes

1 1-inch piece fresh ginger, peeled and minced

2 shallots, sliced

1 sweet onion, cut into thick rings, separated

Salt and pepper

1 small butternut squash, peeled, seeded, cut into thin half rings

2 medium carrots, cut in ¼-inch slices

Juice from 1 orange

2 baby bok choy, cut in half lengthwise

1 broccoli crown, florets separated

12 small shiitake mushrooms, tough stems removed and discarded

1 12-ounce package organic firm tofu, drained and cut into small cubes

1 7-ounce bag organic baby spinach

½ cup tamari sauce

1 tablespoon toasted sesame oil

3 cups cooked organic brown rice, wheat berries, quinoa, or black beans

1. Heat the oil in a wok or a large, deep skillet over medium-high heat, but do not allow to smoke. Add the garlic, red pepper flakes, ginger, shallots, and onion. Sprinkle with salt and pepper. Using two large spoons, toss the ingredients to coat with the oil. Cook for about 2 minutes, tossing frequently to mix until the onions are softened. Add the butternut squash, carrots, and orange juice. Toss to combine.

2. Cover the wok and cook for about 10 minutes, tossing frequently until crisp and not quite tender. Add the baby bok choy, broccoli florets, and mushrooms, tossing to combine. Cover and cook for about 3–5 minutes, tossing frequently, until the vegetables are just tender. Add the tofu, spinach, tamari, and sesame oil and toss to combine. Cook, uncovered, for about 2 minutes until the tofu is heated through. Taste for seasonings. Serve over brown rice or other good grains or beans.

Curried Mixed Vegetables with Peaches and Chickpeas V GF

The produce used in this recipe is at its peak during the summer months, which makes summer the perfect time to take advantage of their freshness. You'll taste the difference in your finished dish.

Serves 4–6

1 tablespoon organic trans fat–free buttery spread

1 tablespoon extra-virgin olive oil

1 large organic red onion, cut into thick slices

1 large organic yellow onion, cut into thick ribs

3 large cloves organic garlic, coarsely chopped

2 medium organic carrots, peeled and cut into ¼-inch diagonal slices

2 teaspoons organic curry powder

½ teaspoon crushed organic red pepper flakes

1 large organic jalapeño pepper, finely chopped (optional)

Sea salt and pepper, to taste

2 small organic zucchini, cut into ½-inch diagonal slices

1 14-ounce can light, pure coconut milk

¼ cup water

1 small head organic escarole, washed well and cut into 2-inch lengths

2 local peaches, fresh or frozen, pitted and each cut into 6 wedges

1 tablespoon freshly squeezed organic lime juice (from about ½ lime)

1 cup cooked organic chickpeas, freshly cooked or canned, drained

¼ cup coarsely chopped organic cilantro

3 cups cooked organic basmati brown rice

1. Heat the spread and the oil in a large, deep skillet over medium heat. Add the onions, garlic, and carrots. Add the curry powder, red pepper flakes, jalapeño pepper, salt, and pepper. Stir to coat the vegetables with the oil and spices. Cover and cook for 15 minutes, stirring occasionally until the onions soften and the vegetables release some of their juices. Stir in the zucchini, coconut milk, water, escarole, peaches, lime juice, and cooked chickpeas. Cover and continue cooking for 10 minutes, stirring occasionally, until the zucchini are tender and the chickpeas are heated through. Stir in the cilantro. Taste for seasonings.

2. Place the cooked rice in the center of a serving bowl. Spoon the curried vegetables and their juices around the rice.

Curried Vegetables with Tofu V GF

We make one curried vegetable dish every day at Claire's, and this one is a favorite because it has a winning combination of tomatoes and coconut milk and it's really tasty.

Serves 4

2 tablespoons grapeseed oil

1 large red onion, cut into thick slices

3 large cloves garlic, coarsely chopped

12 grape tomatoes, halved

2 scallions, white part and 4 inches green, cut into ¼-inch diagonal slices

12 baby carrots, cut into ¼-inch diagonal slices

2 large golden beets, peeled and cut into small dice

2 teaspoons curry powder

½ teaspoon crushed red pepper flakes

Salt and pepper, to taste

1 small zucchini, cut into ½-inch diagonal slices

1 14-ounce can light, pure coconut milk

¼ cup water

1 3-ounce package enoki mushrooms, trimmed and separated into small bundles

1 tablespoon freshly squeezed lime juice (from about ½ lime)

12–16 ounces firm tofu, cut into small cubes

¼ cup coarsely chopped cilantro

3 cups cooked jasmine or other rice

Heat the oil in a large, deep skillet over medium heat. Add the onion, garlic, tomatoes, scallions, carrots, and beets. Sprinkle with the curry powder, red pepper flakes, salt, and pepper. Stir to coat the vegetables with the oil and spices. Cover and cook for 15 minutes, stirring occasionally, until the onions soften and the vegetables release some of their juices. Stir in the zucchini, coconut milk, water, mushrooms, and lime juice. Cover and continue cooking for 10 minutes, stirring occasionally, until the beets are just tender. Stir in the tofu and cilantro. Cook for 1 minute until the tofu is heated through. Serve over jasmine or other rice.

Tomato-Coconut Curry with Yellow Squash, Corn, and Kale V GF

This flavorful dish celebrates our summer vegetables and local tree fruit, stewed in a curry-flavored broth of coconut milk. The basmati rice has an interesting, nutty flavor and is a nice pairing for this traditional Indian dish.

Serves 6

3 tablespoons extra-virgin olive oil

1 large sweet organic onion, cut into thick ribs

2 large cloves organic garlic, chopped

3 large organic tomatoes, cut into thick wedges

4 organic yellow summer squash, cut into thick slices

1 small hot pepper, minced

1 small bunch organic kale, Toscano or other

2 cups fresh corn kernels, from about 2 ears of corn

1 1-inch piece fresh ginger, peeled, and minced

Salt and pepper

1 teaspoon ground turmeric

1 tablespoon curry powder

2 cups light coconut milk

1 ripe organic peach, pitted and chopped

1 medium organic apple, Granny Smith or other, cored and chopped

½ cup chopped almonds

1½ cups cooked organic basmati brown rice

Heat the oil in a large, deep skillet over medium heat. Add the onion, garlic, tomatoes, squash, hot pepper, kale, corn, ginger, salt, pepper, turmeric, and curry powder. Stir to coat. Cover and cook for about 15 minutes, stirring occasionally until the vegetables have softened and released some of their liquids. Add the coconut milk, peach, apple, and almonds. Cook, uncovered, at a low-medium boil for about 10 minutes, stirring frequently, until the vegetables are softened to your preference. Taste for seasonings. Serve over the cooked basmati rice.

Claire's Classic

Eggplant Veracruz

This is our Mexican version of the ever-popular eggplant parmigiana. Try with Claire's Classic Salsa (page 138).

Serves 8

2 cups flour (or more) for dredging

6 eggs

3 tablespoons chopped Italian flat-leaf parsley

Salt and black pepper, to taste

½ cup soybean or vegetable oil for frying

1 large eggplant, peeled and sliced lengthwise into ⅛-inch pieces

3 cups salsa

8 ounces shredded Monterey Jack cheese

1. Preheat the oven to 375°F. Measure the flour into a shallow bowl and set aside. In a separate bowl, beat together the eggs, parsley, salt, and pepper. Set aside.

2. Heat the oil in a large nonstick skillet over medium heat. Dredge the eggplant slices one at a time in the flour to coat both sides. Shake off the excess. Dip each slice into the beaten eggs. Lightly shake off the excess. Place the eggplant in the hot oil, filling the skillet without overlapping. Cook each side until golden brown, 1 minute or more. Drain the eggplant slices on a plate lined with a double thickness of paper towels. Repeat with remaining eggplant slices. If the oil begins to smoke or foam, heat fresh oil and try the remaining eggplant slices.

3. Spread 1 cup salsa in a rectangular glass baking dish. Stack the eggplant slices evenly in the dish. Pour the remaining salsa on top. Sprinkle with the cheese. Bake for 30 minutes, until the salsa is hot and the cheese has melted.

side dishes

My mom's favorite way to eat was the traditional Italian way. To her, that meant eating several small amounts of vegetables, some pasta, and usually a bean dish, too. She referred to meat and a vegetable or two as "Americana" or "Blue Plate," and she never ate that way or fed us that way. And because I loved my mother's kitchen so much, I follow that principal in my kitchens both at home and at Claire's. So my side dish section is huge and it's the way our customers like to eat, too.

Years ago, when I started to offer our entrees in appetizer portions, Frank thought I had lost my mind and was trying to put myself out of business. I reminded him that my mother was always right and that she had said, "Doing the right thing is always the best way to run your business." I knew that people wanted smaller portions sometimes as a snack and sometimes as their meal. And it's better to eat a little less than we often do, anyway. Luckily, my mom and I were right.

I recommend that you enjoy several dishes, using various vegetables simply prepared. By doing this, you can try new things and eat a wide range of healthful ingredients. I might make double batches of Moroccan Sautéed Spinach with Dried Apricots, Pine Nuts, and Preserved Lemons; Sweet Carrots; and Black Beans and Peppers in Rum Barbecue Sauce one day so that I'll have leftovers for another supper a few days later, at which time I'll only have to make one or two side dishes. Or I might make Sweet and Sour Red Cabbage, Roasted Tri-Colored Bell Peppers, and Sweet Onions, New York Style to serve alongside pan-grilled tofu hot dogs.

A healthful goal is to enjoy seven to nine fruits and vegetables every day, and by serving several side dishes as a meal or one or two as a snack, you can get to your goal—deliciously.

Hot Antipasto

This is a version of a perennial favorite at Claire's, first shared with us by Mrs. "Sav," whose three wonderful daughters worked with us back in the early days. It's my "go-to" dish for holiday meals and summer picnics because it's healthful and great served either hot from the oven or at room temperature.

Serves 8

4 ribs organic celery, including leaves, cut into ½-inch slices

2 broccoli crowns, cut into thick spears with florets

1 large red onion, cut into thick ribs

1 medium organic zucchini, cut into 1-inch slices

5 cloves garlic, sliced

2 large organic bell peppers, seeded and cut into thick ribs

16 button or cremini mushrooms

16 olives, pitted, or ¼ cup sliced black olives

1 14-ounce can artichoke hearts, drained and cut in half, or left whole if small

3 tablespoons extra-virgin olive oil

¼ cup plain bread crumbs

¼ cup grated pecorino Romano cheese

½ teaspoon dried oregano

½ teaspoon crushed red pepper flakes

Sea salt and pepper, to taste

1. Preheat the oven to 350°F.

2. Place all the ingredients into a bowl and, using your hands, toss to combine. Taste for seasoning. Spray a large, glass baking dish with olive oil spray. Turn into the prepared baking dish, cover with foil, and bake for about 45 minutes, until the vegetables are crisp-tender, then remove the foil, stir the vegetables, and continue baking for 10–15 minutes until the vegetables are tender to your preference. Serve hot or at room temperature.

Stuffed Artichokes

When I was a child, artichokes were reserved for holiday meals. This was mainly due to their high cost, but also to their limited availability. In our family of six, artichokes were a rare but adored treat, generally served only on Easter Sunday. Things have changed, and today artichokes are available several times a year, with the biggest (and best) crops harvested in late March and April. These are cultivated mostly in California, Italy, Spain, and France, although more and more home gardens are including artichokes, particularly throughout parts of the country that benefit from a longer growing season.

Globe artichokes, the ones with the luscious leaves and delectable heart—the ones I love to stuff and steam—are thistle plants, and the artichoke is really the flower bud. Frank and I once grew artichokes in our backyard garden; most were really tough, even after cooking for a long time, so we decided to let our next crop grow out and flower. Then I dried the stalks with their flowers for decoration. The artichoke grows on a long stalk, and if you don't cut the "bud," which has the petal-shaped leaves, the bud will bloom into a gorgeous but inedible flower, with the most beautiful deep purple thistles and a center of bright yellow thistles. If we ever grow artichokes again, I'll grow them in a flower bed rather than in my vegetable gardens.

Stuffed Artichokes (page 278) are a favorite in our family and something I continue to serve on holidays, particularly on Easter Sunday. Today I stuff my artichokes with whole wheat panko crumbs because they are crispier and stay firmer than the usual dried, store-bought crumbs. I combine them with pecorino Romano cheese, slices of healthful garlic, a little extra-virgin olive oil, and parsley—simple yet delicious. Also, I use a lot less stuffing than usual to save calories. (Really, the artichoke is so very delicious that a little stuffing is all you need to enjoy both the stuffing and the artichoke.) Artichokes are so healthy for you, too. They are loaded with vitamin A and fiber and are reputed to be terrific for digestion.

How do you eat a cooked artichoke? Gently pull off one leaf at a time. Then, while holding the tip end of the leaf, put the other end in your mouth and gently bite down as you draw the leaf through your teeth to remove the yummy, soft part of the leaf. When you get to the thorny "choke," just take a spoon and scrape and discard the choke and savor the heart, which is at the base. Serve a plate for scraps with every artichoke.

Stuffed Artichokes

Used as a base for the stuffing in this delectable recipe, panko bread crumbs are available in supermarkets and other food emporiums.

Serves 2 (can be doubled, tripled, or multiplied by any quantity you choose)

Stuffing:

½ cup whole wheat panko or other bread crumbs

2 tablespoons grated pecorino Romano cheese

2 tablespoons coarsely chopped organic Italian flat-leaf parsley

2 small cloves garlic, sliced thin

Black pepper

1 tablespoon water

1 tablespoon plus 1 teaspoon extra-virgin olive oil

Artichokes:

1 organic lemon, cut in half

1 clove garlic, peeled and sliced

1 tablespoon extra-virgin olive oil

Sea salt and pepper

2 large artichokes

1. To prepare the stuffing, measure the bread crumbs, grated cheese, parsley, and garlic into a bowl. Sprinkle with a little pepper. Using a spoon, stir to combine. Drizzle the water evenly over the bread crumb mix, then stir to coat. Drizzle the olive oil evenly over the top, then stir to combine. Taste for seasonings. Set aside while you prepare the artichokes for stuffing and cooking.

2. To prepare the artichokes, select a pot with a tight-fitting cover. You'll need a pot that's large enough to fit the artichokes; they should stand upright with a little space in between, but not so large that the artichokes will wobble about the pot, tipping over. Next, add enough water to later reach about one-fourth of the way up the artichokes. Squeeze the lemon halves into the water, then drop them in. Add the sliced garlic, 1 tablespoon of olive oil, and a little salt and pepper. Set this pot on the stove, but don't turn on the heat yet.

3. Lay the first artichoke on its side on a cutting board. Using a sharp knife, cut off the stem, then peel it. Drop the stem into the lemon-water mixture on the stove.

4. Repeat with the remaining artichoke.

5. Next, while holding the first artichoke on its side, slice off and discard the top ½-inch of thorny leaves (the tip of the artichoke). Using sharp scissors, cut off the thorny, pointed tips from the remaining leaves one at a time, removing about ¼ inch. Stand the artichoke upright, stem end down. Hold the stem end of the artichoke in one hand and smash the other end on a counter. Using your fingers, open the leaves, exposing the center leaves. Twist and pull out the very pale inner leaves, enough to create a cavity to stuff. Repeat with the remaining artichoke.

6. One at a time, spoon about half the stuffing into the cavity of the artichoke and in between some of the leaves. Pack it loosely, not tightly, or else the stuffing will be tough. After you stuff the artichoke, set it, upright, in the lemon-water mixture. Repeat with the remaining artichoke. Cover the pot, turn the heat to high, and bring the water to a boil. When it reaches a boil, in a few minutes, reduce the heat to medium. Cook the artichokes in the liquid at a low-medium boil, covered so that the leaves above the boiling liquid are steamed. Cook for about 45–60 minutes, until a leaf can be easily tugged out and is tender to the teeth when tested for doneness. Serve hot, at room temperature, or chilled. Serve the stems alongside the artichokes; they are really yummy, too.

"Years ago, I 'borrowed' Claire's Corner Copia Cookbook from my sister. I had never been to Claire's but it became my go-to cookbook. So, when I moved to New Haven, the first place my sister and I went to was Claire's. I still haven't given her back the cookbook!"

—Rena Leddy, a frequent Claire's customer

Confetti Vegetable Slaw V GF

I often stock a bag of the broccoli cole slaw mix from the supermarket and it's "bailed me out" so many times when I'm home alone and busy in the office and just don't want to stop to cook. I enjoy a big bowl of this slaw and it satisfies me. I feel good knowing I'm eating broccoli, cabbage, and carrots, all ingredients in this pre-shredded slaw mix. Of course, it's a welcome addition to any picnic, too.

Serves 4

1 12-ounce bag broccoli cole slaw mix, or 5 cups shredded broccoli stems, carrots, and red cabbage

¼ cup chopped cilantro

2 tablespoons organic apple cider vinegar

2 tablespoons mayonnaise or dairy-free mayonnaise

2 tablespoons organic soy milk or dairy milk

Sea salt

White pepper

1. Place the broccoli cole slaw mix and the chopped cilantro in a bowl. Using tongs, toss the vegetables to mix.

2. Into another bowl, measure the vinegar, mayonnaise, milk, a little sea salt, and a little white pepper. Whisk to combine. Taste for seasonings. Pour evenly over the vegetables, using a rubber spatula to scrape the bowl of all the dressing. Using the tongs, toss the salad to coat with the dressing. Taste for seasonings.

Braised Greens and Cabbage V GF

Pair this winning combination with veggie burgers for a quick and healthful weeknight supper.

Serves 6

1 tablespoon extra-virgin olive oil

1 organic shallot, finely chopped

1 medium head organic Savoy cabbage, cored and coarsely chopped

1 large bunch organic Swiss chard, stems cut into medium slices, leaves coarsely chopped

Sea salt and pepper

1 tablespoon apple cider vinegar

Heat the oil in a pot over medium heat. Add the shallot, cabbage, and stems from the Swiss chard. Sprinkle lightly with sea salt and pepper. Cover and cook for about 10 minutes, stirring occasionally until the vegetables are barely tender. Add the Swiss chard leaves and the cider vinegar, then stir to combine. Cover and continue cooking for about 5 minutes, stirring occasionally until the vegetables are tender to your preference. Taste for seasonings.

Braised Dandelion Greens ⓥ

We never spray any chemicals on our small lawn at home. I love the yellow color from the dandelions (not so much love for this from my husband, but it allows me to enjoy the fresh dandelion greens right from my back yard). Or I buy plenty from our local farms to braise, to put in a salad, or to add to any vegetable soup.

Serves 4–6

3 tablespoons organic canola oil

1 large organic spring onion, or 2 medium, sliced into thin rings, separated

2–3 strips meatless soy bacon or smoked organic tempeh, cut into 1-inch pieces

Sea salt and pepper, to taste

1 large bunch organic dandelion greens, washed well, bottom 2 inches of stems cut off and discarded, remaining leaves and stems cut in half, lengthwise

¼ cup freshly squeezed orange juice (from about ½ orange)

1 cup cooked organic chickpeas; if using canned, rinse and then drain before adding

Heat the canola oil in a large, deep skillet over low-medium heat. Add the onion, soy bacon, salt, and pepper. Stir to coat with the oil. Cover and cook for about 10 minutes, stirring occasionally until the onions have softened. Add the dandelion greens and a little more salt. Using tongs, toss the greens to coat. Cover and cook for about 8–10 minutes, stirring occasionally until the greens have wilted. Add the orange juice and chickpeas. Cook, uncovered, for about 5 minutes, stirring occasionally until the chickpeas are heated through. Taste for seasonings.

Roasted Smokey Onions and Sweet Potatoes

This side dish has lots of sweet and smokey flavors, caramelized onions, and healthful organic sweet potatoes. It's loaded with vitamins A and C, fiber, and antioxidants, things we can all use to build our immune systems—deliciously!

Serves 4

1 extra-large onion or 2 large onions, cut in half, then each half into thick ribs, separated

2 large organic sweet potatoes, cut into half, then each half cut into 4 wedges

3 tablespoons extra-virgin olive oil

5 tablespoons water

2 teaspoons smoked sweet paprika

¼ teaspoon smoked hot paprika (optional)

Sea salt, to taste

1. Preheat the oven to 425°F.

2. Spray a large glass baking dish or sheet pan with olive oil spray. Place the onions and the sweet potatoes into a bowl. Drizzle the olive oil and water evenly over the top and toss to coat the vegetables. Sprinkle the paprika and sea salt over the vegetables, and toss to coat. Turn the vegetables into the prepared pan. Use a rubber spatula to scrape the bowl of all the juices and spices and to spread the vegetables evenly.

3. Bake in the preheated oven for about 50 minutes, occasionally stirring the vegetables to cook evenly, until the potatoes are tender and the onions soft and caramelized. Taste for seasonings.

Candied Sweet Potatoes V GF

Thanksgiving just wouldn't be the same without this side dish, made using my mother's recipe. I can close my eyes and transport back to my childhood, watching as my mother lovingly tended to what remains my favorite Thanksgiving vegetable.

Serves 6

3 tablespoons butter or trans fat–free margarine

3 large sweet potatoes, cut into 1-inch rounds

1 cup water

½ cup firmly packed brown sugar

1 tablespoon cinnamon

1 tablespoon pure vanilla extract

Salt

1. Melt the butter in a medium skillet with 2- to 3-inch-high sides, over low-medium heat. Add the sweet potatoes, fitting as many as you can in a single layer. Then arrange another layer over the first. Pour the water evenly over the potatoes. Sprinkle the brown sugar and cinnamon evenly over the potatoes. Drizzle the vanilla evenly over the potatoes. Sprinkle lightly with salt. Cover the skillet and cook over low-medium heat at a low-medium boil for 25 minutes without stirring.

2. Turn the potatoes over, using a fork, rotating the top layer to the bottom, turning those potatoes over as well to cook the other side. Keep in mind while turning that both sides of each slice need a turn on the bottom in the center of the skillet to caramelize properly. Cover and continue to cook for about 15 minutes, turning the potatoes over to coat with the syrupy cooking liquid until the potatoes are tender when tested with a fork.

Pan-Fried Zucchini Rounds with Lemon and Parmesan GF

This is how my mother prepares these delicious rounds of zucchini every summer, but really, nothing ever tastes as good to me as when my mother makes it.

Serves 6

4 small organic zucchini

Sea salt and pepper

2–3 tablespoons extra-virgin olive oil

1 wedge of lemon, about ¼ lemon

1–2 tablespoons freshly grated Parmesan cheese

1. Slice the zucchini into ¼-inch rounds and separate the pieces. Place them in a bowl and sprinkle lightly with sea salt and pepper, tossing to coat. Heat a large skillet over medium heat, then add 1 tablespoon of the olive oil, swirling to coat the skillet. Arrange as many zucchini rounds as you can without overlapping.

2. Set a large plate by the stove. Cook the rounds for about 5–6 minutes, until the underside is golden brown. Using two forks or tongs, turn to cook the other side for about 5 minutes, until golden brown. Transfer the browned zucchini to a plate, overlapping slightly as you form a circular patter. Add another tablespoon of the olive oil and continue cooking the zucchini, adding another tablespoon of the oil if needed, until all the zucchini are pan-fried. Squeeze the lemon over the zucchini, then sprinkle with the Parmesan cheese. Taste for seasoning. Serve hot, at room temperature, or chilled.

Summer Squash with Heirloom Tomatoes and Sweet Onions V GF

Serve this lovely little side dish with any summer meal for a delicious dose of vitamins A and C and many protective antioxidants.

Serves 4–6

2 tablespoons extra-virgin olive oil

2 cloves fresh organic garlic, sliced

1 large sweet organic onion, cut into thick ribs, separated

2 small-medium organic yellow summer squash, cut into ½- to ¾-inch slices, separated

1 small-medium organic green zucchini, cut into ½- to ¾-inch slices

3 large organic heirloom tomatoes, cored and cut into thick wedges

Sea salt and pepper

1 tablespoon fresh organic oregano leaves

3 tablespoons white wine

4–6 large fresh organic basil leaves

Heat the oil in a large skillet over medium heat. Add the garlic, onion, yellow squash, zucchini, and tomatoes. Sprinkle with salt and pepper. Stir to coat the vegetables with the oil. Cover and cook, stirring occasionally, for about 10 minutes, until the zucchini is barely tender. Add the oregano and the white wine and stir to mix. Cook, uncovered, for about 3–5 minutes, stirring occasionally until the zucchini is tender. Stir in the basil leaves. Taste for seasonings.

> **"Wherever you live, you always have that special place. For me, Claire's is that place. There's a reason why Claire's Corner Copia is world renowned. As we locals like to say—you haven't been to New Haven, until you've been to Claire's."**
>
> **—Todd Leddy, a Claire's customer and Rena's husband (page 279)**

Maple-Roasted Butternut Squash V GF

This dish contains only two ingredients and it exemplifies the essence of goodness, pure and simple. It's naturally fat-free, loaded with vitamins A and C, and will please everyone.

Serves 6–8

2 medium local butternut squash

½ cup pure maple syrup

1. Center the oven racks. Preheat the oven to 425°F.

2. While carefully holding the squash secure on its side, and using a heavy, sharp knife, carefully trim off the top (stem part). This will make cutting it in half easier. Stand the squash upright, placing the knife on top of the center of the squash. Carefully using one hand to hold the knife handle and the other hand on top of the end, close to but not on the tip, push through the squash, cutting it in half. Use a spoon to scoop out the seeds and the fibrous part of the cavity.

3. Arrange the squash halves cut side up in a large, 2-inch-deep glass baking dish. Pour about 1½ tablespoons of the maple syrup into the cavity and about ½ tablespoon of the syrup over the entire top of each squash half. Pour hot water into the baking dish, around (not over) the squash, to a depth of about ½ inch. Tightly cover the pan with foil. Bake in the preheated oven for about 45 minutes, until the flesh and the skin of the squash are tender-soft when tested with a fork. Using a spoon, carefully "bathe" the top of each squash half with the syrup from the cavity, leaving very little syrup remaining in each cavity. Transfer the squash halves to a platter. Cut each half in half lengthwise and serve warm or at room temperature.

Tip: You can rinse the seeds and roast them. They are yummy and healthful just lightly salted, for a snack or a salad topping.

Mashed Butternut Squash and Apples V GF

Serve this side dish with any entree, and also think about leftovers for a healthful snack or a dessert.

Serve 6

2 medium butternut squash, peeled, seeded and coarsely chopped

4 organic apples, cored and coarsely chopped

3 tablespoons organic trans fat–free margarine or butter

3 tablespoons local, pure maple syrup

¼ teaspoon cinnamon

¼ teaspoon ground ginger

¼ cup walnut pieces

Sea salt

Bring a large covered pot of water to a boil over high heat. Add the butternut squash, cover, and cook for about 15 minutes or until not quite tender. Add the apples, cover, and cook for another 5 minutes, or until the squash is tender-soft. Drain and return the squash and apples to the cooking pot. Add the margarine, the maple syrup, cinnamon, ginger, walnut pieces, and a little sea salt. Using a potato masher, mash until chunky-smooth. Taste for seasonings.

Pumpkin Squash with Broccoli Rabe V GF

This colorful dish combines two of my all-time favorites, which also happen to be two of the healthiest vegetables, each loaded with vitamins A and C and sure to bring antioxidant power to your diet. Serve it as a side dish, or toss it with whole wheat pasta for a scrumptious entree.

Serves 4–6

3 tablespoons extra-virgin olive oil

4 large cloves garlic, chopped

1½ pounds pumpkin squash, cut into 1-inch cubes

1 small bunch broccoli rabe, bottom 3 inches of tough stems cut off and discarded, remaining rabe cut into 2-inch pieces

Salt and pepper, to taste

¼ cup water

¼ cup basil leaves

½ teaspoon crushed red pepper flakes

1 tablespoon fennel seeds

Heat the oil in a heavy pot over low-medium heat. Add the garlic and the squash. Stir to coat with the oil. Cover and cook for 10 minutes, stirring occasionally, until the squash just begins to soften. Add the broccoli rabe, salt, pepper, water, basil leaves, pepper flakes, and fennel seeds. Stir to mix. Cover and cook for about 15 minutes, stirring occasionally, until the squash is cooked to your preference. Taste for seasonings.

Mashed Potatoes and Carrots V GF

Local potatoes and carrots are just perfect for the best flavors possible. They need little embellishment; their pure flavors will shine through.

Serves 6

Sea salt

3 large, local organic potatoes, peeled and diced

3 medium local organic carrots, coarsely chopped

2 teaspoons extra-virgin olive oil

Pepper

Bring a medium covered pot of lightly salted water to a boil over high heat. Add the potatoes and the carrots. Cover and boil the vegetables for about 18 minutes, until tender-soft when pierced with a fork. Drain, then return the vegetables to the pot. Drizzle the olive oil evenly over the top. Sprinkle lightly with pepper. Using a potato masher, mash slightly, leaving some of the potatoes and carrots in tiny pieces for texture. Taste for seasonings.

Purple Potato Mash V GFO

Purple potatoes make a stunningly beautiful presentation, and they are a nice change from the usual white or golden-colored potatoes. And children just love the color!

Serves 4

3 medium purple potatoes, unpeeled

¼ cup plain soy milk

1 teaspoon extra-virgin olive oil

2 cloves garlic, coarsely chopped

Salt and pepper, to taste

Cook the potatoes in lightly salted boiling water for 25–30 minutes, or until soft when pierced with a fork. Meanwhile, measure the soy milk, olive oil, and garlic into a pot. Sprinkle with salt and pepper. Place over low heat and cook, just below a simmer, for about 15 minutes to soften the garlic, while the potatoes cook. Remove from the heat and set aside while the potatoes continue cooking. Before draining the potatoes, reserve ¼ cup of the cooking liquid. Drain the potatoes and turn into a bowl. Add the reserved cooking liquid, the heated soy milk mixture, and salt and pepper to taste. Mash to your favorite consistency. Taste for seasonings.

Tip: Use gluten-free soy milk to make this recipe gluten free.

Roasted Beets and Potatoes with Maple Syrup V GFO

This beautiful salad is perfect for any time you can source local beets and potatoes, particularly during the cooler months.

Serves 4

3 large unpeeled organic potatoes, cut into wedges

4 medium organic beets, peeled and cut into wedges

1 large yellow onion, cut into thick ribs, separated

4 large cloves garlic, peeled

2 large organic oranges, 1 juiced (reserve the juice) and 1 skinned and cut into wedges

2 tablespoons organic extra-virgin olive oil

¼ cup pure maple syrup

2 tablespoons organic balsamic vinegar

Sea salt and pepper, to taste

1. Preheat the oven to 400°F.

2. Place the cut potatoes, beets, onions, garlic, and orange wedges into a bowl. Toss to mix. In a separate bowl, whisk together the reserved orange juice, olive oil, maple syrup, vinegar, and a little salt and pepper. Taste for seasonings. Pour this over the cut vegetables. Toss to coat.

3. Spray a large rectangular glass baking dish with olive oil spray. Turn the vegetables into the prepared baking dish. Using a rubber spatula, scrape the bowl of the juices, pouring them evenly over the vegetables. Cover the baking dish tightly with foil. Bake the vegetables for about 30–45 minutes, or until they are fork-tender to your preference.

Tip: Use gluten-free balsamic vinegar to make this recipe gluten free.

Afghani Pickled Carrots V GF

One of the most wonderful things about being a part of a world-class city is getting to meet people from all parts of our world—and sharing their family recipes with others.

Serves 4–6

4 cups white vinegar

2 cups water

1 bay leaf

1 teaspoon raw sugar

1 pound locally grown organic carrots, trimmed and cut into ¼-inch diagonal slices

2 cloves organic garlic, cut into thin slices

1 organic jalapeño pepper, thinly sliced

2 tablespoons fresh dill, finely chopped

Sea salt, to taste

Measure the vinegar and water into a medium-size pot. Add the bay leaf and the sugar. Cover and bring to a boil over high heat. Add the carrots and the garlic. Cook at a boil for 3 minutes, then add the jalapeño pepper. Continue cooking for about 2 minutes, until crisp-tender. Remove from the heat and turn into a bowl. Let it sit out for about an hour, to cool to near room temperature, then stir in the dill and the sea salt to taste. Serve at room temperature or cover and refrigerate for up to 3 days, then serve chilled.

> I have thirty years of memories of good food, good times, and good friends at Claire's. Whatever job I have had in New Haven, I have always found my way there for delicious soup, warm bread, or a scrumptious salad, as well as an occasional piece of Lithuanian Coffee Cake. Claire's is like a beautiful quilt . . . the fabric weaves the best of New Haven, community, and family.
>
> —Dorothy Weston-Murphy, vice president of donor and professional services at the Community Foundation for Greater New Haven

Sweet Carrots V GF

This is a fat-free way to enjoy beta-carotene-rich carrots, and the vanilla adds just the right surprise.

Serves 6

8 medium carrots, cut on the diagonal into ¼-inch slices

3 cups organic apple juice or cider

2 bay leaves

2 tablespoons brown sugar

½ teaspoon cinnamon

1 teaspoon pure vanilla extract

Salt and pepper

1. Place the carrots in a small pot. Add the apple juice, bay leaves, brown sugar, and cinnamon. Stir to combine. Cover and bring to a boil over high heat, then lower the heat to medium and remove the cover. Cook at a low boil, uncovered, for about 4 minutes, until just fork-tender. Stir in the vanilla, and add salt and pepper to taste. Taste for seasonings.

2. Using a slotted spoon, transfer the carrots to a shallow bowl. Raise the heat to medium-high and bring the cooking liquid to a boil. Cook at a medium boil for about 15 minutes, until the liquid reduces into a syrupy consistency. Remove the bay leaves. Pour this liquid over the carrots.

Sweet Onions, New York City Style V GF

I love this topping for my tofu dogs. It reminds me of the topping offered by the hot dog vendors in New York. My husband says it's every bit as delicious!

Makes about 4 cups

2 teaspoons extra-virgin olive oil

3 cloves garlic, coarsely chopped

2 large, sweet onions, cut in half, then into thick ribs, and separated

6 scallions, coarsely chopped

Salt and pepper

1 tablespoon paprika

1 tablespoon tomato paste

½ cup water

1 teaspoon naturally milled cane sugar, honey, or maple syrup

Heat the oil in a 4-quart pot over low-medium heat. Add the garlic, onions, scallions, and salt and pepper to taste. Stir to coat the onions with the oil. Cover and cook for 10 minutes, stirring occasionally, until the onions are softened and have released some of their liquids. Stir in the paprika, tomato paste, water, and sugar, mixing well to combine. Cover and continue cooking, stirring occasionally, for an additional 20 minutes, or until the onions are soft. Taste for seasonings.

Braised Kale, Carrots, and Shiitake Mushrooms V GF

If there is a healthier combination, I don't know of it. And it's delicious—easy to eat.

Serves 4

1 bunch (about 1¼ pounds) organic kale

2 tablespoons extra-virgin olive oil

5 cloves garlic, sliced

4 medium carrots, cut on the diagonal into ¼-inch slices

15 medium shiitake mushrooms (about 4 ounces), stems removed and caps sliced into thirds

Sea salt

White pepper

½ teaspoon crushed red pepper flakes, divided

2 tablespoons freshly squeezed lemon juice (about ½ lemon)

1. Set a large bowl in the sink and fill it two-thirds with cool water.

2. Hold 1 stalk of kale at a time in your hand and fold the leaves in half lengthwise, over the stem. Using your other hand, starting at the top of the stem, gently but firmly tug the leaves down and away from the stem. Using both hands, tear the leaves into medium-size pieces and drop them into the bowl of water. Discard the stripped stems or save them for a broth. Repeat with the remaining stalks of kale.

3. Set a large bowl near the sink. Swish the kale around in the prepared bowl of water to remove any dirt. Using your hands, lift out a double handful of kale. Shake off the excess water, allowing most of the water to drip into the sink, leaving just the water that clings to the leaves. Set this in the bowl you put by the sink. Lift out and shake off excess water from the remaining kale. Set aside.

4. Heat the olive oil in a heavy pot over medium heat. Add the garlic, carrots, and the shiitake mushrooms. Sprinkle lightly with sea salt, white pepper, and ¼ teaspoon of the red pepper flakes. Add the kale and sprinkle lightly with sea salt, white pepper, and the remaining ¼ teaspoon red pepper flakes. Cover the pan. Cook, covered for 10–12 minutes, until the kale is wilted. Using two wooden spoons, toss the vegetables to combine. Cover and continue cooking for about 5 minutes, or until the kale is tender to your preference. Drizzle the lemon juice over the top of the vegetables and toss lightly to coat. Taste for seasoning.

Kale

Kale is a "super-food"—that is, it's a food that is loaded with nutrients. This leafy green vegetable is available nearly year round, and whether you choose the curly green kale, mixed leaf kale, or the Toscano kale, it's loaded with beta-carotene, calcium, folate, iron, and fiber, as well as the antioxidant vitamins A, C, and E—nutrients we can all use to help build our immune systems.

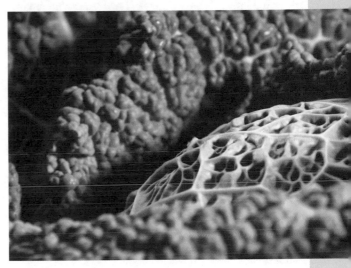

Kale is a member of the cabbage family so it might protect us from some cancers. If you are not yet a fan, I suggest you come on board to this wonderful leafy green vegetable. Besides, it's a joy to use. You can eat it raw in a salad. Just remove the thick stem, then slice the leaves into thin strips, add some raisins and chopped walnuts, and toss it with a little toasted sesame oil, fresh lemon juice, and sea salt. You'll end up with a beautiful and delicious salad. You can chop the kale and add it to any bean and/or vegetable soups, any stir-fry or roasted vegetables—it's that versatile. You'll find kale in the produce section of most supermarkets and farm markets.

When buying kale, look for deep, dark green leaves that are not yellow or wilted—a sign that it is past its prime. When you get it home, wrap it in a kitchen towel and refrigerate for up to 3 days. Always wash the leaves well before using in lots of cool water with as many changes as needed to remove any grit. (Greens can be gritty, especially when they've been harvested during rain.) Please consider growing kale in your garden this summer. It's a vegetable to be reckoned with!

Braised Swiss Chard V GF

Swiss chard is a member of the beet family. It has large green, red-tinged, or rainbow-color crinkly leaves, depending on the variety, and pale green celery-like stalks. The entire leaf and stalk are edible, but the stalks should be cooked longer than the tender leaves. Avoid wilted leaves and bunches with any yellow spots, which are telltale signs of aging. Like other vegetables, try to use Swiss chard the day you buy it, or store it gently wrapped in a clean kitchen towel in the refrigerator for up to 3 days. Swiss chard is a cruciferous vegetable and a good source of antioxidants, vitamins A and C, and iron. Your body metabolizes iron better when combined with vitamin C, so try adding a squeeze of fresh lemon or orange juice for a brighter flavor and extra antioxidants.

Serves 4–6

---

2 tablespoons extra-virgin olive oil

2 cloves local organic garlic, sliced

1 local organic onion, cut into thick ribs, separated

1 bunch local organic Swiss chard, about ¾ pound, well washed and drained, stems separated and cut into ½-inch pieces, and leaves coarsely chopped and stored separately

Sea salt and pepper

1 teaspoon smoked paprika

2 tablespoons freshly squeezed organic orange juice (from about ½ orange)

Heat the oil in a large skillet over medium-high heat. Add the garlic, onion, and chopped Swiss chard stems. Sprinkle lightly with sea salt and pepper. Stir to coat. Cook for about 4 minutes, stirring frequently until the stems have softened. Add the chopped Swiss chard leaves and the smoked paprika. Stir well to combine. Cook for about 2 minutes, stirring frequently until the leaves are tender to your preference. Stir in the orange juice. Taste for seasonings.

Moroccan Sautéed Organic Spinach with Dried Apricots, Pine Nuts, and Preserved Lemon

The sweet and tart combination is magic! Use Preserved Organic Lemons (page 307) for the lemon peel.

Serves 3–4

2 teaspoons extra-virgin olive oil

3 cloves organic garlic, sliced

7 ounces organic baby spinach, about 3 cups

¼ teaspoon dried cumin

½ teaspoon smoked paprika

2 tablespoons pine nuts

2 dried apricots, cut into thin strips

Preserved lemon peel from ¼ preserved lemon, cut into very thin strips

Sea salt

Heat the oil in a large skillet over medium heat. Add the garlic and cook for about 2 minutes, stirring frequently, until the garlic softens and is golden but not burned. Add the spinach, cumin, paprika, pine nuts, and apricot strips. Using tongs, turn the spinach to coat with the oil. Cook for about 2 minutes, stirring frequently, until the spinach wilts. Stir in the preserved lemon peel. Taste for seasoning before adding salt, if needed.

Sauté of Greens with Garlic Chips V GF

Serve this delicious and vitamin-rich side dish (loaded with vitamins A and C) with any entree, or toss it with cooked white beans and pasta, and maybe a little grated Asiago cheese, for a lovely entree.

Serves 4–6

1 small head escarole

1 small bunch Toscano or other kale

3 tablespoons extra-virgin olive oil

5 large cloves garlic, sliced

¼ teaspoon crushed red pepper flakes

¼ cup raisins

2 tablespoons capers, drained

Salt and pepper, to taste

1 tablespoon grated orange zest

1. Cut off and discard the bottom 1 inch of the escarole, then tear the leaves in half. Cut off and discard the tough stems from the kale, then tear the leaves in half. Wash the escarole and kale in plenty of water to remove any sand, changing the water as many times as needed until no grit or sand remains. Drain. Heat the oil in a heavy pot over low-medium heat. Add the garlic and cook for about 1 minute until just golden. Add the red pepper flakes, raisins, and capers. Add the escarole and kale leaves with any water clinging to their leaves. Sprinkle with salt and pepper. Using tongs, turn the greens to coat with the oil.

2. Cover and cook, using the tongs to turn the greens frequently until they shrink and are tender to your preference, about 10 minutes. Stir in the grated orange zest. Taste for seasonings.

Sautéed Escarole with Sun-Dried Tomatoes V GF

Escarole is a member of the endive family and it has big, dark green leaves with pale yellow inner leaves. My mother always reserved the inner leaves for salads. She would dress them with extra-virgin olive oil and freshly squeezed lemon juice, add a little salt, and that's it! Escarole has a mild, slightly lemony flavor and it is rich in vitamin A and fiber.

Serves 6

4 tablespoons extra-virgin olive oil

6 large cloves garlic, sliced

2 shallots, sliced

2 medium yellow onions, cut in half, then into thin ribs

2 sun-dried tomatoes, cut into thin strips

½ teaspoon crushed red pepper flakes

1 teaspoon fennel seeds

Salt and pepper

2 large heads escarole or chicory, well washed and coarsely chopped

1. Heat the olive oil in a large, deep skillet over medium heat. Add the garlic, shallots, onions, and sun-dried tomatoes, the red pepper flakes, and fennel seeds. Sprinkle lightly with salt and pepper.

2. Cook for about 5 minutes, stirring occasionally, until the onions have softened. Add the escarole, and sprinkle lightly with salt and pepper. Cover and cook for about 5 minutes, then using tongs, turn the escarole to coat with the oil. Cover and continue cooking for about another 10 minutes, stirring occasionally, until the escarole is tender to your liking. Taste for seasonings.

> "Claire's Corner Copia represents all that is wonderful about local businesses: Claire Criscuolo has a deep love for New Haven, a broad acquaintance with its people, and a strong commitment to the welfare of both. Claire's both draws from and contributes to the strength of New Haven. It's one of those places you return to when you want to recapture your times in New Haven, and one of the places you first go when you are getting to know the place. Claire's is living proof that a business can be local, green, socially responsible, profitable, and cherished by its customers and business partners alike."
>
> **—Abigail Rider, a Claire's devotee**

Orange and Sesame Roasted Brussels Sprouts V GF

Brussels sprouts are so healthy and cute, too. The orange and sesame combination adds a lovely accent to the strong cabbage flavor of the brussels sprouts. Even our customers who claim not to like brussels sprouts enjoy these.

Serves 4–6

16 medium brussels sprouts
(about ¾ pound)

Juice from 1 seedless orange
(about ⅓ cup)

2 teaspoons sesame oil

Sea salt and pepper

1. Center the oven rack. Preheat the oven to 450°F.

2. Rinse and then drain the brussels sprouts. Trim a thin slice of the dry bottom from the brussels sprouts, then turn them into a bowl. Drizzle the orange juice and the sesame oil evenly over the brussels sprouts. Sprinkle with sea salt and pepper. Toss to coat. Spray a glass baking dish with olive oil spray. Turn the brussels sprouts and the juices into the prepared baking dish.

3. Bake in the preheated oven for about 20 minutes, using tongs to turn them once or twice during roasting for even doneness. Test using a paring knife inserted into the center of one brussels sprout; it should be just tender and have a nice glazed exterior. Serve hot or chilled.

Stewed String Beans with Tomatoes

Serve this lovely one-dish supper with good crusty Italian bread to sop up the luscious juices.

Serves 6

3 tablespoons extra-virgin olive oil

3 large cloves garlic, sliced

1 large yellow onion, cut into thick ribs

¾ pound string beans, stems trimmed, cut in half

1 ripe tomato, coarsely chopped, including juices

Sea salt and pepper

1 6-ounce can tomato paste

3 cups water

⅛ teaspoon ground cloves

⅛ teaspoon ground cayenne pepper

5 large fresh basil leaves

1. Heat the oil in a heavy 4-quart pot over medium heat. Add the garlic, onion, string beans, tomato, salt, and pepper. Stir well to coat with the oil. Cover and cook, stirring occasionally, for 10 minutes, or until the vegetables have softened and released some of their juices.

2. Add the tomato paste, water, cloves, and the cayenne, stirring well to mix thoroughly. Coarsely chop the basil, then stir it into the string bean mixture.

3. Cover and bring to a medium-high boil. Cook, stirring occasionally, for 15 to 20 minutes, or until the string beans are tender. Taste for seasonings.

Roasted Tri-Color Bell Peppers V GF

I love roasted bell peppers and make them nearly every Saturday, my day off. Frank and I eat them for lunch or before dinner, with some Italian bread and chunks of pecorino Romano cheese. Or sometimes I'll puree them in the processor and toss them over penne pasta for a room-temperature pasta dish. The peppers keep well for up to 3 days in the refrigerator, so why not make a double batch?

Serves 6–8

1 each large organic red, yellow, and orange peppers (about ½ pound each)

3 small cloves garlic, cut into thin slices

2 teaspoons extra-virgin olive oil

2 tablespoons small capers, rinsed, and squeezed with your hand to remove excess liquid

1 teaspoon dried oregano

Sea salt and pepper

Tip: Don't worry if a little non-charred skin is left behind, it's fine, and it's also rich in fiber.

1. Center your oven rack and preheat the broiler to high.

2. Rinse the peppers. Set them on their side on a cookie sheet lined with parchment paper, allowing at least an inch in between them for even broiling. Broil for about 5 minutes if you keep the oven door closed or about 15–20 minutes if you broil with the oven door ajar. The outside of the skin should be blackened, somewhat charred, and blistered, fairly uniformly; it should not be completely charred deep within the flesh of the peppers. Using long tongs (you might want to wear mitts, too), turn the peppers over to blacken the other side for about 5–10 minutes. Continue turning the peppers to blacken the skin on all sides, including the bottom and the top of the peppers, for about 5 minutes or so per side. Remove the peppers from the oven. Using the tongs, transfer them to a large bowl. Cover the bowl with a kitchen towel (over the bowl, not touching the peppers, then top with a tight-fitting plate to keep the steam from the peppers in the bowl. This will "cook" the peppers, making them tender, and it will help loosen the charred skin, making for easier removal.

3. After about 20 minutes, or when the peppers are cool enough to handle, transfer 1 pepper at a time to a plate. Gently twist the stem to loosen the top. Try to lift out the stem and as much of the seed "pouch" as you can. Discard the stem and the seeds. Using your fingers, peel back and slip off as much of the charred skin as you can, and use a paring knife to remove the remaining skin. Using your fingers, tear the pepper in half. Remove and discard any seeds and ribs, as they are bitter-tasting. Tear each half into strips, about ¼ to ½ inch wide, and put them in a shallow bowl. Repeat the process with the remaining peppers. Add the garlic, olive oil, capers, and oregano, then sprinkle lightly with sea salt and pepper. Using two wooden spoons, toss to combine. Taste for seasonings.

Champagne Vinegar-Roasted Baby Bellas V GF

The vinegar adds just the right edge to the rustic flavor of baby portobellos, and mushrooms are so rich in antioxidants that there's every reason to enjoy them as often as possible. And, these are also delicious served chilled, which makes them perfect to take along on a picnic at your local green during a concert.

Serves 4

1 pound baby portobello mushrooms (about 16 mushrooms)

2 teaspoons avocado oil or extra-virgin olive oil

1 tablespoon champagne vinegar

Sea salt and pepper

1. Center the oven rack. Preheat the oven to 450°F.

2. Rinse the mushrooms to remove any sand. Drain and turn into a bowl. Drizzle the oil and the vinegar evenly over the mushrooms, then sprinkle them with sea salt and pepper. Toss to coat. Spray a glass baking dish with olive oil spray. Turn the mushrooms and the juices into the prepared baking dish. Bake in the preheated oven for about 12–14 minutes, until fork-tender. When cooled enough to taste, taste for seasonings. Serve hot or chilled.

Baked Beans V

Homemade baked beans taste so much better than any store-bought beans. You can make them on your day off and reheat them within 3 days for convenience in a pinch.

Serves 6

1 12-ounce can organic Great Northern beans

1 tablespoon extra-virgin olive oil

1 medium sweet organic onion, coarsely chopped

3 strips meatless smoked bacon, chopped

2 tablespoons organic brown sugar

¼ cup organic blackstrap molasses

2 tablespoons pure maple syrup

1 tablespoon coarse deli mustard, or other

1 organic orange, Valencia or other

Sea salt and pepper

1. Preheat the oven to 350°F.

2. Drain the beans and rinse under cold water, then drain again. Turn them into a bowl. Add the olive oil, chopped onion, meatless bacon, brown sugar, molasses, maple syrup, and mustard. Grate the zest from about one-third of the orange and add about a tablespoon of the orange zest to the bowl. Into a separate bowl, squeeze the juice from the orange, picking out any seeds, then add the juice to the bowl with the beans. Sprinkle lightly with sea salt and pepper. Toss well, using two wooden spoons to combine. Taste for seasonings.

3. Spray a 3-quart glass baking dish with olive oil or organic canola oil spray. Turn the bean mixture into the prepared baking dish. Cover the dish tightly with foil. Bake in the preheated oven for about 45 minutes, until beans are hot and bubbling.

Black Beans and Peppers in Rum Barbecue Sauce ⅴ

Our customers love black beans, and we're always trying new ways to serve them. This is a lovely combination that pairs nicely with tofu dogs cooked on the grill or pan-fried in a little olive oil.

Serves 6

2 tablespoons extra-virgin olive oil

1 large sweet onion, cut into ½-inch ribs

3 large organic bell peppers, red and yellow, seeded and cut into large dice

2 strips smoked soy bacon, chopped

¼ cup water

1 12-ounce can organic black beans, drained

3 tablespoons rum (optional)

3 tablespoons organic brown sugar

1 cup bottled organic barbecue sauce

Salt and pepper, to taste

Heat the olive oil in a large skillet over medium-high heat. Add the onion, peppers, and soy bacon strips. Cover and cook for about 10 minutes, stirring frequently, until the onions and peppers are barely tender. Add the water and stir in the black beans, rum (if using), brown sugar, and barbecue sauce, mixing well to combine. Stir in salt and pepper to taste. Continue cooking, uncovered, for about 5–7 minutes, stirring occasionally until the beans are heated through and the sauce thickens slightly. Taste for seasonings.

Hearty Chili Dog Topping V GFO

For a delicious and satisfying entree, just double the recipe and serve it with baked tortilla chips or warm corn or flour tortillas.

Makes about 5 cups

2 teaspoons extra-virgin olive oil

1 medium sweet onion, coarsely chopped

4 cloves garlic, coarsely chopped

2 medium bell peppers, seeded and coarsely chopped

1 large poblano chile or other minimally hot green pepper, seeded and coarsely chopped

1 small jalapeño pepper, finely chopped

Salt and pepper, to taste

1 16-ounce can vegetarian baked beans

¼ cup bottled barbecue sauce

2 tablespoons Dijon mustard

2 veggie burgers, crumbled (any brand found in the produce section or the frozen foods section of your supermarket is fine)

Heat the oil in a 4-quart pot over low-medium heat. Add the onion, garlic, peppers, salt, and pepper to taste. Cover and cook, stirring occasionally, for about 15 minutes, until the vegetables are just tender and have released some of their liquids. Add the baked beans, barbecue sauce, mustard, and crumbled veggie burgers. Stir well to combine. Cover and continue cooking for about 3 minutes, stirring occasionally until heated through. Taste for seasonings.

Tip: Use gluten-free beans and barbecue sauce to make this recipe gluten free.

Red Cabbage and Onion Sauerkraut V GF

Make this topping for your next cookout and enjoy the flavors while knowing that you're eating a healthful dose of antioxidants, too.

Makes about 8 cups

2 teaspoons extra-virgin olive oil

1 medium red onion, cut in half and sliced thin

½ small head red cabbage, cut in half, cored, and sliced thin

1 tablespoon whole caraway seeds

Salt and pepper

¼ cup Dijon mustard

2 pounds sauerkraut, packaged or canned, including juice

Heat the oil in a 4-quart pot over medium heat. Add the red onion, cabbage, caraway seeds, and a little salt and pepper. (Make sure you use only a little salt; the sauerkraut that you'll be adding later is salty.) Stir to coat the vegetables with the oil. Cover and cook for about 10 minutes, stirring occasionally until the cabbage and onions are wilted but still have a crunch. Stir in the mustard, mixing well. Add the sauerkraut and stir to combine. Cover and continue cooking for about 4 minutes, stirring occasionally, until heated through. Taste for seasonings.

Sweet and Sour Red Cabbage V GF

Cabbage is so healthful, and when you pair it with tomatoes, lemons, and raisins, the flavors and healthful ingredients multiply.

Serves 6–8

3 tablespoons extra-virgin olive oil

4 medium sweet onions, cut in half, then crosswise into thick ribs, separated

1 large head red cabbage, cut into quarters, cored, then cut into ½-inch slices

1 28-ounce can organic chopped tomatoes in juice

1½ cups water

½ cup firmly packed brown sugar

Juice of 2 lemons (about $1/3$ cup juice)

½ cup organic raisins

Salt and pepper

Heat the oil in a large pot over low-medium heat. Add the onions and cabbage. Stir well to coat with the oil. Cover and cook for 10 minutes, stirring occasionally, until the onions and cabbage are wilted. Add the tomatoes and water. Stir well to combine. Raise the heat to high. Cover and bring to a boil, then lower the heat to low-medium and continue cooking, covered, for about 30 minutes, stirring occasionally. Stir in the brown sugar, lemon juice, raisins, salt, and pepper to taste. Mix well to combine. Taste for seasonings.

Vegetable and Fruit Chow Chow V GF

For this recipe, you may find it helpful to work with a julienne peeler, which makes easy work of preparing julienne carrots and other vegetables. You can buy a julienne peeler in most kitchen-ware shops.

Makes about 4 quarts

1 quart apple cider vinegar

½ cup granulated sugar

¼ teaspoon sea salt

Freshly ground black pepper, to taste

5 whole cloves

1 large head Savoy cabbage

3 carrots

3 ears sweet corn, kernels cut, about 3 cups

1 medium red onion

1 large organic red bell pepper

¼ large pineapple

1. Measure the cider vinegar, sugar, sea salt, pepper, and cloves into a pot. Bring to a simmer over medium heat, stirring occasionally until the sugar dissolves.

2. Meanwhile, core, slice, and coarsely chop the cabbage. Add this to a large bowl. Cut the carrots into thin julienne slices and add them to the bowl. Cut the kernels from the ears of corn and add them to the bowl. Peel and cut the onion in half, then cut each half into thin slices and separate them; add them to the bowl. Seed and coarsely chop the pepper and add to the bowl. Trim the pineapple, then cut into slices; cut the slices into small cubes and add them and any juices to the bowl. Using your hands or two wooden spoons, toss the vegetables and pineapple to combine.

3. Once the cider vinegar brine is hot and the sugar is dissolved, pour it evenly over the tossed vegetables and pineapple. Using two wooden spoons, toss to coat thoroughly. Taste for seasonings. Serve warm or cool to room temperature, tossing frequently to coat with the brine. After it has cooled to room temperature, cover and store in the refrigerator for up to a month. Toss again just before serving.

Preserved Lemons

Lemons are indispensable in the kitchen. When you add the freshly grated yellow zest or the freshly squeezed juice of a lemon to foods, you add a bright, fresh citrus flavor and a healthful dose of vitamin C. There are countless ways to use lemons: in a dressing or a sauce, in a dip or a sandwich spread, in a fruit smoothie, or in a cupcake batter or frosting. And summers wouldn't be the same without fresh lemonade, would

they? Lemons have a subtle yet distinctive impact on so many foods.

But lemons have another side, too. They can be preserved in salt and take on a completely different flavor and texture. This method has been used in Moroccan and African cooking for hundreds of years. It's so easy to preserve lemons and much less expensive than buying them already preserved. You simply salt washed lemons that have been cut into wedges and pack them into a clean jar. It takes about a month for the lemons to preserve, but once you preserve a jar, you can leave it in your refrigerator to use as needed, for up to 6 months.

The flavor is so potent that just a little bit of the preserved skin of the lemon goes a long way. I like to preserve lemons when they are a little lower in price, usually during July and August. Slice off the skin from about a quarter of a preserved lemon and cut it into very thin slices. Add this to any green salad or a simple rice dish, couscous, pasta salad, or potato salad, and you'll give the dish an interesting flavor that people usually cannot identify, but often find really delicious. I like to add thin slices of preserved lemon to Moroccan Sautéed Organic Spinach with Dried Apricots, Pine Nuts, and Preserved Lemon (page 295).

Preserved Organic Lemons V GF

These preserved lemons last for 6 months. The flavor is potent, so use no more than a wedge per 4 servings at first; you can always add more to your taste.

Makes 9 preserved lemons

9 organic lemons

3 cups plus 2 tablespoons salt

Tip: Experiment with using the skin and the pulp. Some people prefer to rinse the lemon before using, but I like it as is. Just remember to taste the food you add it to before adding any salt.

1. Wash and dry a glass jar with a tight-fitting lid. Set a bowl and a ⅓-cup measure on the counter where you will be working. Wash and dry the lemons. Hold a lemon upright. Using a sharp knife, carefully cut the lemon in half, but not all the way through. Cut about three-fourths of the way; you want to create a "blossom," not separate wedges. (Don't fret if you do cut all the way through—it will still work; just try not to cut through the next one.) Cut the lemon in half again, going three-fourths of the way through, not all the way. You'll have 4 attached wedges like a "blossom." Measure ⅓ cup of salt. Hold the cut lemon over the bowl and carefully pour most of the salt, a little at a time, over the cut sides of the lemon wedges, allowing excess to fall into the bowl. Pour the remaining salt, also using any salt that has fallen into the bowl, over the outside of the lemon. Place the salted lemon into the clean jar, laying it on its side and pushing slightly to allow some of the juice to fall into the jar.

2. Repeat the process with 7 more lemons, saving the last one. Cut the last lemon into the same 4-wedge "blossom" as the others, but before salting it, squeeze the juice into the jar, over the other salted lemons. Now salt the final lemon and add it to the jar. Pour about 2 tablespoons of the remaining salt over the salted lemons in the jar. Cover tightly and turn the jar upside down to allow the juices to flow over the lemons.

3. Label and date the jar. Leave the jar on the counter for a day, turning it over whenever you pass by it or think of it, at least three times. The next day, put the jar in the refrigerator. Store for about 30 days, turning it over to distribute the juices once or twice a day, or more if you remember. After 30 days, the lemons will darken slightly, their skin will soften, and you can begin to enjoy them in your favorite foods.

desserts

When my dear friend Phyllis Jacks was working on her PhD, she learned to cross-stitch and I was one of the lucky ones to get a piece she made. It had the message that remains our mantra: Life is uncertain, eat dessert first!

And everyone who comes to Claire's knows that our desserts are not to be missed. There is a counter that runs the length of most of the restaurant, and it's covered with cakes, cookies, pies, cobblers, tarts, scones, muffins, sweet breads, and so many other baked goods that we make in house and bake all day and evening. Sometimes a cake right from the oven gets bought off the shelf before it has a chance to cool enough for us to frost, so we give the customer the frosting on the side. And, because we fully believe that there is room for indulgence in every healthy diet, we have a lot of fun baking and decorating our desserts. Everyone on staff takes part in this, and often our customers can watch the process and even taste the frostings and fillings while we're making them. It's not unusual for someone to pass around "taster sticks" with a new frosting or filling we're trying. After all, it's for them and we love their input. And who doesn't like to taste?

Lithuanian Coffee Cake is our signature cake. It's a streusel-filled sour cream coffee cake that we've been making for decades. We get letters and comments about "Lithuanian Coffee Cake love" all the time, and we love this! Once, when I asked long-time staffer Brenna Harvey if she ever tires of our Lithuanian Coffee Cake, she responded with "Lithuanian Coffee Cake is a love whose flame cannot die." I guess that says a lot. I know I still love the cake, too.

I think part of the reason that our desserts are so popular is because we follow our same commitment to quality and love that we use in everything else we do at Claire's. We use King Arthur flour, pure butter, pure vanilla, organic eggs, and other fine ingredients even when the costs are really high—we just do.

So many parents order cupcakes and cakes for birthday celebrations for their children, and they tell us it's because we use the same care and love that they would. I am forever proud of this.

I hope you'll enjoy baking treats from Claire's and sharing these desserts with people you love. That's how we do it at Claire's.

Barley, Pumpkin, and Blueberry Pudding V

This is a delicious pudding that is also loaded with beta-carotene and many other rich antioxidants.

Serves 6

1 16-ounce can (about 2 cups) pumpkin

½ cup firmly packed brown sugar

1 teaspoon cinnamon

½ teaspoon ground cardamom

1 teaspoon almond extract

¼ teaspoon ground nutmeg

6 organic eggs or equivalent egg substitute

4 cups organic dairy or soy milk

1 cup cooked hulled barley

¼ cup dried blueberries

1. Preheat oven to 350°F.

2. Combine the pumpkin, brown sugar, cinnamon, cardamom, almond extract, and nutmeg in a large bowl. Mix thoroughly with a whisk. Add the eggs and soy milk, and whisk to blend. Add the cooked barley and the blueberries. Spray a 3-quart glass baking dish with canola oil spray. Turn the barley pudding into a prepared dish, using a rubber spatula to scrape the bowl.

3. Bake in the preheated oven for about 1½ hours until set. Test for doneness by scooping a spoonful of pudding from the center. The eggs should be fully cooked and set. Serve warm or chilled.

Dairy-Free Lemon Mousse with Fresh Berries V

"Creamy and rich, smooth and delicious" is how our customers at Claire's Corner Copia describe this wonderful dessert. "Quick and easy" are the words you'll add. And the bright lemon flavor is a perfect way to celebrate spring and Earth Day.

Serves 4 (¹/₂-cup servings)

½ cup organic granulated sugar

½ cup organic soy milk

2 tablespoons cornstarch

Finely grated zest from 1 organic lemon

3 tablespoons fresh lemon juice (from about 1 lemon)

1 12-ounce package plain silken organic tofu, drained

½ pint organic raspberries

Honey for drizzling

Measure the sugar, soy milk, and cornstarch into a small pot and whisk well to mix. Place over a low-medium heat for a few minutes, whisking constantly, until it thickens. Remove from the heat and whisk in the lemon zest and lemon juice. Place the tofu in a blender cup. Add the thickened soy milk mixture, using a rubber spatula to scrape the pot. Cover and blend on high speed for 15 seconds or until smooth, stopping to scrape the sides as needed. Turn into dessert cups, using a rubber spatula to scrape the sides of the blender cup. Serve warm or refrigerate to chill before serving. To serve, scatter raspberries over the top and drizzle with honey.

Hot Mulled Cider V GF

Fall is the time to buy freshly pressed cider from locally grown apples. Enjoy with warm muffins on a cool fall afternoon.

Makes a gallon

1 gallon freshly pressed local cider

1 cinnamon stick

2 whole cloves

1 1-inch piece fresh ginger, peeled and finely minced

Combine the ingredients in a pot and heat to just boiling over high heat. Serve the hot cider immediately or cool to room temperature and store in the refrigerator for up to 3 days, heating a cupful as needed.

Fresh Blueberry Lemonade V GF

When I was growing up, my mother always kept dozens of lemons on hand and would make us fresh lemonade. As a result, I'm a big fan of lemonade. At Claire's we initially reserved lemonade for summers only, but then we realized that if we drink cold water during the winter, why not lemonade?

Makes about 1 quart

1/3 cup local honey

1 cup hot water

1 cup local blueberries

¾ cup freshly squeezed lemon juice, from about 4 lemons

4 ice cubes, plus additional for serving

2½ cups cold water

Measure the honey and hot water into a blender cup. Cover and blend on high speed for 15 seconds or until well blended. Add the blueberries, lemon juice, and 4 of the ice cubes. Cover and blend on high speed for about 45 seconds until well blended. Pour into a pitcher, then stir in the remaining cold water. Serve over additional ice cubes.

Frozen Strawberry Lemonade V GF

Bump up the flavor and the vitamin C with this refreshing and incredibly delicious summer drink! It will be the hit at every party, too.

Serves 6

½ cup raw sugar

½ cup hot water

Juice of 8 lemons (about 1½ cups)

8 cups cold water

1 quart frozen strawberries

6 mint leaves

Place the sugar and the hot water in a blender cup. Cover and blend on high speed for about 10 seconds to dissolve the sugar. Add the lemon juice and the cold water. Cover and blend for a few seconds to mix. Add the frozen strawberries, cover, and blend for about 20 seconds until the mixture is icy and like slush. Pour/spoon into stemmed glasses. Garnish each with a mint leaf.

Anonna's Limoncello V GFO

For this recipe, I use 2-cup Ball jars; they're easy to shake because of their good seals, and also, I think they're adorable.

Makes a little less than a quart

6 organic lemons, washed

1¾ cups grain alcohol

2 cups granulated organic sugar

2 cups water

Tip: Use gluten-free alcohol to make this recipe gluten free.

1. Using a sharp hand peeler, remove the rind from the lemons, peeling off as little of the white pith as possible. (Don't worry, a little won't matter much.)

2. Place the peel in a clean 2-cup jar that has a tight-fitting lid, packing lightly. Pour the grain alcohol over the peel to cover completely, filling the jar to the top. Cover tightly. Label and date the jar. Set on the counter in a place where you'll remember to shake it at least a few times a day. (I leave mine by the sink.) Give the jar a shake, turning it upside down, at least twice a day, for 2 weeks or longer. I've left a batch macerating (steeping) for up to 2 months—the longer you leave it, the stronger the lemon flavor, but 2 weeks will produce a good flavor, too. As the days pass, you'll notice that the color of the alcohol changes from clear to a cloudy pale yellow color. Be patient. After 2 weeks to 2 months, the lemons will have flavored the alcohol and you can proceed with the recipe.

3. Measure the granulated sugar and the water into a small pot and set it over a high heat. Bring it to a boil, stirring occasionally until the sugar is dissolved. Remove the pot of sugar-water (the mixture is called simple syrup) from the stove and set it on a trivet on the counter to cool to room temperature. When cool, set a strainer over a medium-sized bowl. Pour the contents of the jar (the lemon peel and alcohol) into the strainer so that the alcohol drains into the bowl and the peel stays in the strainer. Pour the simple syrup over the peel and allow it to sit, draining, for a few minutes. Using the back of a wooden spoon, press out as much alcohol and simple syrup as you can. You now have limoncello. You can discard the peels or you can candy them—but remember, they're not for kids!

4. Using a whisk, beat the limoncello to completely combine. Taste it for sweetness. It's always as I like it, but if you prefer a sweeter version, you can always make a little more simple syrup, cool it, and add it to the limoncello. Pour your limoncello into clean jars or bottles. Label and date the jars. It's ready right now, but if you can wait a couple of weeks, the flavors will meld nicely. Store your limoncello in the freezer because it's best when it's icy cold.

Limoncello

Smells can evoke vivid memories. For me, the smell of lemons transports me back to my grandmother's house, Anonna's, a place where she surrounded us with love. In Anonna's house, like my mom's, love was always served on plates and in cups and in the kitchen. I do the same thing today at home and in my profession. At Anonna's house I first

discovered limoncello, the classic drink that my grandmother made every year, the drink made famous in Amalfi, Italy, and loved throughout the world.

These days I make Christmas and Hanukkah gifts of my beloved limoncello, an Italian liquor made using fresh lemon peels, grain alcohol, and simple syrup (a mixture of sugar dissolved in boiling water). Limoncello makes a wonderful and thoughtful present and, as with everything else homemade, always tastes better than a store-bought counterpart. You can buy pretty bottles for your limoncello, tie each with a ribbon, and add a homemade gift tag. Present a bottle as a host/hostess gift, and for everyone else who you think will enjoy this lovely drink. (Don't forget to keep a bottle for yourself.) Store limoncello in the freezer (it won't freeze because of the high alcohol content) and drink it icy cold. Limoncello is also delicious when brushed on slices of sponge cake, with a dollop of whipped cream on top and a sprinkling of chopped almonds and pomegranate seeds for a lovely holiday dessert.

Please note that limoncello is powerful stuff, and you should serve it in little cordial glasses or demitasse cups, and only in sensible servings—say, no more than 2 ounces—because it's so strong.

Enjoy sending out this delicious, easily made gift to friends and family. I hope that, as it does for me, limoncello stirs lovely memories in all of you.

Dark Chocolate–Dipped Walnut-Coated Apricots VO GFO

Feel the dried apricots in their bag before buying, and choose a bag with apricots that feel soft and tender rather than hard and leathery. They will be easier to chew.

Makes 16

¼ cup (about 1½ ounces) dark chocolate chips

16 dried apricots

¼ cup finely chopped black walnuts

1. Line a cookie sheet with parchment and set it on the counter by your microwave oven. Place the chocolate chips in a 1-cup glass bowl. Place the apricots on a plate and the chopped walnuts in a small, shallow bowl. Set the plate and bowl on the counter by the lined cookie sheet. Place the glass bowl with the chocolate chips into the microwave oven and set the controls for 1 minute at high speed. After a minute, carefully (the bowl will be hot) remove the chocolate chips from the microwave oven. They won't be completely melted but they will have softened. Using a metal spoon, stir the softened chips until they melt and are smooth.

2. Working quickly, hold one end of an apricot and dip the other end into the melted chocolate, coating it about halfway up on both sides, then dip the chocolate end into the chopped walnuts to cover the chocolate. Set the coated apricot on the lined cookie sheet. Continue to dip and coat the remaining apricots. Serve immediately or place in the refrigerator for up to 3 days.

Tips: Use vegan chocolate chips to make this recipe vegan. Use gluten-free chocolate chips to make this recipe gluten free.

Grilled Apricots with Fresh Goat Cheese, Blueberries, and Honey GF

Because we try to serve as many fruits to our customers as we can, we try a lot of new combinations. This one is both beautiful and yummy!

Serves 4

2 large ripe apricots, cut in half and pitted

1 teaspoon walnut oil

½ cup fresh goat cheese, crumbled (or substitute hand-packed ricotta cheese)

1 cup blueberries

3 tablespoons honey

Mint leaves for garnish, if desired

1. Heat a grill pan over medium-high heat. Using your hands, rub the apricots all over with the oil. Grill, cut side down, for about a minute, until golden brown grill marks are visible when apricots are lifted with a spatula. Turn and grill the other side for about 25 seconds, or until brown grill marks are visible when lifted. Transfer to a platter, cut side up.

2. Divide the crumbled goat cheese evenly on top of each apricot half. Scatter the blueberries on and around the apricots. Drizzle with the honey. Garnish with mint leaves if desired. Serve immediately or within a couple of hours.

Maple Mascarpone–Stuffed Pears GFO

This elegant dessert pairs the warm flavors of pears with the richness of creamy mascarpone cheese, and it will be a huge hit for your fall and winter entertaining. Select sweet and juicy Bartlett pears or crisp, russet-color Bosc pears. Look for smooth skin, free from any soft spots.

Serves 4

½ cup mascarpone cheese

3 tablespoons pure maple syrup, divided

2 cups white grape juice

¼ cup golden balsamic vinegar or apple cider vinegar

1 cinnamon stick

4 ripe pears

1. Combine the mascarpone with 1 tablespoon of the maple syrup, and stir to combine. Set aside. Measure the white grape juice, the remaining 2 tablespoons of maple syrup, and the golden balsamic vinegar into a pot large and deep enough to fit 4 pears upright. Add the cinnamon stick. Stir to combine. Cover and bring to a boil over high heat. Meanwhile, peel the pears; then, using a corer, core out the center seeds and stem. When the white grape juice mix reaches a boil, stir in 1 tablespoon of the mascarpone, stirring to combine. Carefully lower each pear into the boiling liquid. Lower the heat to medium. Cover and cook at a medium boil, using a spoon to occasionally baste the pears with the cooking liquid, for about 10 minutes, until fork-tender.

2. Using a slotted spoon, carefully remove the pears and arrange them in a shallow bowl in a single layer. Set aside to cool to room temperature. Lower the heat to medium-low. Continue cooking the liquid, uncovered, at a low boil for about 25 minutes, stirring occasionally, until it looks like thin caramel and lightly coats a spoon. You'll have about ¾ cup. Remove from the heat. If you have a pastry bag fitted with a round tip, fill it with the remaining mascarpone and maple syrup mixture; as an alternate, use a tiny spoon like an espresso spoon to fill each of the 4 cored pears with the mascarpone mixture. Spoon the warm cooking liquid around and over the pears. Serve warm.

Tip: Use gluten-free vinegar to make this recipe gluten free.

Prosecco and Cinnamon Poached Apples with Mascarpone `GF`

In our family and in our other New Haven restaurant, Basta Trattoria, we like to welcome our guests with a glass of Prosecco, the sparkling Italian wine from Veneto. It also makes a lovely base for poaching apples. I like to use Gala apples for their floral notes, but really, all fresh apples have a wonderful flavor—mix it up.

Serves 4–6 as a dessert, or up to 12 as a topping for Butternut Squash Pancakes (see page 238)

¼ cup local maple syrup

2½ cups Prosecco

½ cup local fresh apple cider

1 cinnamon stick

2 tablespoons mascarpone cheese or local cream cheese

5 locally grown apples, cored, cut in half, and each half cut into 4 wedges

1. Measure the maple syrup, Prosecco, and cider into a medium pot. Add the cinnamon stick. Cover and bring to a boil over high heat. Stir in the mascarpone cheese. Add the apple wedges and lower the heat to medium. Stir to combine. Cover and cook at a low boil for about 10 minutes, until tender to your preference, stirring occasionally.

2. Using a slotted spoon, transfer the apples to a shallow bowl. Raise the heat to high and cook the remaining liquid, uncovered, at a rapid boil for about 5 minutes, stirring frequently, until it has reduced to a slightly thicker consistency. Pour this over the apples.

Summer Strawberry Island Dessert ▣

For a quick dessert, toss antioxidant-rich local strawberries with a little pure rum extract, then toss them in an island-inspired mixture of bread crumbs, coconut, raw cane sugar, crunchy almonds, and cinnamon. Serve this dessert in martini glasses for an elegant appearance, or on your favorite plate for a casual feel. Served plain or topped with a dollop of organic vanilla yogurt, organic crème fraîche, or whipped organic cream.

Serves 4–6

Bread Crumb Mixture:

½ cup organic dry bread crumbs

3 tablespoons organic turbinado sugar

3 tablespoons sliced toasted almonds, plus additional for scattering on top, if desired

2 tablespoons organic unsweetened shredded coconut

¼ teaspoon cinnamon, freshly ground if available

Strawberries:

1 heaping quart fresh local strawberries, about 4 cups

1½ teaspoons pure organic rum extract

1. To prepare the bread crumb mixture, combine the ingredients in a small bowl and stir to mix. Set aside.

2. Prepare the strawberries just before you're ready for dessert. To do so, rinse the strawberries, then drain them on paper towels or on a kitchen towel that you don't mind staining with the juice. Hull the strawberries. Place on a plate. Drizzle the rum extract evenly over the berries, then turn the berries into a bowl. Using your hands, toss gently but thoroughly to coat.

3. To assemble the dessert, add the bread crumb mixture to the strawberries. Using your hands or two wooden spoons, toss to coat. Divide the berry-crumb mixture into serving glasses or plates. Top each with a dollop of yogurt, crème fraîche, or whipped cream, if desired. Scatter a few sliced almonds on top of each. Serve immediately.

Lemon Shortcakes

Soft and tender, these lightly sweetened biscuits are good enough to serve warm from the oven all by themselves, and they also make a most wonderful strawberry shortcake. But don't stop there. Switch to blueberry shortcake or peach shortcake as the summer harvest progresses—or the mood strikes.

Makes 6 biscuits

1 pint fresh organic strawberries

4 tablespoons turbinado sugar

1 cup unbleached all-purpose flour

1 cup whole wheat flour

¼ teaspoon salt

1 tablespoon baking powder

Finely grated zest from 1 lemon

¼ cup plus 2 tablespoons organic trans fat–free shortening (I like to use Spectrum® brand), chilled

1½ cups chilled half-and-half

1 cup heavy cream

1. Rinse the strawberries, then remove the green caps. Slice into a bowl. Sprinkle with 1 tablespoon of sugar. Toss gently. Set aside to macerate.

2. Center your oven rack. Preheat the oven to 450°F.

3. Sift the flours, sugar, salt, and baking powder into a bowl. Add the lemon zest. Using your fingers, toss to combine. Break off pieces of the shortening and scatter them over the dry ingredients. Using your fingers, rub the shortening into the dry ingredients, until the mix resembles medium crumbs. Add the half-and-half. Using your hand, mix to combine. Spray a cookie sheet with canola oil spray or line it with parchment paper.

4. Using a ½-cup measuring cup, drop ½-cups of the batter onto the prepared cookie sheet, allowing a couple of inches in between for even baking. Bake on the center rack of the preheated oven for about 20 minutes, until biscuits are golden brown and a cake tester inserted into the center of one comes out clean.

5. While the shortcake biscuits are baking, you can whip the cream until soft peaks form, making sure that cream and beaters are cold.

6. When the shortcake biscuits are done, remove the tray from the oven and set it on a heat-resistant surface to cool slightly. Just before serving, cut each shortcake biscuit in half. Spoon some of the strawberries and their juices onto the bottom half of the biscuit, then spoon a dollop of whipped cream over the strawberries. Cover with the top biscuit. Continue filling the remaining biscuits.

Irish Soda Bread

Makes 1 loaf, serves 6–8

2 cups flour

¼ cup plus 2 tablespoons sugar, plus an additional teaspoon for topping the bread

1 teaspoon baking soda

⅛ teaspoon salt

2 tablespoons butter, cut into small cubes

1½ teaspoons caraway seeds

¼ cup plus 2 tablespoons raisins

½ cup plus 1 tablespoon buttermilk, plus an additional teaspoon for topping the bread

1. Center the oven rack. Preheat the oven to 375°F. Into a medium bowl, measure the flour, sugar, baking soda, and the salt. Whisk to combine. Add the cubes of butter, and using your fingertips, rub the butter into the flour mixture, pressing the butter with the flour, until you have small crumbs. Add the caraway seeds and the raisins and using two spoons or your fingers, toss to combine. Pour the buttermilk over the flour mixture, and using your hand, mix to combine.

2. Then using your hands, knead the mixture right in the bowl, pushing the dough into the dry ingredients to collect any dry bits of flour and to mix them into the dough. Knead for about a minute until the dough is smooth. It will be a little sticky, but fine.

3. Line a cookie sheet with parchment paper or spray it with organic canola oil spray. Transfer the dough to the prepared cookie sheet and gently pat into a round shape about 6-inch diameter. Using a sharp knife, cut an X about half way down into the dough. Bake centered in the preheated oven for about 40 minutes or until the bread is a deep golden brown. To test for doneness, remove the bread from the oven, and turn the bread onto a plate (or right onto your hand if you are wearing an oven mitt). Turn the bread over and using your fist, tap on the underside of the bread and if it makes a hollow sound it's done.

4. Turn the cooked bread back onto the cookie sheet, then brush the top with the remaining teaspoon of buttermilk, and sprinkle it with the remaining teaspoon of sugar. Bake for a minute just to give the top a shine. Remove from the oven. Turn onto a plate, right side up. Cool slightly before serving. Store any leftovers tightly wrapped in foil on the counter for up to 2 days. Serve plain or with a little butter on top.

Vegan Irish Soda Bread V

My niece Carolyn keeps a vegan diet. She has always loved Irish soda bread, which challenged me to make this one for her, our other vegan friends, and everyone else who enjoys a good Irish soda bread.

Makes 1 loaf, serves about 8

1½ cups plain organic soy milk

1 tablespoon organic apple cider vinegar

¼ teaspoon sea salt

4 cups organic all-purpose flour

½ cup organic granulated sugar

1 teaspoon baking soda

1½ teaspoons caraway seeds

1/3 cup raisins

¼ cup organic non-dairy buttery spread
   (I like to use Earth Balance® brand),
   melted

1 teaspoon organic plain soy milk

1 teaspoon organic granulated sugar

1. Center the oven rack. Preheat the oven to 375°F. Measure the soy milk, cider vinegar, and salt into a bowl. Whisk to combine. Set aside for 10 minutes. (It will begin to look like it has separated a bit.)

2. Into a big bowl, measure the flour, sugar, baking soda, and caraway seeds. Whisk to combine. Stir in the raisins. Add the melted buttery spread to the soy milk and vinegar mix, and whisk to combine. Pour the liquids all at once over the flour mixture, and use a rubber spatula to scrape the bowl of liquids. Stir the mixture several times to mix the liquid and dry ingredients. Right in the bowl, start kneading the dough, pushing the dough into the dry ingredients to collect any dry bits of flour and mix them into the dough. Knead for about a minute, until the dough is smooth.

3. Spray a 9-inch-round and 2-inch-deep pan with organic canola spray. Transfer the dough to the prepared pan and gently pat it to fit into the pan. Using a sharp knife, cut an X about halfway down into the dough. Bake in the preheated oven for about 50 minutes or until the bread is golden brown. To test for doneness, remove the bread from the oven and turn onto a plate (or right onto your hand if you're wearing an oven mitt). Using your fist, tap on the underside of the bread; if it makes a hollow sound, it's done.

4. Turn the cooked bread back into the pan, then brush the top with the remaining teaspoon of soy milk, and sprinkle it with the remaining teaspoon of sugar. Bake for a minute just to give the top a shine. Remove from the oven. Turn onto a plate, right side up. Cool slightly before serving. Store any leftovers tightly wrapped in foil on the counter for up to 2 days. Serve plain or with a little buttery spread on top.

Pumpkin Spice Bread

This is a perennial favorite in my house and it can be baked up to 2 days in advance. After it cools from the oven, wrap it in foil and leave on the counter for snacking. This bread is delicious alone, but for a more festive presentation you can top it with a dollop of organic vanilla yogurt and a sprinkle of candied ginger pieces.

Makes a 9 x 5-inch loaf

1 cup organic whole wheat flour

1 cup organic unbleached all-purpose white
    flour

2 teaspoons baking powder

¼ teaspoon baking soda

½ teaspoon salt

¼ teaspoon ground ginger

¼ teaspoon ground cloves

¼ teaspoon ground cardamom

¼ teaspoon ground allspice

¼ teaspoon ground cinnamon

¼ cup chopped pecans

¼ cup dried cranberries

2 organic eggs

1 cup organic granulated sugar

¼ cup organic soybean oil

1 cup canned organic pumpkin puree

¼ cup buttermilk

1. Center the oven rack, then preheat the oven to 375°F. Spray a 9 x 5-inch loaf pan with nonstick cooking spray.

2. Place the flours, baking powder and soda, salt, and spices in a large bowl. Whisk to combine, then stir in the pecans and cranberries.

3. In another large bowl, combine the eggs, sugar, soybean oil, pumpkin puree, and buttermilk. Whisk together until fully blended.

4. Add the liquid mixture to the dry mixture all at once and mix gently with a large spoon until just combined.

5. Turn the batter into the prepared loaf pan, using a rubber spatula to scrape the bowl and to smooth the top of the batter. Bake on the center rack of the preheated oven for about 1¼ hours, until a cake tester inserted into the center comes out clean. Allow the bread to set for 5 minutes before turning out onto a cake plate. Cool slightly before serving. Serve plain or with a dollop of organic vanilla yogurt with candied ginger on top.

Claire's Classic

Dairy-Free Gingerbread V

This is one of my favorite desserts, and one of the oldest I know—I've seen recipes dating back to the early fifteenth century. I love molasses and am especially happy to eat a calcium-rich treat with the added benefit of tofu. I prefer my gingerbread plain, but when I was growing up, my neighbor Millie Ricitelli used to serve her gingerbread with a lemon topping, and the combination is quite popular. Try it with my Lemon Glaze (page 346).

Serves 8 (1 8-inch pan)

1½ cups flour

1 teaspoon ground ginger

¼ teaspoon salt

¼ teaspoon cinnamon

1 teaspoon baking powder

¼ cup hot water

3 tablespoons softened trans fat–free organic margarine

1 teaspoon baking soda

¼ cup soft tofu

1 cup blackstrap molasses

1. Preheat the oven to 350°F.

2. Measure the flour, ginger, salt, cinnamon, and baking powder into a bowl. Whisk together to mix well. Put the hot water, margarine, baking soda, tofu, and molasses in a blender. Cover and blend on high speed for 30 seconds, until blended well. Pour this mixture all at once over the dry ingredients, using a rubber spatula to scrape the blender. Stir the ingredients together using a wooden spoon for about 1 minute, until all the ingredients are blended.

3. Spray an 8-inch glass pan with nonstick cooking spray. Pour the batter into the prepared pan, using a rubber spatula to scrape the bowl. Smooth the top using the spatula. Bake for 40–45 minutes, until a tester inserted into the center comes out clean. Serve warm or at room temperature.

Dessert Crepes with Apple Filling

These dessert crepes are enriched with almond meal to add fiber and antioxidants along with a lovely, subtle flavor of almonds. I like to fill them and then fold them over into triangles, which reminds me of the *fazzoletti* (handkerchiefs) that my grandmother carefully ironed with me at her side.

I fill crepes with a variety of things, sometimes sautéed bananas with a bit of maple syrup, a reduction of Frangelico, or a reduction of blackberry brandy with organic strawberries. For this recipe, I use a filling of chopped organic apples sautéed in a bit of butter with apple cider vinegar, maple syrup, honey, and a sprinkle of cinnamon. The juxtaposition of sweet honey against sweet-tartness from the cider vinegar is terrific.

Makes 19–20 crepes, perfect for a party

Crepes:

1¾ cups unbleached all-purpose flour

½ cup almond meal (found in the baking section of most supermarkets)

3 tablespoons sugar

4 eggs

2 cups water

½ teaspoon orange blossom water, almond extract, or other flavor of your choice

1 tablespoon melted butter

Filling:

2 tablespoons butter

4 organic apples, cored and sliced, then cut into small cubes

¼ cup organic apple cider vinegar

2 tablespoons pure maple syrup

1 tablespoon honey

1 shake (about ¼ teaspoon) cinnamon

Confectioners' sugar for dusting the finished crepes before serving

1½ cups plain, fat-free Greek yogurt

1. To prepare the crepes, combine the flour, almond meal, and sugar in a large bowl, whisking to blend. In a separate bowl, combine the eggs, water, orange blossom water, and melted butter, whisking well to blend. Pour the liquid mixture over the flour mixture, using a spatula to scrape out the bowl and whisking until the consistency is of pancake batter. Line a cookie sheet with parchment paper. Heat a 6-inch skillet over medium heat, then carefully spray with cooking spray. Pour about 2 tablespoons of the batter into the center of the skillet, then quickly tilt to spread the batter, coating the entire bottom of the skillet. Cook for 1–2 minutes, or until the crepe looks set and the underside is golden brown. Turn the crepe over and cook the other side for about a minute, or until golden brown. Transfer the crepe to the lined cookie sheet and continue cooking the remaining crepes.

2. To prepare the filling, melt the butter in a large skillet over medium heat. Add the apples and stir to coat. Cook for about 2 minutes, frequently moving the pan back and forth until the apples have softened a bit. Add the apple cider vinegar and cook at a simmer for about 3–5 minutes, frequently moving the skillet back and forth until the apples are crisp-tender.

3. Add the maple syrup and the honey, and sprinkle with the cinnamon. Cook for about 2–3 minutes, moving the skillet back and forth to cook the apples evenly until they're tender and the liquid has reduced to about a couple of tablespoons. (It should be a medium caramel color.) Test the apples for tenderness, using a fork to pierce a cube of the apple. Carefully (it's going to be really hot) taste for tenderness and for sweetness. I prefer my filling moderately tart-sweet, but if you want yours sweeter, stir in another spoon of maple syrup or honey.

4. To assemble the dessert, lay a crepe on a plate. Place a heaping tablespoon of the filling (with any juices clinging to the apples) onto the center of the crepe. Fold in half, then in half again, to form a thick triangle. Transfer the filled crepe to a platter and continue with the remaining crepes. Dust with powdered sugar and serve with the yogurt.

Note: You can make the crepes a day in advance. Wrap the tray in foil and keep them in the refrigerator until you need them. Then heat them briefly in a preheated 350°F oven for just a few minutes, right from the fridge and still wrapped in foil, until they are warm. Prepare the filling, sit back, and enjoy the crepes with your guests.

Cider Donut Holes

I feel compelled to warn you that these are highly addictive and to confess that we've eaten too many of these spiced little donut balls in the kitchen before they ever made it to our customers—oops!

Makes about 6 dozen little donut holes

1 cup cider

3½ cups unbleached all-purpose flour

2 teaspoons baking powder

1 teaspoon baking soda

½ teaspoon cinnamon

¼ teaspoon salt

½ teaspoon ground cardamom

1/8 teaspoon ground nutmeg

¼ cup organic trans fat–free shortening,
    plus 2 cups for frying

1 cup granulated sugar

2 eggs

½ cup buttermilk

½ teaspoon finely grated lemon zest

    Cinnamon-Sugar Coating:

1/3 cup granulated sugar

½ teaspoon cinnamon

1. Measure the cider into a small pot and bring to a boil over high heat. Boil for about 12–15 minutes until it reduces to ¼ cup. Meanwhile, measure the flour, baking powder, baking soda, the cinnamon, salt, cardamom, and nutmeg into a bowl, then sift it into another bowl. Set aside.

2. Measure the shortening into a medium-sized bowl. Add the sugar. Using a hand mixer set on medium speed, cream the shortening and sugar for about a minute until the sugar is incorporated into the shortening. Add the eggs and beat on medium speed for about 2 minutes, until creamy, stopping once or twice to scrape the sides of the bowl with a spatula. Add the buttermilk, the reduced cider, and the grated lemon zest, and beat on medium speed for about a minute until smooth and creamy. Add the sifted flour mixture all at once. Using a spoon, stir until the flour mixture is completely blended in. The batter will be quite thick, so after you've stirred the mixture for a minute of so, you can just use your hand, turning and "kneading" to incorporate all the flour into the creamed mixture until no unmixed flour remains.

3. To prepare the cinnamon-sugar coating, measure the sugar and cinnamon into a medium-size bowl and, using a whisk, blend to combine. Set aside.

4. Line a cookie sheet with parchment paper and line another with a brown paper bag or a double layer of paper towels to drain the donut holes after frying. Scoop a heaping teaspoon of the batter into your hand and roll into a ball. Continue with the remaining batter. Set the lined cookie sheet by the stove and get a slotted spoon handy, too. Measure the remaining 2 cups of shortening into an 8-cup heavy pot. Attach a thermometer to the pot. Heat the shortening to 325°F over medium heat. After the shortening is heated, carefully drop 4–5 balls into the hot shortening. Fry the donut holes for about a minute, turning them to cook evenly until golden brown.

5. Using a slotted spoon, transfer the cooked donut holes to the lined cookie sheet. Continue frying the remaining donut holes, adjusting the heat to keep the temperature around 325°F. Place 1–2 donut holes into the cinnamon-sugar mixture and toss to coat. Transfer to a platter and continue coating the remaining donut holes. Eat warm or at room temperature. Store, covered tightly with foil, on the counter for up to 3 days. There are plenty to share!

Open Apricot Tart

This lovely tart is easier than double-crust pies because you make a free-form crust. The combination of rich and creamy mascarpone cheese paired with sweet apricot preserves is, as they say, a marriage made in heaven.

Makes a 10-inch tart

1 recipe Flaky Piecrust dough

Flour to dust rolling pin and counter

5 tablespoons mascarpone cheese

½ cup apricot preserves

1 egg, lightly beaten

1 teaspoon granulated sugar

1. Prepare the Flaky Piecrust (page 334). Then roll out the dough on a lightly floured counter to form a 12-inch circle.

2. Center the oven rack. Preheat the oven to 425°F.

3. Spray a cookie sheet with canola oil spray. Carefully transfer the pie dough circle to the prepared cookie sheet. Using a rubber spatula, spread the mascarpone evenly over the inner 8 inches of the circle, leaving a 2-inch border. Spread the apricot preserves evenly over the mascarpone, leaving a 2-inch border around the preserves. Carefully lift the surrounding pie dough over some of the preserves, folding the dough as you lift and leaving most of the filling exposed. Don't worry about it being perfectly round; a free-form shape gives it an attractive and rustic appearance. Using a pastry brush, carefully brush the beaten egg on the crust that surrounds the preserves. Take care not to allow the egg to drip, as this would cause the tart to stick to the pan. Sprinkle the sugar evenly over the crust. Bake in the center of the preheated oven for about 25 minutes, or until the crust is golden brown. Serve hot or at room temperature.

Pear, Apple, and Pomegranate Cobbler [V]

The tastes and textures of antioxidant-rich, flavorful Bosc pears, Bartlett pears, and several varieties of apples make this dessert special. And the pomegranate juice lends its bright red hue to the cobbler, which is a nice match for the juice's robust flavor.

Serves 8

Filling:

6 organic apples (use a variety of apples), cored and cut into fairly thin slices

¼ cup pomegranate juice

6 pears (a combination of Bosc and Bartlett), cored and cut into fairly thin slices

¼ cup packed brown sugar

¼ cup pure maple syrup

1 teaspoon cinnamon

1 teaspoon ground cardamom

Topping:

1½ cups organic rolled oats

1½ cups organic whole wheat flour

1 cup organic sugar

1 tablespoon baking powder

¼ teaspoon cinnamon

¼ teaspoon ground cloves

½ cup trans fat–free organic buttery spread (I like to use Earth Balance® brand), melted

½ cup pomegranate juice

½ cup milk (or substitute ½ cup soy milk)

1. Preheat the oven to 350°F.

2. To prepare the cobbler filling, in a large bowl combine the apples, pomegranate juice, pears, brown sugar, maple syrup, cinnamon, and cardamom. Toss well to combine. Turn into a rectangular glass baking dish.

3. To prepare the cobber topping, in another bowl combine the oats, flour, sugar, baking powder, cinnamon, and cloves. Toss to combine. Drizzle the melted buttery spread, pomegranate juice, and milk evenly over the top. Mix well with a spoon to combine.

4. To assemble the cobbler, drop spoonfuls of the topping evenly on the fruit mixture. Bake for 1½ hours, or until the fruit is softened to your liking and the top is a red-golden brown. Serve hot or at room temperature.

Flaky Piecrust V

This recipe for delicious, flaky crust calls for organic, trans fat–free shortening, so you can enjoy your next pie or quiche with less guilt. Our customers do: We've been voted Best Quiche by the readers of *Connecticut Magazine* many times, and I'm sure that our lovely crusts contribute to this honor.

Makes a 10-inch deep-dish pie or open tart

2 cups unbleached all-purpose flour, plus additional for rolling out dough

¼ teaspoon sea salt

½ teaspoon baking powder

½ cup plus 2 tablespoons organic trans fat–free shortening (I like to use Spectrum® brand), chilled in the refrigerator for 1 hour

6–7 tablespoons ice-cold water

1. Measure the flour, salt, and baking powder into the bowl of a food processor fitted with a metal blade. Cover and pulse 5 times. Using your fingers, scoop out 15 small pieces of the cold shortening and scatter them over the flour. Cover and pulse about 10 times until the mixture looks like coarse cornmeal. Sprinkle 6 tablespoons of the cold water evenly over the mixture, cover, and pulse eight to ten times until the mixture comes together.

2. Remove the cover. Using your hand, squeeze the dough between your fingers; if it holds together, it's ready. If it's too dry and it crumbles, add another tablespoon of cold water, cover, and pulse another two to three times. Remove the dough from the processor and fold it over two to three times, kneading two to three times. Form into a 6-inch disc and wrap in plastic. Refrigerate at least an hour until firm or overnight. This lets the gluten relax, making it easier to roll out.

3. Before rolling, let the dough sit at room temperature for about 20 minutes, until it softens slightly. Dust a countertop lightly with flour. Unwrap the dough. Using a rolling pin lightly dusted with flour, "whack" the dough several times, first in a horizontal direction, then in a vertical one, to form a circle. Roll the dough into a 12-inch circle, adding a bit more flour if the dough sticks. Try not to add too much flour, or the dough will be dry.

Claire's Classic

Apple-Crumb Pie vo

There may be little to add to what's already been said in praise of apple-crumb pie, but we can never make too many of these beauties at Claire's. As quickly as we can peel the apples and bake the pies, that's how quickly they sell. Apple pie is surely one of our national treasures. Bake one for your family or friends as soon as the organic Pink Lady, McIntosh, Rome, or Braeburn apples are available.

Makes a 9-inch pie

Pie:

8 apples, cored, peeled, and sliced about ¼ inch thick (about 8 cups)

Juice of 1 lemon

¾ cup packed dark brown sugar

1 teaspoon cinnamon

½ teaspoon ground nutmeg

Crumb Topping:

½ cup packed dark brown sugar

½ cup unbleached flour

¼ cup rolled oats

½ teaspoon cinnamon

4 tablespoons (½ stick) butter, brought to room temperature

1 9-inch unbaked piecrust (store-bought is fine)

1. Preheat the oven to 375°F.

2. Combine the apples and lemon juice in a bowl, tossing to coat well. Add the brown sugar, cinnamon, and nutmeg. Toss again to coat well.

3. To prepare the topping, in a bowl combine the brown sugar, flour, oats, and cinnamon, tossing well. Add the butter and work in, using your fingers, until the mixture resembles coarse crumbs.

4. Lift the apples out of the bowl and mound them in the piecrust, using your hands so that most of the liquid remains in the bowl. Sprinkle the topping evenly over the apples.

5. Bake the pie, centered in the oven on a cookie sheet, for about 1 hour, until the crumbs are browned and the apples are tender when tested with a fork. Remove from the oven and let stand for 15 minutes before serving.

Tip: Use a vegan buttery spread instead of butter to make this recipe vegan.

North Carolina Pecan Pie

Our pecans come from Elbie Powers, who grows them on his farm in North Carolina. They are truly enormous, meaty, and amazing! Pure indulgence!

Makes a 9-inch pie

4 eggs

¼ teaspoon salt

1 cup granulated sugar

1⅓ cups light corn syrup

4 tablespoons (½ stick) butter, melted

1 teaspoon pure vanilla extract

1 cup pecan halves

1 9-inch prebaked piecrust (trans fat–free store bought will work in a pinch)

1. Center the oven rack. Preheat the oven to 400°F.

2. In a bowl, combine the eggs, salt, and sugar. Whisk well. Add the corn syrup, melted butter, and the vanilla. Whisk well. Set the prebaked piecrust on a cookie sheet to collect any spills. Spread the pecans evenly on the bottom of the prebaked piecrust. Ladle the filling over the pecans. Bake in the preheated oven for 15 minutes, then lower the heat to 350°F and bake for another 30–35 minutes, until the center is just set. Let stand for 15 minutes before serving.

"While at Yale, I was constantly writing papers. The source of my inspiration: Claire's cakes! Every week I came to Claire's, my home away from home, to muscle through paper after paper with a pen in one hand and a fork in the other. I don't know how I would have graduated without the support of the Claire's family (and Corner Copia food)! When people ask me what I'm going to miss the most about Yale, I always say Claire's!"

—David Washer, Yale University, Class of 2011

Peach-Oat Crumb Pie V

The quintessential summer pie for us is a peach pie. I hope it will become yours, too.

Serves 6

Filling:

8 medium peaches, pitted and sliced ¼-inch thick

Juice of 1 lemon

¼ cup packed brown sugar

¼ teaspoon cardamom

¼ teaspoon cinnamon

¼ cup sliced almonds

Topping:

½ cup packed brown sugar

¼ cup unbleached organic flour

¼ cup organic whole wheat flour

¼ cup organic rolled oats

½ teaspoon cinnamon

¼ cup butter or trans fat–free buttery spread (I like to use Earth Balance®), brought to room temperature

1 9-inch unbaked trans fat–free piecrust (store-bought is fine)

1. Center the oven rack. Preheat the oven to 375°F. Line a sheet pan with parchment paper or spray with nonstick oil spray for an easy cleanup later.

2. To prepare the pie filling, combine the peaches and lemon juice in a bowl and toss to coat. Add the brown sugar, cardamom, cinnamon, and almonds. Toss to coat.

3. To prepare the oat crumb topping, in a bowl combine the brown sugar, flours, oats, and cinnamon, and toss to combine. Add the butter and work in, using your fingers, until the mixture resembles coarse crumbs.

4. To assemble the pie, set the piecrust on the prepared sheet pan. Lift the peaches out of the bowl and mound them in the piecrust, using your hands so that most of the liquid remains in the bowl. Sprinkle the oat crumbs evenly over the peaches.

5. Bake the pie in the preheated oven for about 1 hour, until the crumbs are browned and the peaches are soft when tested with a fork. Remove from the oven and cool for 20 minutes or so before serving—the peaches will be really hot.

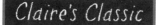

Claire's Classic

Pumpkin-Walnut Pie

Everyone loves this Grand Marnier–flavored pumpkin pie.

Makes a 9-inch pie

1 cup chopped walnuts

1 cup packed dark brown sugar

1½ teaspoons cinnamon

1 9-inch unbaked piecrust
   (store-bought is fine)

3 eggs

1 cup evaporated milk

¼ teaspoon salt

½ teaspoon ground ginger

⅛ teaspoon ground cloves

Pinch of ground nutmeg

1 cup pumpkin puree, canned or fresh

2 tablespoons Grand Marnier liqueur

1. Preheat the oven to 375°F.

2. In a small bowl, combine the walnuts, ¼ cup of the brown sugar, and ½ teaspoon of cinnamon. Spread evenly on the bottom of the piecrust. In a separate bowl, whisk the eggs for about 30 seconds. Add the evaporated milk, the remaining 1 teaspoon cinnamon, salt, ginger, cloves, nutmeg, the remaining ¾ cup of brown sugar, pumpkin, and Grand Marnier. Whisk for about 30 seconds, until smooth. Pour over the walnuts in the piecrust.

3. Bake on a cookie sheet for 40–45 minutes, until the center is set. Remove from the oven and let stand for 15 minutes before serving.

Claire's Classic

Anginettes

Anginettes are delicious cookies with a citrus glaze. They were always present on major occasions at our house. You'll find them at traditional Italian bridal showers, weddings, and christenings, as well as at Christmas and Easter celebrations. They keep well in a covered tin, but don't expect them to last, especially if your family takes to them as much as mine has.

Makes about 10 dozen (recipe can be halved)

Cookies:

1 pound butter, softened to room temperature

3½ cups sugar

6 eggs

4 teaspoons vanilla extract

2 pounds ricotta cheese

8 cups unbleached all-purpose flour

2 teaspoons baking powder

2 teaspoons baking soda

2 teaspoons salt

Glaze:

2½ cups confectioners' sugar

3 tablespoons orange juice

2 tablespoons milk

1. To prepare the cookies, place the softened butter in a large bowl. Beat until smooth, using a hand mixer on low speed. Add the sugar. Beat well on medium speed for about 3 minutes or until well blended, stopping once or twice to scrape down the sides of the bowl with a rubber spatula. Add the eggs, 2 at a time, beating on low speed for 1 minute after each addition. Add the vanilla and the ricotta. Mix on low speed for 1–2 minutes, or until blended.

2. Preheat the oven to 350°F.

3. Measure the flour, baking powder, baking soda, and salt into a bowl. Stir to combine. Add this all at once to the creamed mixture. Using a wooden spoon, stir until all the flour is mixed into the creamed mixture. The batter should be fairly stiff. Drop teaspoons of batter onto ungreased cookie sheets, leaving about 1½ inches of space between the cookies to allow for spreading. Bake for about 10 minutes, then rotate the cookie sheets from top to bottom and front to back. Continue baking for another 10 minutes, or until the cookies are golden brown and firm to the touch. Let cool to room temperature before glazing.

4. To make the glaze, sift the confectioners' sugar into a small bowl. Add the orange juice and milk. Beat until soft and creamy.

5. Drizzle the glaze evenly over the cooled anginettes.

Blueberry Ricotta Cookies

These tender little gems make a great treat for company and are perfect for your Easter baking.

Makes 5 dozen

1 cup organic trans fat–free shortening

1¾ cups organic granulated sugar

3 organic eggs

1 teaspoon pure almond extract

1 cup ricotta cheese

4 cups organic white whole wheat flour

1 teaspoon baking powder

1 teaspoon baking soda

1 teaspoon salt

1 cup fresh blueberries

1. Place the shortening in a large bowl. Using a hand mixer on low speed, cream the shortening until fluffy. Add the sugar. Beat well for 3 minutes, until blended, stopping once or twice to scrape down the sides of the bowl with a rubber spatula. Add the eggs and beat on low speed for a minute until blended. Add the almond extract and the ricotta. Mix on low speed for a minute until blended.

2. Preheat the oven to 350°F. Measure the flour, baking powder, baking soda, and salt into a bowl. Whisk to combine. Add this all at once to the creamed mixture. Using a wooden spoon, stir until well blended. Stir in the blueberries.

3. Line cookie sheets with parchment paper or spray with nonstick canola spray. Drop teaspoons of the batter onto prepared cookie sheets, leaving about an inch of space between the cookies for spreading. Bake for 10 minutes, then rotate the cooking sheets from top to bottom and front to back. Continue baking for another 10 minutes, or until the cookies are golden brown and firm to the touch.

Chocolate Chip Cookies with Cranberries, Dates, and Apricots

These rich and buttery cookies will make a delicious and welcome indulgence.

Makes about 27 cookies

1¾ cups organic all-purpose flour

1½ teaspoons baking soda

½ teaspoon salt

¾ cup organic butter, softened

½ cup organic granulated sugar

¾ cup brown sugar, packed

2 organic eggs

2 tablespoons organic milk

1 teaspoon organic vanilla

½ cup chocolate chips

1/3 cup fresh or frozen cranberries

¼ cup finely chopped dried pitted dates

¼ cup finely chopped dried apricots

1. Preheat the oven to 350°F. Center the oven racks.

2. Measure the flour, baking soda, and salt into a medium-size bowl. Whisk to combine. Measure the softened butter into a separate medium-size bowl. Cream the butter using a hand mixer set on medium speed. Add the sugars and beat with the mixer set on medium speed for about a minute, until well blended. Add the eggs, milk, and vanilla, then beat the mixture at medium speed, for about a minute until well blended, stopping once or twice to scrape the sides of the bowl with a rubber spatula. Pour this mixture over the flour mixture, using a rubber spatula to scrape the bowl.

3. Using a wooden spoon, stir to combine until all the flour is mixed in. Stir in the chocolate chips, cranberries, dates, and apricots until well mixed. Line two cookie sheets with parchment paper or spray them with canola oil spray. Drop heaping tablespoons of the batter (or use a ¾-ounce scooper) onto the prepared cookie sheets, allowing about an inch of space between cookies to allow for spreading. Bake in the preheated oven for about 22 minutes until golden brown. Remove the cookies and set aside to cool to room temperature. The cookies will be soft to the touch when you first remove them from the oven but will firm up as they cool. Allow them to cool before transferring them to a plate. Store in a covered container for up to 3 days.

Soft and Chewy Coconut Cookies

These soft, chewy cookies are a coconut lover's dream, and they're made using olive oil and toasted walnut oil for those good monounsaturated fats.

Makes about 5 dozen

2 cups unbleached all-purpose flour

1 tablespoon baking powder

6 eggs

4 cups sugar

¼ cup organic olive oil

1 tablespoon organic toasted walnut oil

1 tablespoon pure rum extract

4 cups shredded coconut

1 cup rolled oats

1. Preheat the oven to 375°F.

2. Sift together the flour and baking powder into a bowl. Set aside.

3. Break the eggs into a large bowl. Using a whisk, beat the eggs for about 1 minute until golden yellow. Add the sugar and whisk for about 1 minute, until well blended. Add the olive oil, walnut oil, and rum extract. Using the whisk, beat well for about a minute to combine. Add the coconut, rolled oats, and sifted flour and baking powder. Using a wooden spoon, stir the ingredients together until they're combined and the flour is completely mixed in. The batter will be fairly loose.

4. Line two or more cookie sheets with parchment paper or spray them with canola or grapeseed oil spray. Scoop heaping tablespoons of the batter onto the prepared cookie sheets, allowing about 2 inches between cookies because the batter will spread as the cookies bake. Bake for about 18 minutes, until just set, creamy in color, and barely golden around the edges. The cookies will be soft when you remove them from the oven, so let them set for 5 minutes until cool enough and firm enough to transfer to a platter. Continue baking remaining batter. These cookies will stay chewy and soft for up to 3 days if you cover the platter tightly with plastic wrap.

Sunflower Seed Butter and Chocolate Chip Cookies V

We are peanut-free at Claire's because we have several children who are very allergic. These cookies make being peanut-free easier—they're quite delicious.

Makes about 50 cookies, plenty for sharing with family and friends

1 cup trans fat–free buttery spread

1¾ cups organic granulated cane sugar

¼ cup organic brown sugar, packed

2 organic eggs or equivalent vegan egg substitute

1 cup organic sunflower seed butter

2 cups organic all-purpose unbleached flour

1 tablespoon baking soda

¼ teaspoon sea salt

1 cup dark or dairy-free chocolate chips

1. Center the oven rack, then preheat the oven to 350°F. Line two cookie sheets with parchment paper or spray them with organic nonstick baking spray.

2. Measure the buttery spread into a large bowl. Using a hand mixer set at medium speed, mix for about 30 seconds until creamy. Add the granulated and brown sugars and the eggs or their equivalent. Mix on medium speed for about 30 seconds until thoroughly combined, stopping once or twice to scrape the sides of the bowl with a rubber spatula. Add the sunflower seed butter. Mix at medium speed for about 30 seconds, until smooth, stopping once or twice to scrape the sides of the bowl.

3. Into a separate bowl, measure the flour, baking soda, and sea salt, then whisk to blend. Add this dry mix to the creamed mixture all at once. Using a large spoon, stir to combine, or use a hand mixer first on low speed to mix in the dry ingredients, then on medium speed for about a minute to combine, stopping once or twice to scrape the sides of the bowl. Stir in the chocolate chips.

4. Roll heaping tablespoons of the batter into balls and arrange them in three rows of four on the prepared cookie sheets, leaving space between cookies to allow for spreading. Bake in the preheated oven for about 17 minutes, until set. Remove from the oven and let cool for about 5 minutes (cookies will be very soft and fragile) before transferring to a platter using a spatula. Let cool for another 20 minutes, until firm, before storing in a covered container. They will keep fresh for up to 4 days.

Vegan Oatmeal Cookies with Cranberries, Carrots, Raisins, and Walnuts V

These chewy cookies are sweetened with pure maple syrup and agave, a liquid sweetener made from the agave plant. Agave has a low glycemic index and a pleasant, sweet flavor that enhances other flavors. You can find agave in the natural foods section at your local supermarket.

Makes about 40 cookies—plenty to share with friends

1 cup drained, crumbled soft organic tofu

1 cup agave

¼ cup pure maple syrup

¼ cup canola oil

1 teaspoon organic vanilla extract

2 cups organic all-purpose flour

2 teaspoons baking powder

1 teaspoon baking soda

1 teaspoon nutmeg

1 teaspoon cinnamon

1 teaspoon ground ginger

¼ teaspoon salt

2 cups rolled organic oats

1 cup fresh or frozen organic cranberries

½ cup grated carrots

1 cup raisins

¼ cup chopped walnuts

1. Center the oven rack. Preheat the oven to 375°F.

2. Combine the tofu, agave, maple syrup, canola oil, and vanilla in a blender cup. Cover and blend on high speed for about 20 seconds, until smooth.

3. Measure the flour, baking powder, baking soda, nutmeg, cinnamon, ginger, and salt into a bowl. Whisk to combine. Stir in the oats. Add the blended liquid ingredients, using a rubber spatula to scrape the blender cup of the liquid. Stir well to combine. Stir in the cranberries, grated carrots, raisins, and walnuts. Line two cookie sheets with parchment paper or spray with canola oil spray. Drop heaping tablespoons of the batter onto the prepared cookie sheets, leaving about ½ inch of space between each cookie.

4. Bake in the preheated oven for about 20 minutes, until the cookies are just firm to the touch and the undersides are deep golden-brown and firm. Remove from the oven and cool for a few minutes, then serve, or cool to room temperature before storing in a covered container for up to 3 days.

Claire's Classic

Brownies

These are the best brownies, the chewiest and richest—a chocolate lover's jackpot.

Makes an 8-inch square pan of brownies

3 ounces semisweet chocolate, chopped

8 tablespoons (1 stick) butter, brought to room temperature

¾ cup unbleached flour

¼ teaspoon baking powder

¼ teaspoon salt

2 eggs

1 cup sugar

1 teaspoon vanilla extract

1. Preheat the oven to 350°F.

2. Combine the chocolate and butter in the top of a double boiler. Set over gently boiling water. Stir frequently until the chocolate and butter melt. Meanwhile, in a large bowl, combine the flour, baking powder, and salt. In a separate bowl, beat together the eggs, sugar, and vanilla extract, whisking well. Add the chocolate mixture to the egg mixture, whisking well to blend. Pour this over the flour mixture and whisk together until all the flour is mixed in.

3. Spray the 8-inch square pan with nonstick cooking spray, or grease and flour the pan. Turn the batter into the prepared pan, using a rubber spatula to scrape the bowl. Smooth the top. Bake in the center of the oven for about 30 minutes, until a cake tester inserted in the center comes out clean. Let stand for 5 minutes before cutting into squares.

> "When I survived my oral exams—four professors grilling me about 120 books—I celebrated with a piece of Lithuanian Coffee Cake. When my adviser nixed the feminist analysis in my dissertation chapter, I consoled myself with a piece of Lithuanian Coffee Cake. Claire's Lithuanian Coffee Cake got me through grad school!"
>
> —Maria Trumpler, PhD, Senior Lecturer, Program in Women's, Gender and Sexuality Studies, Yale University

Almond Glaze VO GFO

For something truly spectacular, try drizzling this glaze over a chocolate cake.

Makes enough to glaze a 9-inch round cake or a 10-cup Bundt cake

1 cup organic confectioners' sugar

½ teaspoon pure organic almond extract

2 tablespoons plus 1 teaspoon organic milk
or soy milk or coconut milk

Sift the confectioners' sugar into a small bowl. Add the extract and the milk. Using a spoon, beat for about 30 seconds until smooth and glossy.

Tip: Use gluten-free almond extract to make this recipe gluten free.

Lemon Glaze VO GF

We use this pretty glaze for cupcakes and cakes, and for cookies, too.

Makes enough to glaze a 10-cup Bundt cake

1 cup organic confectioners' sugar

¼ teaspoon pure organic lemon extract

2 tablespoons plus 1 teaspoon organic milk
or soy milk or coconut milk

Sift the confectioners' sugar into a small bowl. Stir in the extract and the milk, and beat by hand for about 30 seconds or until smooth and glossy.

Orange-Pear Cupcakes

Frost these tender, yummy cupcakes with Rich and Fluffy Chocolate Caramel Frosting (page 359) or Fluffy Pumpkin Spice Frosting (page 358), or serve them dusted with confectioners' sugar. Any way you top them, they're delicious.

Makes 12 cupcakes

½ cup buttery spread (I like to use Earth Balance® brand), brought to room temperature

1 cup organic sugar

2 local eggs

1 tablespoon organic orange extract

1 cup plain low-fat organic yogurt

1 cup organic unbleached flour

1 cup organic whole wheat flour

1 teaspoon baking soda

1 teaspoon baking powder

1 local Bosc pear, peeled, cored, and minced

1. Center the oven rack. Preheat the oven to 350°F.

2. Cream the buttery spread and sugar in a mixing bowl, using a hand mixer on medium speed for 45 seconds, stopping once or twice to scrape the bowl with a rubber spatula.

3. Add the eggs and beat on medium speed for 30 seconds until light and fluffy, stopping once to scrape the bowl. Add the orange extract and the yogurt. Beat on low speed for 30 seconds until smooth, stopping once to scrape the bowl. In a separate bowl, measure the flours, baking soda, and baking powder. Sift this mixture over the creamed mixture. Mix on low speed for 30–45 seconds, stopping once or twice to scrape the bowl, until well blended. Stir in the minced pear. Spray the cupcake tins with nonstick cooking spray. Divide the batter evenly among the tins, about a heaping ¼ cup in each.

4. Bake in a preheated oven for about 20 minutes, until a cake tester inserted into the center of a cupcake comes out clean. Let set for a few minutes, then turn out onto a platter to cool before frosting.

Lemon-Almond Polenta Cake

This is a lovely cake served alone, dusted with a little powdered sugar, or topped with a dollop of plain whipped cream. Often we surround the cake with fresh berries or fruit salad, because the cake is even more delicious if you pair it with fruit.

Makes a 9-inch-round, 2-inch-thick cake; serves 12–14

2 cups organic all-purpose flour

½ cup organic cornmeal

1 tablespoon organic baking powder

¼ teaspoon sea salt

1 cup (2 sticks) organic butter, brought to room temperature

1½ cups organic sugar

4 organic eggs

¼ teaspoon pure organic lemon extract

Grated zest of 1 organic lemon

2 tablespoons freshly squeezed lemon juice (from about ½ organic lemon)

½ cup sliced almonds

1. Center the oven rack. Preheat the oven to 350°F. Spray a 9-inch-round, 2-inch-deep pan with nonstick baking spray. Set aside.

2. Measure the flour, cornmeal, baking powder, and sea salt into a bowl, then whisk until blended. Set aside. Place the softened butter into a medium-large mixing bowl. Using a handheld mixer, beat on low-medium speed for about a minute until smooth and creamy. Add the sugar, then beat on low-medium speed for about a minute, until well blended, stopping two or three times to scrape the sides of the bowl. Beat in the eggs, one at a time, on low-medium speed for about 30 seconds, until all the eggs have been added and the batter is well blended. Add the lemon extract, zest, and juice, then beat on medium speed for a few seconds until blended.

3. Scrape down the sides of the bowl. Add the dry mixture. Beat on low speed for a minute, stopping once or twice to scrape down the sides of the bowl. Then beat on medium speed for about 2 minutes, until all the dry ingredients are well blended into the batter, stopping a couple of times to scrape the sides of the bowl. The batter will be thick. Stir in the almonds.

4. Spoon the batter into the prepared pan, then use a rubber spatula to scrape the bowl and to smooth the top of the batter in the pan. Bake on the center rack in the preheated oven for about 45–50 minutes, until a cake tester inserted into the center comes out clean. Turn the cake onto a plate to cool to room temperature and glaze with Lemon Glaze (page 346), if desired.

Blueberry Ricotta Cake

Serve this pretty cake with a Lemon Glaze (page 346) or with a little fresh whipped cream or crème fraîche for a special dessert.

Makes a 10-cup Bundt cake, serves 12–14

3 cups organic all-purpose flour

1 tablespoon organic baking powder

¼ teaspoon sea salt

1 cup (2 sticks) organic butter, softened to room temperature

2½ cups organic sugar

½ cup organic ricotta cheese

4 organic eggs

½ cup organic milk

1 teaspoon pure organic lemon extract

Grated zest of 1 organic lemon

1 cup fresh or frozen organic blueberries

1. Center the oven rack. Preheat the oven to 350°F. Spray a 10-cup Bundt pan with nonstick cooking spray. Measure the flour, baking powder, and sea salt into a bowl, then whisk to combine. Set aside.

2. Place the softened butter into a large bowl. Using a hand mixer, cream the butter on low-medium speed for about 30 seconds, stopping to scrape the sides of the bowl, until the butter is creamy smooth. Add half the sugar, then beat on low-medium speed for about a minute until it is well blended, stopping once or twice to scrape the sides of the bowl. Add the other half and mix on medium speed for about a minute, until well blended, stopping once or twice to scrape the sides of the bowl.

3. Into a small bowl, measure the ricotta, eggs, milk, lemon extract, and lemon zest, then whisk them together. Add the ricotta mixture to the creamed mixture. Mix on medium speed for about a minute, until well blended, stopping once or twice to scrape the sides of the bowl. Add the flour mixture, then mix first on low speed for about a minute, then on medium speed for about 2 minutes, stopping once or twice to scrape down the sides of the bowl, until blended and all the flour is mixed into the batter. Stir in the blueberries.

4. Turn the batter into the prepared pan, using a rubber spatula to scrape the batter from the bowl and to smooth the top once it's in the pan. Bake on the center rack of the preheated oven for about 1 hour and 25 minutes, until a stick inserted into the center comes out clean. Allow to sit at room temperature for a few minutes, then turn out onto a platter. Cool to room temperature before icing, if desired.

Carrot Cake

I remember my surprise when my Aunt Jerry, one of the best bakers I know, served a carrot cake to our family many years ago. Although my aunt's culinary talents were well known, I wasn't so sure I wanted a vegetable in my dessert. What a delicious revelation! Each day at Claire's we bake a number of moist carrot cakes packed with pineapple and vitamins.

Serves 12–14

1½ cups unbleached flour

1½ cups sugar

1 teaspoon salt

2 teaspoons baking soda

2 teaspoons cinnamon

½ teaspoon ground nutmeg

3 eggs

¾ cup soybean or vegetable oil

1 cup drained crushed pineapple

¾ cup grated carrots

¾ cup grated walnuts

1/3 cup raisins

1. Preheat the oven to 350°F.

2. In a large bowl, whisk together the flour, sugar, salt, baking soda, cinnamon, and nutmeg. In a separate bowl, beat the eggs for 1 minute using a hand mixer. Add the oil and mix on medium speed for 1 minute. Stir in the drained pineapple. Pour this mixture all at once over the dry ingredients and mix lightly to combine. Stir in the carrots, walnuts, and raisins. Mix just to combine, using a spoon.

3. Prepare a 10-cup Bundt pan with nonstick cooking spray, or grease and flour the pan. Pour the batter into the prepared pan. Bake on the center rack of the preheated oven for about 1 hour and 10 minutes, or until a cake tester inserted in the center comes out clean. Remove from the oven and let stand for 5 minutes, then turn out and cool to room temperature before frosting with Buttercream Frosting (page 358).

Claire's Classic

Chocolate Cake

This cake is wonderful and a big success any way we present it at Claire's. We serve it plain or with our Buttercream Frosting (page 358) or other imaginative frostings and glazes. Or we spoon sunflower seed butter or raspberry preserves over the top of the batter just before baking. Or we slice a fresh banana and push the slices into the batter before baking. We use about 20 quarts of this batter every day and it has only gotten more popular over the past thirty-five years.

Serves 12–14

8 tablespoons (1 stick) butter, brought to room temperature

1½ cups sugar

3 eggs

1¹/₈ teaspoons vanilla extract

2 cups flour

¾ cup unsweetened cocoa powder

½ teaspoon salt

1¹/₈ teaspoons baking soda

1¹/₈ teaspoons baking powder

½ cup buttermilk or sour milk

1. Preheat the oven to 350°F.

2. Cream the butter in a mixing bowl, using a hand mixer. Add the sugar and beat on medium speed, scraping the sides of the bowl as needed, until well blended, about 1 minute. Add the eggs and vanilla extract and continue to beat on medium speed about 30 seconds, until well blended.

3. In a separate bowl, sift together the flour, cocoa powder, salt, baking soda, and baking powder. Spoon all of the creamed mixture onto the sifted dry ingredients. Pour the buttermilk over the top. Using a hand mixer on low speed, mix for about 1 minute, scraping down the sides of the bowl two or three times.

4. Spray a 10-cup Bundt pan with nonstick cooking spray, or grease and flour the pan. Spoon the batter into the prepared pan, scraping the sides of the bowl. Smooth the batter. Bake in the center of the oven for about 50 minutes, or until a cake tester inserted in the center comes out clean.

5. Remove from the oven and let stand for 5 minutes, then invert onto a cake dish.

Claire's Classic

Lithuanian Coffee Cake

This is our most popular cake at Claire's. After thirty-five years, it's still the splurge of choice for many.

Serves 12–14

Filling:

¼ cup packed dark brown sugar

2 tablespoons granulated sugar

1 teaspoon cinnamon

1 tablespoon ground coffee (not brewed)

¼ cup chopped walnuts

¼ cup raisins

Cake:

8 tablespoons (1 stick) butter,
   softened to room temperature

1 cup granulated sugar

2 eggs

1 tablespoon brewed coffee, chilled

1 teaspoon vanilla extract

1 cup low-fat sour cream

2 cups unbleached flour

1 teaspoon baking soda

1 teaspoon baking powder

1. Prepare the filling by combining the filling ingredients in a small bowl. Stir to combine well. Set aside. Preheat the oven to 350°F.

2. For the cake, cream the butter and sugar in a mixing bowl, using a hand mixer on medium speed for 45 seconds. Scrape the sides of the bowl with a rubber spatula. Add the eggs and beat for 30 seconds. Scrape the sides of the bowl. Add the coffee, vanilla extract, and sour cream. Beat on low speed for 30 seconds, until well creamed. Scrape the sides of the bowl. In a separate mixing bowl, sift together the flour, baking soda, and baking powder. Pour the creamed mixture over the top of the flour mixture, scraping the bowl well. Mix on low speed for 45 seconds just to combine, stopping to scrape the sides of the bowl.

3. Prepare a 10-cup Bundt pan, either by thoroughly spraying with nonstick cooking spray or greasing with shortening and flouring the pan. Pour in half the batter. Sprinkle half the filling evenly over the top of the batter. Pour the remaining batter evenly over the filling. Use a rubber spatula to scrape the batter from the bowl and smooth the batter. Sprinkle the remaining filling evenly over the batter.

4. Bake in the center of the oven for 50–55 minutes, until a cake tester inserted in the center comes out clean. Remove the cake from the oven and let it cool in the pan for 5 minutes, then turn it out onto a plate. Serve warm or cooled to room temperature, drizzled with a glaze, frosted with Buttercream Frosting (page 358), or sprinkled with powdered sugar.

Parsnip Cake

Parsnips are wonderfully old-fashioned, and right now "old school" is hot! Serve this lovely cake with just a dusting of confectioners' sugar or with Spice Frosting (page 359) or other frosting for a wonderful indulgence.

Serves 12–14

¾ cup unbleached all-purpose flour

¾ cup whole wheat flour

1½ cups organic pure cane sugar

1 teaspoon salt

2 teaspoons baking soda

1 teaspoon cinnamon

1 teaspoon ground allspice

3 organic eggs

¾ cup organic soybean oil

1 teaspoon pure vanilla

1 cup thinly sliced organic bananas
    (about 2 medium bananas)

¾ cup shredded parsnips

¾ cup sliced almonds

1. Center the oven rack. Preheat the oven to 350°F.

2. In a large bowl, whisk together the flours, sugar, salt, baking soda, cinnamon, and allspice. In a separate bowl, beat the eggs for 1 minute, using a hand mixer at medium speed. Add the oil and vanilla and mix on medium speed for 1 minute. Pour this mixture all at once over the dry ingredients, using a rubber spatula to scrape the bowl. Using a wooden spoon, stir to combine. Stir in the bananas, parsnips, and almonds, mixing just to combine.

3. Spray a 10-cup Bundt pan with nonstick cooking spray. Pour the batter into the prepared pan, using a rubber spatula to scrape the bowl. Bake on the center rack of the preheated oven for about 1 hour and 10 minutes, or until a cake tester inserted into the center comes out clean. Remove from the oven and let stand for 5 minutes, then turn out and cool to room temperature before frosting.

Dark Chocolate Almond Cake with Rich Dark Chocolate Espresso Glaze Ⓥ

This delicious cake is also dairy-free, which will please anyone who keeps a vegan diet or is lactose intolerant. It is a delight with or without the glaze.

Serves 12–16

Cake:

2¼ cups organic unbleached all-purpose flour

4 teaspoons organic baking powder

¼ teaspoon sea salt

1²/₃ cups organic pure cane sugar

1 cup unsweetened dark cocoa powder

½ cup organic soybean or canola oil

²/₃ cup silken organic tofu, drained and crumbled

1½ cups organic plain soy milk

1 teaspoon organic almond extract

1 cup sliced almonds

Glaze:

1 cup confectioners' sugar

½ cup dark unsweetened cocoa powder

1 tablespoon ground espresso (not brewed)

¼ cup plain organic soy milk

1. Preheat the oven to 350°F.

2. To prepare the cake, measure the flour, baking powder, salt, sugar, and cocoa into a bowl, then sift it into another bowl. Measure the oil, tofu, soy milk, and almond extract into a blender container. Cover and blend on medium speed for about 30 seconds, until blended smooth. Pour the blended ingredients over the dry ingredients all at once.

3. Using a wooden spoon, stir the ingredients to combine, then beat for about 10 seconds until smooth. Stir in the sliced almonds. Spray a 12-cup Bundt cake pan with nonstick cooking spray. Turn the batter into the prepared pan, using a rubber spatula to scrape the bowl and to spread the batter smooth. Bake for about 50 minutes, until a cake tester inserted into the center comes out just clean. Remove from the oven and let stand for about 2 minutes, then turn out onto a cake dish. Allow to cool to room temperature.

4. Meanwhile, to prepare the glaze, sift the confectioners' sugar and cocoa powder into a bowl. Stir in the ground espresso. Add the soy milk all at once and, using a spoon, beat until smooth.

5. Drizzle glaze over the top of the cooled cake, using a rubber spatula to scrape the bowl.

Tangelo Orange Cake with Blueberries

This lovely cake is tender and light, and the flavor from the tangelos, well, it tastes like "sunshine," and we love it. If tangelos are out of season, you can use another really fragrant orange such as Honeybell or Valencia. Serve the blueberries alongside the cake or scatter them on top of the Orange Buttercream Frosting (page 357). It's a delicious way to add fiber and antioxidants to your dessert.

Makes 2 9-inch layers

2/3 cup trans fat–free shortening (I like to use Spectrum® brand)

1¾ cups sugar

3 eggs

1 tablespoon grated tangelo orange zest

¾ cup tangelo orange juice (from 1½–2 big tangelos)

2¼ cups unbleached all-purpose flour

1 teaspoon baking powder

¼ teaspoon baking soda

¼ teaspoon sea salt

1 recipe Orange Buttercream Frosting

1 cup fresh blueberries

1. Center the rack in your oven. Preheat the oven to 350°F. Spray two 9-inch layer cake pans with canola oil spray.

2. Measure the shortening and the sugar into a large mixing bowl. Using a hand mixer, beat on medium speed for about 1 minute, stopping once or twice to scrape the sides of the bowl with a rubber spatula, until the sugar is well blended with the shortening. Add 1 egg and beat on medium speed for 1 minute, stopping once to scrape the sides of the bowl. Add the second egg and continue beating for another minute, stopping once to scrape the sides of the bowl, until the mixture is light and creamy. Add the third egg and continue beating for another minute, stopping once to scrape down the sides of the bowl, until the mixture is light and creamy. Add the grated orange zest and the juice. Beat for 1 minute, until smooth and combined, stopping once to scrape the sides of the bowl. The mixture will appear curdled, but don't worry—it will be fine.

3. Measure the flour, baking powder, baking soda, and salt into a separate bowl, then sift twice. Add this to the creamed mixture all at once. Beat on low speed for about a minute, until smooth and creamy, stopping two or three times to scrape the sides of the bowl and to blend in the flour.

4. Divide the batter among the prepared pans, using a rubber spatula to scrape the bowl and to smooth the top. Bake on the center rack in the preheated oven for about 30 minutes, until a cake tester inserted into the center comes out clean.

5. When the cake layers are done baking, invert, separately, onto cooling racks or a platter large enough to hold the cakes in a single layer. Set aside until they are completely cooled to room temperature before frosting. Serve the blueberries alongside the cake.

Orange Buttercream Frosting ▣

Originally, I made this delicious, fluffy, and creamy frosting for my Tangelo Orange Cake with Blueberries (page 356), but I soon discovered that it's also a perfect topping for plain pound cake, angel food cake, and chocolate cake. It's vegan and delicious, so you might want to use it for a vegan cake, too.

Makes 4 cups

1 tablespoon grated orange zest, from about 1 orange

1 cup freshly squeezed orange juice (from about 2 sweet oranges; I like to use tangelos, Honeybells, or Valencia), including the pulp

¾ cup trans fat–free organic shortening

½ cup organic trans fat–free buttery spread (I like to use Earth Balance® brand)

4 cups confectioners' sugar, sifted

¼ teaspoon pure orange extract

2 tablespoons plain whole soy milk

1. Measure the orange zest and the orange juice into a small pot. Set the pot on the stove over medium heat. Cook at a low boil for about 15 minutes, occasionally moving the pot in a circular motion, until the juice reduces to about ⅓ cup and has a syrupy consistency.

2. Measure the shortening and the buttery spread into a large mixing bowl. Using a hand mixer, beat it at medium speed for about 30 seconds, until the mixture is creamy and well combined, stopping once or twice to scrape the sides of the bowl with a rubber spatula. Add the sifted confectioners' sugar, the reduced orange juice, the orange extract, and the soy milk. Continue mixing on medium speed for about 2 minutes, stopping two to three times to scrape the sides of the bowl with a rubber spatula, until the mixture is fluffy and the confectioners' sugar is completely mixed in.

Claire's Classic

Buttercream Frosting

This frosting is the fluffy white cream that is generously spread on the delicious cakes that have been our trademark at Claire's since 1975.

Makes enough to frost a large Bundt cake

4 tablespoons (½ stick) butter, brought to room temperature

4 tablespoons (½ stick) organic, trans fat–free margarine substitute, brought to room temperature

2 cups confectioners' sugar, sifted

1 teaspoon vanilla extract

Using a hand mixer on medium speed, beat together the butter and the margarine substitute for about 3 minutes, or until light and creamy. Scrape down the sides of the bowl with a rubber spatula as needed. Add the confectioners' sugar ½ cup at a time, beating about 2 minutes after each addition, until light and creamy. Beat in the vanilla extract.

Fluffy Pumpkin Spice Frosting V GFO

This fall-flavored frosting is terrific any time of year.

Makes 2 cups

½ cup trans fat–free shortening

3 tablespoons trans fat–free margarine or spread

2 cups confectioners' sugar, measured and then sifted

1 teaspoon pumpkin pie spice

2 tablespoons local apple cider

¼ cup organic dairy milk or organic plain soy milk

Measure the shortening and the margarine into a mixing bowl. Using a hand mixer set on medium speed, cream this mixture for about 30 seconds, stopping once or twice to scrape the bowl. Add the remaining ingredients. Using a hand mixer set on low speed, beat this for about a minute, stopping once or twice to scrape the bowl. Raise the speed to medium-high and beat for an additional 2–3 minutes, until light and fluffy, stopping a few times to scrape the bowl.

Tip: Use gluten-free milk or gluten-free soy milk to make this recipe gluten free.

Spice Frosting V GF

We make a variety of frosting flavors at Claire's and often let our customers pick their favorite to top their cake or cupcake. Wouldn't it be fun to have a party and do the same thing? They are so quick to prepare, too.

Makes enough to frost a Bundt cake

1 stick butter or ½ cup trans fat–free margarine, brought to room temperature

2 cups organic confectioners' sugar, sifted

1 teaspoon cinnamon

½ teaspoon nutmeg

1 tablespoon organic blackstrap molasses

Place the butter in a medium bowl. Using a hand mixer on medium speed, beat the butter for about 3 minutes, until light and fluffy, stopping once or twice to scrape the sides of the bowl with a rubber spatula. Add the powdered sugar, cinnamon, nutmeg, and molasses. Beat on low speed for about 2 minutes, then on high speed for about 3 minutes, stopping a couple of times to scrape down the sides of the bowl, until light and creamy.

Rich and Fluffy Chocolate Caramel Frosting V GFO

Sometimes we put this frosting into a pastry bag and pipe it into cupcakes for a nice little surprise for our beloved customers.

Makes about 2 cups

½ cup trans fat–free shortening

3 tablespoons trans fat–free margarine or buttery spread (I like to use Earth Balance® brand)

2 cups confectioners' sugar, sifted after you measure it

1 cup cocoa powder, sifted after you measure it

1 teaspoon chocolate extract

2 tablespoons caramel flavor shot

⅓ cup organic dairy milk or organic plain soy milk

Measure the shortening and the margarine into a mixing bowl. Using a hand mixer set on medium speed, cream this mixture for about 30 seconds, stopping once or twice to scrape the bowl. Add the remaining ingredients. Using a hand mixer set on low speed, beat this for about a minute, stopping once or twice to scrape the bowl. Raise the speed to medium-high and beat for an additional 2–3 minutes, until light and fluffy, stopping a few times to scrape the bowl.

Tip: Use a gluten-free caramel flavor shot to make this recipe gluten free.

Rich and Indulgent Chocolate Ganache GF

Like anything else you prepare, the finished results will be only as good as the quality of your ingredients. That being said, experiment with different types of chocolate, right from your supermarket. Just recently I used Ghirardelli 60 percent cacao bittersweet chocolate and we all really liked it—a lot! But I've often used Hershey's semi-sweet milk chocolate chips, and the results are creamy and yummy, too. Try out some different types of chocolate, and have fun!

Makes enough to frost a Bundt cake or a two-layer 9-inch round cake, or plenty for dipping fresh fruits for 10 people

1 11.5-ounce bag (about 2 cups) chocolate chips

1 cup heavy whipping cream

1. Place the chocolate chips in a medium bowl. Have a lid ready to cover the bowl later in the recipe. (The lid to a pot will do fine.) Heat the heavy cream in a small pot over high heat until it just comes to a boil. Pour the hot cream over the chocolate chips all at once, then cover the bowl with a lid.

2. Set aside for 2 minutes, then whisk the mixture until the chocolate chips melt and the mixture is creamy and smooth.

   Tip: Of course, this luscious ganache is heaven atop a cake, but it's also a crowd-pleaser when paired as a dip with fruit. Try it with a platter of assorted fruits at your next gathering. I like to use organic strawberries; bananas; dried apricots; and dried, pitted dates.

Dairy-Free Chocolate-Cinnamon Ganache V GFO

Your vegan friends will love you for making this for them. While this dairy-free ganache is not as creamy as our Rich and Indulgent Chocolate Ganache (page 360), which is made with heavy whipping cream, the cinnamon flavor with the rich chocolate really is delicious, so please give it a try. Spread this ganache over cupcakes, cakes, vegan "ice cream," or cookies, or enjoy it as a dip for your favorite fresh or dried fruits. It's even yummy drizzled over lemon Italian ice—try it!

Makes 1 cup of ganache, enough to frost 12 cupcakes or serve with a tray of organic strawberries or apricots

2/3 cup dairy-free chocolate chips (I like to use Tropical Source Chocolate Chips, available at many supermarkets)

1/3 cup plus 2 tablespoons organic rice milk

A sprinkle of good cinnamon

1. Measure the chips into a small bowl. Have a lid ready to cover the bowl later in the recipe—a lid from a pot will work fine. Bring the rice milk to a boil in a small pot over high heat. Pour the boiling milk over the chocolate chips all at once and cover the bowl with a lid.

2. Set aside for about 2 minutes. Then, using a whisk, mix the chips and the hot milk for about a minute, until the chips are melted and the sauce is smooth. Whisk in a sprinkle of cinnamon until fully blended. Let set for about 15 minutes until it thickens a bit, then refrigerate, covered, for about 40 minutes until it is firm enough for dipping or spreading onto cupcakes, cookies, cake, or slices of fruit.

Tip: Use gluten-free chocolate chips to make this recipe gluten free.

Honey-Cinnamon Tortilla Snacks `VO` `GFO`

I like to keep a supply of these treats around the house because they're delicious and because they're a guiltless indulgence.

Serves 4

2 teaspoons organic free-flowing brown sugar

1 teaspoon cinnamon

Canola oil spray

2 8-inch sprouted wheat tortillas or other whole wheat tortillas

2 teaspoons local honey

1. Preheat the oven to 400°F.

2. Combine the brown sugar and cinnamon in a bowl and whisk to combine. Set aside. Spray two cookie sheets with canola oil spray.

3. Cut tortillas into 16 pieces (first cut each tortilla in half, then each half in half, then each quarter in half). Place in a medium bowl. Spray 5 or 6 3-second sprays of the canola oil evenly over the tortilla pieces, using your hands to toss them to coat evenly with the oil. Drizzle the honey evenly over the tortilla pieces; again, using your hands, toss to coat. Sprinkle evenly with the brown sugar mixture. Toss to coat evenly. Turn the coated tortilla pieces onto the prepared cookie sheets, arranging them in a single layer.

4. Using your hands, sprinkle any remaining brown sugar mixture onto the tortillas. Bake in the preheated oven for about 10 minutes until crisp. Serve warm or at room temperature. After cooling to room temperature, store any leftovers in a sealed container for up to 2 days.

Tips: Use agave instead of honey to make this recipe vegan. Use gluten-free tortillas to make the recipe gluten free.

metric conversion tables

Approximate U.S.–Metric Equivalents

LIQUID INGREDIENTS

U.S. Measures	Metric	U.S. Measures	Metric
¼ tsp.	1.23 ml	2 Tbsp.	29.57 ml
½ tsp.	2.36 ml	3 Tbsp.	44.36 ml
¾ tsp.	3.70 ml	¼ cup	59.15 ml
1 tsp.	4.93 ml	½ cup	118.30 ml
1¼ tsp.	6.16 ml	1 cup	236.59 ml
1½ tsp.	7.39 ml	2 cups or 1 pt.	473.18 ml
1¾ tsp.	8.63 ml	3 cups	709.77 ml
2 tsp.	9.86 ml	4 cups or 1 qt.	946.36 ml
1 Tbsp.	14.79 ml	4 qts. or 1 gal.	3.79 lt

DRY INGREDIENTS

U.S. Measures		Metric	U.S. Measures	Metric
17 ³/₅ oz.	1 livre	500 g	2 oz.	60 (56.6) g
16 oz.	1 lb.	454 g	1¾ oz.	50 g
8⅞ oz.		250 g	1 oz.	30 (28.3) g
5¼ oz.		150 g	⅞ oz.	25 g
4½ oz.		125 g	¾ oz.	21 (21.3) g
4 oz.		115 (113.2) g	½ oz.	15 (14.2) g
3 ½ oz.		100 g	¼ oz.	7 (7.1) g
3 oz.		85 (84.9) g	⅛ oz.	3½ (3.5) g
2 ⁴/₅ oz.		80 g	¹/₁₆ oz.	2 (1.8) g

acknowledgments

I can never say thank you enough to everyone who has helped to make this book possible. There have been so many people who over the years have led me on this path that I love, the path that now has led to this very book.

First and foremost, I always give thanks and praise to God!

My beloved mother, Anna, passed away before this book was published, but I am grateful to know that she is forever proud of me for my work—really, an extension of her work. Her recipes, her love, her smile, memories of all the delicious smells from her kitchen, even the inflection in her voice when she would ask "Did you wash those greens thoroughly?" will be what helps to sustain me without her.

My mother raised my brothers and me to know the difference between good and not-so-good food. She spoiled us with really good, homemade food. We started our day with freshly squeezed orange juice and a cooked breakfast of either hot cereal like oatmeal or farina, or poached or olive oil–fried eggs with toasted slices of Italian bread—crostini, often topped with apricot preserves or ricotta, sliced banana, and honey. Lunches, whether at home during days off from school or packed for school days, always meant cooked foods. Even sandwiches were made with braised broccoli rabe, peppers, and eggs, or maybe sautéed escarole. They were soggy by lunchtime but so delicious that other classmates, usually those who brought in cold-cut sandwiches, "offered" to trade. No, thank you! Suppers included so many vegetables alongside a pasta dish or perhaps a little meat that during the editing of my first cookbook, my editor called several times to ask, "Exactly how many vegetables did your mother make at supper?" And, if my mother couldn't pronounce any ingredient, we didn't eat it, which meant there was little opportunity for any preservatives to get to us. That philosophy also extended to her backyard garden. I am forever grateful for this, too. The bar for good food was set high from early on.

I am forever grateful also to my staff, who allow Claire's to succeed each and every day whether I'm there or not, and I love them dearly. Past notables who contributed to our early success include Rose (Naclerio) Albin, Sara (Sylvester) Hernandez (namesake of the ever-present menu item Sara's Dream), Don Jackson, Javier Lopez, Anita Lawrence, Sally Tessler, Mary-Ellen Eises, Chrissy and Lori Savastano, Wendy Read, and Kathleen Whipple, among others. It's been thirty-five years, so please forgive me if I've forgotten to mention you, and accept my deepest gratitude. More recent special staff at Claire's include Juana Lopez, who is an amazing cook and for more than ten years has looked out for me like a best friend, and I love her for her loyal devotion! Gerardo Meneses has worked with us since 1997 and never has anyone made more beautiful piecrusts for us, and he's amazing in so many other areas, too. Erin Guild has worked at Claire's since 2003 and in addition to being a really good cook, she knows how to vacation well (I tease that I live my vacation life vicariously through her). And Brenna Harvey has since 2005 loved our Lithuanian Coffee Cake more than anyone I know—no easy feat. I recently asked her, "Do you still love our Lithuanian Coffee Cake as much?" and she answered, "Lithuanian Coffee Cake is a love whose flame cannot die." While that alone is enough to endear her to me forever, Brenna also adds her creative genius to drink signs and our website. Margie Cancel has been a manager at Claire's since 2005, and she is a fantastic cook, a wonderful person, and an old friend (my husband has known her since she was a kid), and she is so much fun to work with, too. Her daughter, Alana, joined our staff in 2006 and added to our cupcake decorating and so much more. Rose Hernandez, our most joyful manager, "beams" as soon as she walks in the door and there is no doubt how much she loves being at Claire's, and for this and her fine cooking I am forever grateful. And, Frank adores her, too. Eduardo Saldana-Pena makes our beautiful breads and many of our cakes, makes sure we always have the finest organic fruits and vegetables, and watches our bottom line too—"This is too much money for a half case of . . . and we can do without it for a while." Chayna Williams makes sure that we are always ready to open and that our dessert section remains amazing! And no one writes a more ambitious projects list—and gets it done! Celestino Romano, Adriana Garcia, and Eufemia Lima help keep everything clean and restocked for us. Adriana's son Angel and Eufemia's daughter Jessica even volunteer each summer for our Alex's Lemonade Stand, and watching them grow up has been a joy, too. Lindsey Eagles helps keep us focused by always asking "How do we make money doing this?" every time I want to host an event or to donate a bit too much, something easy to do given the opportunities we have to help in our city. Hyacynth Pearson, Carl Akins, Jose Alonso, Alyse Guild, Kiley Harvey, Carolyn LaPia (my niece) Felix Lara, and Terrance Paige, newer members of our staff, are a joy to have on our team and in our family at Claire's, and I am grateful to them for their help in our continued success.

Bobbi Dunne has been our office manager since 2005 and I cannot imagine what our books and many of our ads and marketing projects would be like without her.

I want to thank each and every one of my beloved customers, because it is you who support this crazy, fun place, the place I find to be a most happy place because of you.

I thank our organic farmers both near and far, who work hard every single day, protecting the land that will grow their crops to feed us well. We could not cook without them!

My brothers, Jim and Paul, and Billy LaPia and my sister-in-law Kathy are all great cooks, and they continue to share their passion for good food during our times together. Right now, Jim and Paul are really into their backyard pizza ovens, and I couldn't be happier. And Kathy is always trying out a new cake on us—always a delicious experience! And I thank my nieces—Lisa, Carley, and Carolyn—and my nephew Brandon for reminding me each year that our traditional Christmas Eve dinner must be at my house! And I love that you always ask for my *Pasta e Fagioli*.

Our vendors, our landlord Yale Properties, our city of New Haven Police and Fire Departments, the Town Green Special Services District, and our hard-working mayor, John DeStefano, keep our city the only place we want to be. Thank you.

Rabbi David Avigdor supervises our restaurant, allowing us to serve an Orthodox Jewish community along with everyone else who comes to Claire's. I love that I can look in my dining room at Claire's and see people from all backgrounds sharing a meal, because I hope that one day, this will lead to peace. Our food connects us to our history and to our culture, and I love that we can share this through the foods we serve at Claire's.

Larry Dorfman, sales manager at Globe Pequot Press, created the conversation that started this project, and he was also involved in my very first writing project, *Claire's Corner Copia Cookbook*. Mary Norris, Katie Benoit, and Gregory Hyman have been the support from GPP that encouraged this entire project. I believe that good editors take a bunch of words and make them better. They do that and so much more, like encourage the best from me, and I am grateful to them.

Rick Sandella, my editor from the *New Haven Register*, has been a generous, wonderful friend. He always gives me good advice and encouragement, along with really good jokes, something I often need because I do tend to get too intense, and I thank him so much for his constant support.

And, speaking of getting too intense, my beloved husband, Frank, the love of my life, keeps me focused and centered, and reminds me to take time for myself whenever I get too intense—I'm working on that. No one could ever love me more than he does.

index

Note: Page numbers in **bold** indicate recipe category lists.

Throughout this book you will see the following symbols next to the recipes. This will guide you as to which recipes are gluten-free, include a gluten-free option, are vegan, or include a vegan option.

GF	**GFO**	**V**	**VO**
gluten-free	gluten-free option	vegan	vegan option